LIVING WITH GRIEF

LOSS IN LATER LIFE

HOSPICE FOUNDATION OF AMERICA

EDITED BY KENNETH J. DOKA

Foreword by U.S. Senator John Breaux,
Chairman, Senate Special Committee on Aging
Introduction by Jack D. Gordon, Chairman, Hospice Foundation of America

LIVING WITH GRIEF

LOSS IN LATER LIFE

EDITED BY KENNETH J. DOKA

Foreword by U.S. Senator John Breaux,
Chairman, Senate Special Committee on Aging
Introduction by Jack D. Gordon, Chairman, Hospice Foundation of America

This book is part of Hospice Foundation of America's
Living With Grief® series.

Support has been provided in part by the Foundation for End of Life Care.

This book is part of HFA's *Living With Grief®* series.

To order contact:
Hospice Foundation of America
2001 S Street, NW #300
Washington, DC 20009
(800) 854-3402
www.hospicefoundation.org

Managing Editor: Judith Rensberger
Copy Editor: Pat Tschirhart-Spangler
Cover Design: Patricia McBride
Typesetting and Design: Pam Page Cullen

Publisher's Cataloging-in-Publication
(Provided by Quality Books, Inc.)
Living with grief : loss in later life / edited by Kenneth J. Doka ; foreword by John Breaux ; introduction by Jack D. Gordon.
p. cm. -- (Living with grief)
Includes bibliographical references.
LCCN: 2001099332
ISBN: 1-893349-03-9

1. Loss (Psychology) in old age. 2. Death--Psychological aspects. 3. Life change events in old age. 4. Adjustment (Psychology) in old age. 5. Aging--Psychological aspects. 6. Aged--Psychology. I. Doka, Kenneth J.

BF724.85.L67L58 2002 155.67
QB102-200091

Dedication

To All Those Killed
in the Terrorist Attacks of
September 11, 2001,
And to All, of Every Age,
Who Mourn Their Deaths

Contents

Foreword

Senator John Breaux,
Chairman, U.S. Senate Special Committee on Aging

The U.S. Senate Special Committee on Aging, which I chair, continues to hold a series of hearings on long-term care, assisted living, family caregiving, and other issues that affect the lives of older Americans. As chairman, I have had the unique opportunity to talk to older people, their families, end-of-life counselors, and health professionals from across the country about the profound impact that loss and grief have on older people and the generations that succeed them. Their countless stories of the injustices suffered because of an often uncaring and ill-equipped long-term care system serve as a constant reminder of the dire need for change.

From committee hearings to my own experiences, I recognize the struggles, concerns, and issues faced by the bereaved and those who care for them. We must learn to better understand and prepare for death in both the emotional and practical sense and begin to recognize the growing need for end-of-life care and grief counseling services for older Americans.

As this book shows us, when a loved one dies we search for meaning in our own lives while struggling to hold onto memories of a precious life lost. Part of this search for meaning leads us to take stock of our accomplishments, relationships, and life experiences, while at the same time trying to make sense of the loss of an important person in our lives. How we as individuals deal with loss varies based on such factors as our relationship with the deceased, our cultural background, and our spirituality.

The issues associated with death and dying are becoming increasingly complex as more and more Americans are living longer. Old age is generally the time in life when death occurs, yet far too often bereavement for older people is misunderstood and ignored. It is important for us to understand that there is no correlation between frequency of loss and intensity of grief following a loss—the fact that death occurs more often in later life does not make the experience any easier to handle.

Coping with profound sadness after the death of a spouse, sibling, or lifelong friend can lead to an overwhelming emotional burden, especially for older persons dealing with multiple losses, their own failing health, and dwindling sources of support and comfort. Today more than ever, it is important to understand how loss and bereavement affect older people. It is important to try to improve the quality and expand the reach of mental health and grief counseling services designed to help them.

Increased longevity, coupled with the wave of 77 million baby boomers approaching retirement age, magnifies the issues of who dies, who grieves, and who cares for the sick and dying. Aging boomers could quite possibly find themselves supporting an adolescent child, caring for a sick spouse, and grieving the loss of an adult child or a parent all at the same time.

I believe this book will serve as a valuable tool for those facing the most difficult time in their lives and will prompt all Americans to lend a helping hand and a sympathetic ear to an older person who is suffering after a painful loss. ■

Senator John Breaux (D-LA) is the Chairman of the Senate Special Committee on Aging. He has used this position to highlight the importance of protecting and strengthening Social Security, Medicare, and other programs that are essential to the health and well-being of older Americans. In 1998, he was selected to chair the National Bipartisan Commission on the Future of Medicare and co-chair the National Commission on Retirement Policy. Senator Breaux also serves as the Chairman of the Subcommittee on Social Security and Family Policy and is a member of the Health Care Subcommittee. Senator Breaux was instrumental in helping forge the compromises that led to passage of the welfare reform and health insurance reform bills in 1996, and, as the leader of the Centrist Coalition of Senate Democrats and Republicans, has sought bipartisan agreements on a balanced budget, welfare reform, and health care reform.

▪ INTRODUCTION ▪

Jack D. Gordon,
Chairman, Hospice Foundation of America

Although hospice care is available to any terminally ill person, the vast majority of patients cared for by hospice each year are older persons. And any examination of information about demographic shifts in the United States over the coming years suggests a phenomenal growth in the aging population. The subject of *Loss in Later Life*, then, seemed an excellent choice to add to the Hospice Foundation of America (HFA) series on *Living With Grief®*. It was in fact a topic that had been suggested by hospice and bereavement professionals over the years.

As in any exploration of loss that HFA undertakes, some issues are relatively obvious—loss of health, of mobility, of independence. Other losses in this particular population are more intangible—loss of community, of social support, of culture. We at HFA were pleased to be focusing our resources on these salient issues.

Then came the terrorist attacks of September 11, 2001. Across the United States and around the world, everything changed. The enormous losses brought about by the events of that terrible day brought grief into every home. Patricia Murphy, a bereavement specialist at University Hospital in Newark, New Jersey, and a past contributor to this book series, told *The New York Times*: "People are understanding the profound effects of loss at a much more visceral level. We've turned into a community of grievers" (Dewan, October 17, 2001).

The editors and authors who contributed to this book already had been focusing on grief and loss from the perspective of the older population. Several chapters had been completed before September 11. We often found ourselves asking, "How do the events of September 11 change what we have been thinking about loss in later life?" Looking at these national losses through the already-defined focus for this book added new dimensions and created new meaning for much of the information we had compiled.

Older Americans have a unique perspective on world events. They have lived through wars and other tragedies that only the oldest age cohorts have experienced. In addition, they have experienced many of the personal losses that are inevitable as one ages.

For several years, Pace University gerontologists Shirlee Stokes and Susan Gordon have been studying healthy adults over the age of 65 who live in non-hospital community settings. The goal has been to learn what most "stressed them out." In 1998 they reported that the second most common stressor experienced by older Americans was "concern for world conditions." It was second only to "slowing down." Older Americans are concerned about the state of the world they are leaving to their grandchildren. I worry about my own grandchildren and what the future holds for them in this new world.

Perhaps because of their age and life experiences, many older people have developed the kind of strength, resiliency, and acceptance that can teach us all. Abigail Trafford, of *The Washington Post*, wrote this about the generation that came of age during and immediately following World War II: "As they contemplate the future for their grandchildren, they exhibit a bittersweet optimism that combines practical strategies for survival and an intimate grasp of the suffering that may lie ahead" (Trafford, October 16, 2001). Although she was writing specifically in the aftermath of September 11, her statement is true on many levels. This message appears again and again in many of the chapters in this book.

The events of September 11 illuminated two more aspects of grief in later life. First, parents do not expect to bury their own children. Yet most of those killed in the terrorist attacks were under the age of 50. One can assume, then, that there are significant numbers of older parents mourning the sudden and unexpected loss of an adult child. This type of loss is similar to that experienced by many parents during wartime; Vietnam, Korea, and World War II give us far too many examples.

Second, television provided us with harrowing images in the course of reporting the attacks. It will be difficult to see a movie in which a person jumps to his death without conjuring up pictures of the people who jumped from the twin towers of the World Trade Center. Traumatic events in our lives may bring flashbacks of the horrific events of September 11, and these will be difficult to handle. This phenomenon is known as post-traumatic stress; its recognition and understanding are the Vietnam veterans' contribution to American medicine.

The aftermath of September 11 underscores the importance of many of the topics in this book, and it enables HFA to contribute to a greater understanding of how persons in later life are affected by losses of all kinds. While the events of September 11 may redefine much of what is thought about death, grief and loss, it is important to remember that those in later life face and grieve a range of losses on an ongoing basis. Kenneth J. Doka, the editor of this book, reported it well: "We do grieve...the tragedy of September 11. But we may also, honorably and necessarily, grieve the still small tragedies that we continue to encounter as we journey through life" (*Journeys*, November, 2001). We at the Hospice Foundation of America know that the chapters in this book will provide new information and practical suggestions for those professionals and families who accompany older men and women as they continue their journeys.

This book brings to all of us, regardless of age, a deeper understanding of the effects of personal grief, as well as general grief, on the older persons in our lives. Knowledge and understanding begin at home, but the lessons we learn have universal applicability, and should be used to respond properly to societal problems.

Acknowledgments

Acknowledgments fall into what might be called circles of support. In one of those circles are our contributing authors, whose experience, knowledge, and wisdom are the heart of this book.

In another circle are officers and staff (present and former) of the Hospice Foundation of America (HFA). Jack Gordon, Board Chairman, contributed the introduction and a *Voices* piece, along with his customary good counsel. David Abrams, President, offered support and helpful suggestions. Our Senior Program Officer, Judith Rensberger, served as Managing Editor, and two former staff members also played key roles. Lisa McGahey Veglahn, Program Consultant, and Michon Lartigue, Editorial Consultant, contributed their vision and experience.

Office Manager Donna Hines kept the Foundation humming as she provided support for all aspects of this production. Communications Director Jon Radulovic contributed ideas for authors and topics. Program Associate Jason Benion handled fact-checking and proofreading. Other key players were Sophie Viteri Berman, HFA's Chief Fiscal Officer, and Latoya Williams in our accounting operation.

Outside our immediate circle are others who shaped the form and content of *Living with Grief: Loss in Later Life.* Pat Tschirhart-Spangler served as lead copy editor. Author Larry Beresford rewrote parts of this book, bringing to bear his expertise in the hospice field. Freelance editors Helen McMahon and Susan Hunt (both with EEI Communications, Inc.) and Joyce Latham provided additional editorial services. Patricia McBride designed our cover, and Pam Page Cullen once again handled page design and typography. The American Geriatrics Society identified potential authors and compiled information for the resource list that appears in the back of the book. As always, I want to acknowledge Cokie Roberts, who moderates our national teleconference each year.

My own circle of support includes numerous colleagues at the Association of Death Education and The International Work Group on Dying, Death and Bereavement. There are others who enrich my professional life and enable me to write. They include administrators and colleagues at The College of New Rochelle: President Stephen Sweeny, Vice-President Joan Bailey, and Dean Laura Ellis. Vera Mezzaucella and Rosemary Strobel provide critical administrative support.

Then there are the family members and friends. They offer support and respite, understand deadlines, and make one's efforts worthwhile. Included here are Kathy Dillon, my son, Michael, and his wife, Angelina, and my Godson, Keith Whitehead and his family. Other members of my special network include my sister, Dorothy, and my brother, Frank, and their families. Still others are Dylan Rieger, Margot and Paul Kimbal, Don and Carol Ford, Allen and Gail Greenstein, Jim and Mary Millar, Fred and Lisa Amore, Eric Schwarz, Lynn Miller and Larry Laterza.

Finally, speaking for our contributing authors, we acknowledge the clients, mentors, and colleagues who have shared their stories and their work. They make life an ongoing, collaborative learning process.

Kenneth J. Doka, Ph.D.
21 December 2001

PART I

Death as a Fact of Later Life

Some years ago, I attended a conference hosted by the Association of Death Education and Counseling. After the conference, a delayed plane left me and several other participants stranded for the evening. As our group enjoyed dinner, we discussed the conference events. We remarked on the fact that although most deaths occur among older persons, not one conference presentation specifically addressed those losses. Nearly all the workshops and lectures focused on either traumatic losses or grief resulting from an out-of-order death, such as the death of a child. To us, this seemed to reflect a larger reality: In grief, older persons often are underserved.

Thanatologists, who study death, often focus on traumatic and out-of-order deaths. It may be the very nature of these losses that engages their interest, encourages their entry into the field, and provides them with most of their analytical and counseling work. Gerontologists, who study aging, often seek to challenge the stereotype of older people as declining and waiting to die. They focus on healthy and active elders.

This book, along with the teleconference it supports, addresses the subject of loss in later life. It seeks to educate a wide range of health care professionals who deal with older individuals and their loved ones.

The author of our opening chapter is Robert Butler, a pioneer in gerontology and the founding director of the National Institute on

Aging. He is credited with originating the concept of life review, which redefined the way we think about reminiscing in later life.

Butler sees looking back on life not as evidence of living in the past, but as an essential ingredient of living later life *in the present.* The point of life review is to examine the past, make sense of life, and affirm that one's life had and still has value. Prompted by the recognition that one's life is nearing completion, life review offers final opportunities for reconciliation and affirmation.

Following some of the substantive chapters in this book are our Practical Suggestions features. The first, by Michon Lartigue, follows Butler's chapter and offers tips to professionals who may wish to help older clients and patients navigate the process of life review.

My own chapter develops the idea that this life review awareness is central to later life. Older persons frequently do have an awareness of being finite and recognize the reality of death even as they seek to live life fully. Their middle-aged adult children, on the other hand, may be struggling with an awareness of their own mortality, brought on in part by the aging of their parents. Thus, while older parents may want or even need to speak of their future deaths, their adult children may want to avoid such discussions at all costs.

Richard Wald pokes fun at this dilemma by recounting an awkward, albeit amusing, conversation with his mother about her funeral plans. His account is one of our first-person essays, collectively known as *Voices,* which describe the authors' personal experiences. Wald's account also models an excellent adaptive mechanism—the use of humor.

Part I of our book concludes with original research conducted and presented by Lin Noyes. Her narrative study suggests that very old persons can be very comfortable discussing death. They seem reconciled to its nearness even as they appreciate the lives they live day-to-day. ■

—Kenneth J. Doka

CHAPTER 1

Age, Death, and Life Review

Robert N. Butler

INTRODUCTION

Fifty years ago people thought that reminiscing was a sign of senility—what we now call Alzheimer's disease. In that era, many geriatrics researchers confined themselves to the study of people who were long-term residents in chronic disease hospitals and nursing homes. The results of these studies only served to reinforce the stereotypes of old people as confused, decrepit, and leading meaningless lives. Their reminiscences confirmed that they were living in the past.

In 1955 I had the great privilege of joining the National Institutes of Health's Laboratory of Clinical Science, where we studied in detail healthy older people, age 65 and above. Somewhat similar studies were conducted at Duke University. Both groups of investigators initiated the first long-term studies of healthy older persons. Healthy old people who lived in the community were found to be mentally alert and active. An interpretive summary of the multidisciplinary studies was published by the *American Journal of Psychiatry* (Butler, 1963). Some researchers suggested we were studying an elite group of "super-healthy" people who were not representative of the true population of old people. Later studies confirmed our work.

Thus, during my years at the National Institutes of Health I spent a great deal of time with a group of vibrant older people. I slowly became aware that they seemed to be going through a profound internal process that focused on reviewing their life and trying to come to terms with everything that had happened to them in the past. I wrote a preliminary article based on these observations and this phenomenon, which I labeled the life review among older persons, entitled "Recall and Retrospection" (Butler, 1963), and a later comprehensive paper entitled "The Life Review: An Interpretation of Reminiscence in the Aged" (Butler, 1963).

For several more years I worked with patients in both individual and group therapy. I concluded that the life review is a normal function of the later years and not a pathological condition. Over time, my patients taught me that memories, reminiscence, and nostalgia all play a part in the process. Far from living in the past or exhibiting "wandering of the mind," as was commonly thought, older people were engaged in the important psychological task of making sense of the life they had lived.

What Is Life Review?

Life review is a personal process by which a person evaluates his or her life as it nears its end. This spontaneous psychological event is seen especially when one is confronted by death or a major crisis, although some individuals may not be fully aware of it and may even deny that it is happening at all. The intensity and emphasis placed on putting one's life in order is most striking in old age.

Aspects of Life Review

People may recall unresolved conflicts that happened many years before. By reexamining what has happened, they may be able to come to terms with their conflicts. This may involve reconciling with a long-estranged relative or friend, or it may simply mean forgiving oneself or the other person and letting go of the negative feelings associated with the memory. Through these efforts, such reminiscence can give new significance and meaning to life and prepare the person for death by lessening anger, fear and anxiety.

In late life, people have a particularly vivid imagination and memory of the past. Often, they can recall with sudden and remarkable clarity early life events. They may experience a renewed ability to free-associate and to bring up material from the unconscious. The life review can occur in a relatively tranquil form, through nostalgia, mild regret, reminiscing, storytelling, and the like. Sometimes, the life story is told to anyone who will listen. At other times it is conducted in private, as a monologue not meant for others to hear. Life reviews are extremely complex, often contradictory, and frequently filled with irony, comedy, and tragedy.

In many ways life review is similar to the psychotherapeutic process. In both instances, a person reviews the past in order to understand the present. In recent years life review has come to be respected as an entity in itself, and a variety of psychotherapeutic techniques have been developed. They include life review therapy (Lewis & Butler, 1974), guided autobiography, described by Birren and Deutchman (1991), and structured life review therapy, (Haight and Webster, 1995).

A variety of life review and family history training manuals have been developed to guide older people on their journey. The Hospice Foundation of America published *A Guide for Recalling and Telling Your Life Story* (2001). In Great Britain, Age Concern has developed *Reminiscence and Recall: A Guide to Good Practice* (Gibson, 1998) and the *Reminiscence Trainer's Pack* (Gibson, 2000), both of which are available through Age Concern's website: http://www.ace.org.uk. Finally, *Handbook for Mortals* offers practical guidance for people facing serious illness, which includes life review (Lynn & Harrold, 1999).

The Purpose of Life Review

The goals of life review include the resolution of past conflicts and issues, atonement for past acts or inaction, and reconciliation with family members and friends. People often reunite with family and friends after years of separation or estrangement, and return to their birthplace for a final visit. Overall, the life review is a necessary and healthy process and should be recognized in daily life as well as used in the mental health care of older people. The strength of life review lies in its ability to help promote life satisfaction, psychological well-being, and self-esteem.

The overall benefit of a life review is that it can engender hard-won serenity, a philosophical acceptance of what has occurred in the past, and wisdom. When people resolve their life conflicts, they have a lively capacity to live in the present. They become able to enjoy basic pleasures such as nature, children, forms, colors, warmth, love, and humor. Creative work may result, such as memoirs, art, and music, and there is a comfortable acceptance of the life cycle, the universe, and the generations.

Memoir as Life Review

Sometimes, life review can take the form of memoir or autobiography. Public personalities write memoirs and autobiographies because they value their lives and feel that they have important ideas or information to convey to others. They also write to set the record straight or get back at an adversary. Robert McNamara's memoir, *The Tragedies and Lessons of Viet Nam* (1996), was an explanation that included an apology to the American people for his role in events that had occurred nearly 25 years before.

Like life review, a memoir does not necessarily represent the unvarnished truth. *Truth and Poetry* was how 19th century writer and philosopher, Johann Wolfgang von Goethe, entitled his own autobiography. He recognized that he was rewriting his life by tinkering with reality and explaining misdeeds, perhaps to lessen his guilt and soften the judgment of others.

As life nears its end, life review—whether written as a memoir, spoken to a trusted health care worker, family member or friend, or whispered in private to the walls—is the last chance to edit a life story and make it come out "right." It is the last effort to explain, integrate and reconcile everything that has happened in the course of a lifetime.

Memory and Life Review

What ignites a memory? A fleeting smell or sound can bring people back to an event that happened when they were children. For that moment, time and space are suspended. Reminiscing about a happy event and savoring the memory of a special moment in time can be a rare and heartfelt joy. Unfortunately, over the course of a lifetime, people also live through experiences that are so grief laden that they are pushed from conscious memory. They remain forgotten until a traumatic event forces them back into consciousness. The recent terrorist attacks on New York and Washington provided one such example. Many older New Yorkers who lived through traumatic wartime trauma were confronted with sights and sounds that rekindled terrible memories. Although many older people who lived near the site exhibited resilience and an impressive resourcefulness, there was a minority for whom the experience brought to consciousness unbearable memories. Workers who came to their aid reported that in addition to physical assistance, they needed to be able to speak to someone who would listen to them and help them integrate what they had experienced in the past with the more recent experiences.

Helping the Patient

A health care professional who approaches the patient with an open mind and a compassionate, listening ear can greatly facilitate the life review process. People who embark on a life review are making a perilous passage, and they need support that is caring and nonjudgmental. Some people revise their stories until the end, altering and embellishing in an attempt to make things better. Pointing out the inconsistencies serves no useful purpose and, indeed, may cut off the life review process.

It is especially important that those who work with the dying not impose their own values on those of a dying person and to understand that each person has his or her own special forms of meaning that must be respected.

While it is important to be receptive and nonjudgmental, the health care professional must also keep in mind that it is often hard to tap into the life review of someone who wishes to be silent or is psychologically isolated. In addition, not all outcomes are favorable, and life review sometimes results in a major depression or a depressive trend. The individual who conducts his or her life review alone is at much greater risk of depression than those who allow another person to share in the process.

Life review therapy is sometimes conducted in a family setting. This has the therapeutic advantage of facilitating consensus and clarification of specific family issues. Visual images such as family albums, scrapbooks, and cherished possessions can be used to evoke crucial memories. In lieu of direct contact with family members, some people write letters to their children or other important persons in their lives. Others might leave an ethical will, as either a letter or tape recording that shares their values, hopes, insights, beliefs, and wisdom.

Life review is selective, and not all past experiences are remembered or shared. For most people, it is a combination of hard objective truths and the softer lens with which they remember their less noble acts. Some memories are recalled with clarity and focus, while others are indistinct and blurry. Sometimes, people entirely forget significant events that are too painful to remember. On the other hand, they may judge themselves harshly for minor hurts they inflicted by word or deed many years before. Individuals may experience a sense of regret that becomes more painful the more they examine their lives. In severe forms, this process can lead to anxiety, guilt, despair, and depression. In extreme cases, if a person is unable to resolve problems or accept them, terror, panic, and suicide can result. The most tragic life review is one in which a person decides that his or her life was a total waste.

Life Review as Oral History

Recollecting historic events and the era in which they occurred are valuable eyewitness accounts of part of a nation's heritage and are one kind of life review. For example, in Britain, Age Exchange has a Reminiscence Theatre company, through which Londoners have shared their memories of living through the blitz in World War II.

In America, obviously only a few hundred of the 200,000 orphaned and poor children who were sent west between 1854 and 1929 are still alive. They meet annually to share remembrances, and their stories are important historical accounts of a little known social experiment.

In the summer of 1976, under the auspices of the Smithsonian Institution Margaret Mead, Wilton Dillon, and I arranged to obtain the stories of visitors to the Mall in Washington, D.C. In 1993, Sarah L. Delany and A. Elizabeth Delany provided a firsthand account of what it was like to live as African-Americans in the United States in the 20th century, when they wrote their life stories, *Having Our Say: The Delany Sisters' First 100 Years.* These life reviews are an important record our nation's heritage from the point of view of the people whose lives were shaped by historic events.

Some consider life review a Western phenomenon because of its focus on the individual, however, a number of research studies have been conducted around the world. Major programs of reminiscence and life reviews are carried out under the auspices of both national organizations and individuals in Japan and Singapore as well as in the United States and the United Kingdom. In 1995, an International Society for Reminiscence and Life Review was established.

Conclusion

The life review, as sometimes manifested by nostalgia and reminiscence, is a natural healing process. It represents one of the underlying human capacities on which all psychotherapy depends. Some of the positive results of a life review can be the righting of old wrongs, making up with estranged family members or friends, coming to accept one's mortality, gaining a sense of serenity, pride in accomplishment, and a feeling of having done one's best.

Yet, notwithstanding the importance of the life review and its acceptance today as a normal developmental process, health care professionals who care for older persons depend far too much on drugs to quiet psychic pain. It is hard to believe that a pill has the power to help an old person get to the bottom of genuine guilt, or the capacity to satisfy the need to share memories with an empathic listener. Along with pain, anger, guilt, and grief, health care professionals at all levels need to listen to their older patients. We must facilitate the opportunity for a person to achieve resolution and celebration, affirmation and hope, reconciliation and personal growth in the final years.

Physician, gerontologist, psychiatrist, public servant, and Pulitzer-Prize winning author, Robert N. Butler, MD, is perhaps best known for his advocacy of the medical and social needs and rights of older persons. In 1975 he became the Founding Director of the National Institute on Aging of the National Institutes of Health, where he remained until 1982. In 1982, he founded the Department of Geriatrics and Adult Development at The Mount Sinai Medical Center, and served as Chairman and Brookdale Professor until 1995. In 1990, he established the U.S. branch of the International Longevity Center and in 1995 he became its full-time President and CEO. In 1976, Dr. Butler won the Pulitzer Prize for his book Why Survive? Being Old in America. *He is co-author of* Aging and Mental Health *and* Love & Sex after 60.

References

Birren, J.E., & Deutchman, D.E. (1991). *Guiding autobiography.* Baltimore: Johns Hopkins Press.

Butler, R.N. (1963). The life review: An interpretation of reminiscence in the aged. *Psychiatry, 26*, 65-70.

Butler, R.N. (1963). Recall and retrospection. *Journal of the American Geriatrics Society, 11*, 523-529. Abstracted in Biological Abstract.

Butler, R.N. (1963). The façade of chronological age: An interpretative summary of the multidisciplinary studies of the aged conducted at the National Institute of Mental Health. *American Journal of Psychiatry, 119*, 721-728.

Delany, S.L., & Delany, A.E. (1993). *Having our say: The Delany sisters' first 100 years.* New York: Kodansha.

Gibson, F. (1998). *Reminiscence and Recall: Second Edition.* United Kingdom: Age Concern.

Gibson, F. (2000). *Reminiscence Trainer's Pack.* United Kingdom: Age Concern.

A guide for recalling and telling your life story. (2001). Washington, DC: Hospice Foundation of America.

Haight, B.K., & Webster, J.D. (Eds.). (1995). *The art and science of reminiscing: Theory, research, methods and applications.* Washington, DC: Taylor & Francis.

Lewis, M.I., & Butler, R.N. (1974). Life review therapy: Putting memories to work in individual and group psychotherapy. *Geriatrics, 29*, 165-69, 172-73.

Lynn, J., & Harrold, J. (1999). *Handbook for mortals: Guidance for people facing serious illness.* New York: Oxford University Press.

McNamara, R. (1996). *In retrospect: The tragedies and lessons of Viet Nam.* New York: Random House.

CHAPTER 2

Practical Suggestions

Life Review: A Rewarding Activity

Michon Lartigue

Our society is geared towards thinking and planning for the future. We map out and experience our lives with a focus on what we want to accomplish and how to meet those goals. But, as we age, there is often a gradual yet steady shift of balance from thinking about our future to reviewing our past. Health care professionals who work with older men and women can use this natural process of life review to help their patients create meaningful experiences for themselves, family members, and friends. Professionals can tap into a variety of ways to tell a life story and adapt them to the needs and desires of their patients and clients.

Life review can be an individual experience, in which a person privately looks back on life and records it at his or her own pace. It also can be an activity to be accomplished with family and friends. Sharing the activity can enrich a story by providing varied viewpoints of life events. A life story can be compiled with the intent to give as a gift, or it can be a group experience, structured into sections where the group accomplishes targeted activities. For example, a nursing home may host a weekly Life Review Hour. Men and women attend knowing that the question for the week is, "What is your favorite memory of your children?" After the session, they are given the question for next week, which allows time for thought. Even when the topic is not relevant, they can skip that particular session and attend the next one.

The actual recording of a life story also offers many options and opportunities for professionals to help their patients and clients. Writing the story can be done by the individual, or for some it may be easier with the help of another person. If available, computers are very useful tools for such a project; however, writing thoughts in a journal, notebook, or specialty workbook is also a nice and helpful way to keep track of thoughts. Using an audiotape cassette recorder that has a microphone or built-in voice activation is another interesting means of recording life events. It adds some flexibility in organizing taped sessions: one week a patient can talk about childhood, and the next week his or her thoughts about aging. Still, the tapes may be labeled and put into chronological order. Taping also adds the benefit of loved ones hearing the patient's voice. If patients are comfortable with being on camera, then video recording is an easy and personal way to capture their words and ideas. For some, creating a companion scrapbook is a creative and touching way to use old photos, cards, letters, invitations, and other personal documents or memorabilia.

Finally, researching and gathering the details of one's life is an important part of the process of life review and is filled with creative possibilities. Brainstorming can be particularly fun, with or without family and friends. Professionals can provide individuals with questions that stimulate memories, or they can tap into memories by using sensory stimulation: "What does this smell remind you of?" "What sounds remind you of childhood?" Individuals can also use other sources such as other autobiographies, historical books that highlight a particular time, or even life review guides.

The following examples, based on the Hospice Foundation of America's book, *A Guide For Recalling and Telling Your Life Story*, highlight one way to divide and section a life story in order to make it easier to research and record events. The sample questions also show how to stimulate memories by asking specific questions. Professionals may use this sample list as a beginning and add or alter questions as they think best suits a particular client or patient, for example, by removing questions about children if they know that a particular client didn't have any children or by adding questions about a patient's professional life or military service. Regardless of how a professional tailors the life review process, helping their patients or clients look back and share special memories can be both rewarding and entertaining.

Suggested Sections For Telling A Life Story

Family

1. What are some of your childhood memories of your parents?
2. What stories have you heard about your great grandparents?
3. What are some of your favorite stories about your brothers and sisters?

Growing Up

1. Where did you live when you were growing up?
2. Can you describe the room you slept in?
3. How did your family observe holidays and special occasions?

Adult Life

1. When did you first consider yourself to be an adult?
2. Describe your first home. What did you like the most about it?
3. What are some of your favorite memories of your children?

Growing Older

1. How old are you? Do you enjoy this age?
2. What have you done since you or your spouse retired?
3. What do you share in common with your friends now?

Reflections

1. The most important people in my life have been…
2. The ideas, books, music, and poetry that have most influenced me are…
3. I would like to be remembered as… ■

Michon Lartigue is a writer and editor based in Washington, DC. She is the former Publications Director for the Hospice Foundation of America, and is the current Managing Editor for the Foundation's bereavement newsletter, Journeys. *She is also the owner of Lartigue's Too, an editorial consulting company, a Managing Editor for PopandPolitics.com, and has written for numerous publications and Internet sites as a freelance writer. She is currently working on her first novel,* Learning This Life.

■ CHAPTER 3 ■

Death In Life

Kenneth J. Doka

"Doctor, Doctor, Will I Die?
Yes My Child, And So Will I."
—Nursery Rhyme

INTRODUCTION

Between those two short lines of the nursery rhyme lies a complex developmental process. Over a lifetime, human beings learn to deal with death through a series of overlapping processes. Children begin by grasping the reality of death, but it is not until midlife that people learn to accept their own mortality. In later life, individuals understand and accept that their life is nearing its end and that death will come soon. These levels of understanding are linked to other processes typical of the developmental stage in which each occurs. This chapter traces the ways in which humans integrate death into their understanding and proposes three overlapping and related processes that occur at different developmental stages. The main focus is on the two later processes, as it is in midlife and later life that adults feel the presence of death more keenly, and this understanding affects their orientation toward life and loss.

Death In Childhood, Adolescence and Early Adulthood

Very young children have a difficult time understanding an abstract term such as death. According to Speece and Brent (1996), children master the concept over time, gradually understanding component concepts such as that death is universal, meaning that it is inevitable, inclusive, unpredictable, and irreversible. Children, too, begin to learn that the dead do not function in a corporal way. Yet as they attempt to develop their own spirituality of death, they may believe that the dead continue in other ways such as in memory or in some sort of afterlife (Lifton and Olsen, 1974). Speece and Brent (1996) also assert that part of understanding death entails a greater comprehension of causality. Children move then from more magical thinking about death to realize notions of the reasons why living things die.

Yet, while the older child is aware of death, the concept of death is often not personalized. The child recognizes that he or she, like all living creatures, will die, but that thought is pushed into a very abstract future. The issue of the inevitability of one's own death is simply not cogent unless provoked by a life-threatening illness (Bluebond-Langner, 1978). The cognitive comprehension of death does not necessarily entail the recognition of personal mortality. There is a great gap between the statements "people die" and "I, too, will die."

While this recognition of death may begin in childhood, developmental issues that arise in adolescence tend to make the awareness of one's own mortality more of a cogent concern. The adolescent is struggling with a number of issues that intersect with death—primarily, the drive to create an individual identity. As the adolescent struggles with this individuality, there can be a growing awareness that death, nonexistence, represents a great threat to that emerging identity. In some cases, this may lead to extensive denial of death or challenges to death that are evident in dangerous behaviors.

The threat of death can also be accentuated by the stress and isolation that the adolescent experiences. In this time of critical reflection and reassessment, previous sources of support, such as religion, may no longer be as viable. With an emerging sense of individuality may come a growing sense of aloneness. "There is no one like me" easily becomes "there is no one who fully understands me." There may be a sense of separation from parents. There may be mourning for the loss of childhood. As Alexander, Colby, and Alderstein (1957) assert, death may become a more significant issue at times in which one's identity experiences psychological and social stress. Their projective testing techniques indicated that death is affect-laden for adolescents, albeit on a less conscious level.

While the awareness of mortality may begin to sharpen during this developmental stage, adolescents are well able to defend against it. One of the major defenses is, simply, that adolescents are very present-oriented. This is clear in Kastenbaum's (1965) work on the meaning of death in adolescence. Kastenbaum found that most of his adolescent participants had little sense of finality. In their present-oriented world, death was simply not a major issue. Only a small minority of his participants thought about death. These results were similar to a much earlier study that found college students relatively unconcerned about death (Middleton, 1936). Similarly, Newman (1987), in a review of literature, found that while adolescents in that era were fearful of nuclear war and environment devastation, they had comparatively few concerns about personal death. Perhaps there is an illusion of invulnerability, emerging from this intense present-orientation, that contributes to that earlier mentioned tendency to challenge death. In summary then, while adolescents may begin to recognize their own mortality, albeit perhaps subconsciously, their intense present orientation makes it unlikely that this awareness will become a significant issue.

Awareness of mortality can also be ignored in early adulthood. Erikson (1963) for example, sees young adults consumed by a quest to consolidate identity and establish intimacy. The young adult is concerned with the external world—establishing intimate relationships, beginning a family, starting a career. Yet there are some dimensions of early adult life that do, at least in a remote way, raise issues of mortality. As young adults begin to accumulate assets and responsibilities, such as for a significant other, spouse, or child, they may begin to execute documents such as wills, advance directives, or guardianships. Such documents involve an implicit recognition of mortality. Similarly, as adults plan to raise children, they consider the spiritual traditions, values, and beliefs that they wish to share with their offspring. This, too, may engender thoughts about the afterlife, again leading to a consideration or mortality. But again, this thinking is remote and episodic.

Midlife: Developing the Awareness of Mortality

The thesis of this chapter, developed from earlier work (Doka, 1988, 1995), is that it is in midlife that individuals develop an *awareness of mortality* and that in later life they develop an *awareness of finitude* (Marshall, 1980). While this generally occurs, either awareness can occur earlier, especially if the context is marked by internal or external events such as war or catastrophe, developmentally unexpected losses, early onset of chronic illnesses, or an expectation of a more limited life span. Nonetheless, these processes typically occur in midlife and later life.

While some psychoanalytic theorists such as Freud (1925) or Weisman (1972) assert that humans can never imagine their own deaths, other development theorists have implied that the full awareness of mortality begins to emerge in middle adulthood. This awareness of mortality is the recognition that one will die, although not necessarily in the immediate future. It is the understanding that there is an end to one's time that is inexorably drawing closer. To many theorists, it is in middle adulthood that the concerns become more internal and introspective. Erikson (1963) characterizes this stage of life as "generativity vs. stagnation." Implicit in his discussion of this stage is an increasing awareness of personal mortality that creates a desire in these adults to "pass on the torch" to a newer generation. The middle adult wants to develop a legacy, a contribution that can be left to establish the significance of his or her life. That desire is fueled by the increasing understanding that there are limits to one's time. Hence, if the person does not use this time productively, there might not be future opportunity. Other theories have seen middle adulthood similarly. For example, although the universality of a midlife crisis is debated, its adherents claim it is the knowledge of future death that provides the impetus for a major reevaluation of one's life (Brim, 1976; Jacques, 1965; Levinson, 1978; Lifton, 1975; Neugarten, 1972; Zacks, 1980). Research by Rothstein (1967) supports the view that death becomes more of a cogent concern in midlife. He interviewed 36 adults, aged 30 to 48. His older respondents (43 to 48) tended to personalize death more than those in the 30 to 42 age groups. Death becomes a more salient issue in midlife, responded to first by shock and then resigned accommodation.

There are a number of conditions and circumstances that contribute to the development of an awareness of mortality in middle adulthood. First, as adults reach their 30s, 40s, and 50s, they begin to experience varied physiological and sensory declines. The recognition of these declines reminds one of the inevitability of aging and eventual death:

> In the late 30s and early 40s a man falls well below his earlier peak levels of functioning. He cannot run as fast, live as much, do with as little sleep as before. His vision and hearing are less acute, he remembers less well. And he finds it harder to learn masses of specific information (Levinson, 1978, p. 213).

Women experience menopause, and both men and women may experience a gradual diminution of sexual prowess. This, too, is a vivid reminder of loss and aging, and, as Kastenbaum and Aisenberg (1976) suggest, there may be an inverse relationship between reproductive capability and a sense of terminus.

Second, there is a dramatic increase in the mortality rate, particularly for those in their 40s. For example, the male mortality rate for men 45 to 64 is six times that for those 25 to 44 (Tamir, 1982). As adults enter midlife, then, they begin to regularly experience the death of peers from causes other than accident or suicide. Stephenson (1985) notes that when a person in midlife experiences loss, there may be both reactive and existential grief. Reactive grief is a response to the loss of a person. Existential grief is the recognition, often prompted by the loss of another, that one will suffer and die. Thus, the loss of others in one's cohort is a vivid reminder of personal vulnerability.

A third factor is that adults in midlife begin to see their own parents and their parents' cohort aging and dying. The previously omnipotent parent increasingly is seen as weak and vulnerable. To Blenkner (1965) this is a significant factor in adult development. Not only does it create a new relationship with an aging parent, it reinforces for midlife adults their own aging and death. This is further underlined by the fact that their children are at the point of establishing their own families and careers, reinforcing the reality that their own cohort is advancing in age toward distant but inescapable death. As Moss and Moss (1983) state:

> The loss of a parent represents the removal of a buffer against death. As long as the parent was alive the child could feel protected, since the parent by the rational order of things was expected to die first. Without this buffer there is a strong reminder that the child is now the older generation and cannot easily deny his or her own mortality. (p. 73)

Other factors in midlife may also increase awareness of mortality. Grandparenthood, which is a midlife experience, is often interpreted by grandparents as a mark of age. Preparing for retirement, even though it is still some time away, reiterates the passage of time. Approaching what is perceived as a significant birthday (40, 50, etc.) may also be considered a mark of age. Finally, a serious operation, a health crisis, or the onset of chronic illness may increase the awareness of mortality.

It would seem, then, that given the differing conditions and circumstances that lead to the awareness of mortality in adults, this awareness can develop gradually, overtime, as a person slowly becomes aware of physical declines and personal vulnerability. In other cases, this awareness may be sudden insight in response to a crisis.

No matter how the awareness of mortality develops, it has certain implications for adult life. First, the middle aged person's sense of time is modified. The child primarily looks toward the future. Time is measured from birth. The older person may be more oriented toward the past. The "time remaining" is considered both cogent and short. Neugarten (1972) theorizes that this restructuring of time occurs in middle age where the increasing awareness of finiteness leads middle agers to think both in terms of time since birth as well as time left to live.

As the recognition of time shifts, there are profound implications for the sense of self. As stated earlier, the recognition of personal mortality leads to a reassessment of identity. Adults in middle age must consider what they have been, what they wished to be, and what they still can become. In essence, they begin to consider what they could leave behind. To use Lifton and Olson's (1974) terminology, there is a search for symbolic immortality in creations or progeny that will remain. As Erikson (1963) states, generality becomes a central issue.

> Generativity…is primarily the concern in establishing and guiding the next generation…and, indeed, the concept "generativity" is meant to include such more popular synonyms as productivity and creativity. (p. 267)

Levinson (1978) describes a similar concern:

> Knowing that his own death is not far off, he is eager to affirm life for himself and for generations to come. He wants to be more creative. The creative impulse is not merely to "make" something. It is to bring something into being. To give birth, to generate life. (p. 222)

This illustrates that there is not a morbid preoccupation with death in midlife. The middle aged person recognizes that he or she is in the prime of life with death likely to be decades away. The recognition that death will come can create a desire to see that the remaining years are well spent.

Awareness of mortality can be life enhancing. Neugarten (1968), for example, sees the awareness of mortality as a prod that adds zest to life.

Koestenbaum (1971) sees the knowledge of finiteness as contributing to a renewed sense of vitality. In understanding one's personal mortality, there is greater appreciation for the tedious and common tasks that contribute to the completion of goals. Life takes on a new perspective. Zacks (1980), too, feels that the recognition of limited time creates an intensified search for self-actualization. In addition, these processes may make the person more inner directed. Faced with finiteness, the constraints placed by others may seem less significant.

While such reassessment represents a symbolic, long-term preparation for death, other preparation may take more mundane forms. Those in middle age become concerned with the practical aspects of death such as obtaining insurance, providing for trusts, and writing their will. This preparation continues to increase with age (Kalish and Reynolds, 1976).

While the awareness of mortality may in some ways enhance the quality of life or ease the impact of a future death, there can be negative aspects as well. The awareness of mortality strikes at a time when that recognition can be quite problematic. Family responsibilities and financial constraints may be at their peak. Career commitments may be at their apex. Life goals, even if reassessed, are likely to be incomplete. Under such conditions, the knowledge that one will die is likely to provoke great anxiety. It could be expected then that death anxiety would be at its highest in midlife as the adult becomes increasingly cognizant of the paradox of both heightened responsibility and limited time.

While it is beyond the scope of this chapter to review the extensive and contradictory research on death anxiety, there is some support for the idea that death anxiety peaks in midlife (Doka, 1988, 1995; Neimeyer, 1994). Nonetheless, the relationship between age and death anxiety is complex and may have different explanations. It may be a statistical artifact, simply reflecting the greater religiosity of older cohorts that seems to reduce death anxiety, or it may reflect other reasons, as well (Kalish and Reynolds, 1976). Perhaps the aged, suffering varied losses, disabilities, and pain, see life as having less value, or perhaps older persons' believe that they have lived their lives and recognize that now, according to the natural state of the world, they are approaching death. Perhaps, as Kalish and Reynolds suggest, older persons may be anticipating and preparing for their own eventual death, which may reduce their overt anxiety.

Middle-aged persons, though, have different concerns. They become aware of death when their commitments and opportunities are extensive. Death becomes the haunting specter that may yet rob them of the opportunity to achieve their goals and enjoy the fruits of their efforts. Death perhaps is the greater terror, stalking midlife, threatening goals and plans, heralding incompleteness, and even, for some suggesting the futility and meaningless of existence.

Perhaps, then, this crisis creates a process of concession to eventual death. This process may entail a reevaluation of life, renewed commitment to the achievement of critical goals, increased focus on health so as to forestall death, and attempts to reduce the uncertainty and impact of death by prudent preparation. There may also be increased concern with spirituality. While the issues of spirituality, religiosity, age, and death anxiety are too complex to consider here, it is not inconsistent with developmental approaches to posit that the recognition of eventual death encourages spirituality, if not religiosity, in older cohorts. Perhaps this crisis forces midlife adults to confront life in order to find meaning so as to avoid the terror of death. In addition, perhaps, the longer one lives side by side with now-recognized death, the less terrifying it becomes.

To summarize, the awareness of mortality may be the most significant psychological event in middle life. As described earlier in the chapter, the awareness of mortality has two major implications for adult life. First, it changes the nature of time. Aware of their mortality, midlife adults constantly struggle with the issue of time remaining. They now see both the finish and starting lines of their life. Their sense of future is now bounded.

This leads to a second implication. An awareness of mortality leads to a quest for finding meaning in one's life. Aware of limited time, even if it is measured in decades, a midlife adult becomes deeply concerned that his or her life has meaning.

Midlife adults reassess where they are in their lives. If they are generally content with their past and present life and content with the direction life seems to be taking, this concern with meaning may not be overly troublesome. They need simply to reaffirm the meaning they have already found and perhaps commit to current goals. Perhaps such persons may reprioritize their goals and themes, for example, deciding to spend more time with family.

Others may not face the future with such equanimity. If a midlife adult's past is problematic, he or she may be concerned about beginning to gain closure, perhaps expressed by entering therapy or confronting past issues and demons. If an individual views the present as troubling or the future as unresolved, awareness of mortality can engender a sense of panic or terror. Perceiving the boundaries of life, the individual becomes aware of the fact that constructing and living a meaningful life may no longer be possible. There may simply not be enough time to find meaning in a heretofore meaningless existence. Perhaps the midlife crisis is a manifestation of this frantic concern to achieve meaning by rearranging one's present and future.

Not everyone, of course, struggles with the issue of meaning. To some, the awareness of mortality is simply too terrifying to confront or the quest to find meaning too difficult to pursue. Such persons may select varied coping mechanisms, such as escapist or denial strategies to avoid confronting one's mortality. In discussing the fear of nuclear holocaust, Lifton and Olson (1974) described a process of psychic numbing, where the threat is so terrible yet pervasive that one becomes psychologically incapable of considering it. Perhaps, for some, the threat of death holds so much terror that it can never truly be faced.

The awareness of mortality becomes the critical defining moment in adult life. It forces individuals to find or to construct significance and meaning in life or to surrender to terror.

DEATH IN LATER LIFE

In time, the recognition of mortality, that is, an understanding that one will eventually die, leads to an awareness of finitude (Marshall, 1980). Awareness of finitude in older persons does not mean that they expect to die immediately but rather that they realize they are in the end part of life. Hence they are reluctant to perceive or plan too far in to the future. Time is now primarily viewed through the past (Neugarten, 1972).

Consistent with the work of Erikson (1963) and Butler (1963), Marshall (1980) sees the awareness of finitude as prompting a life review process. Here, the individual reviews past life to affirm that his or her life had meaning and value. To Erikson (1963), a successful life review means that the older person can view life with a sense of ego integrity, that is, a sense that he or she has lived a worthwhile life, or as Marshall (1980) states, one's life is a "good story." If the life review is not successful, an individual may perceive that his or her life has been wasted, yielding to a sense of despair.

Like the awareness of mortality, precisely when the awareness of finitude develops is inexact. Certainly, events such as nursing home institutionalization, illness, or frailty can accelerate it. Then, too, a chronic illness or condition that leads to an expectation of a shortened life span or an early and imminent death can create an awareness of finitude and subsequent life review even in the very young (Bluebond-Langner, 1978).

In addition to prompting life review, the awareness of finitude often engenders a concern with a good, appropriate death (Marshall, 1980; Weisman, 1972). This means that the person wants to die in a way consistent with his or her values, wishes, or earlier life. On a practical level, that might mean that older persons are intent on instructing their adult children about their estate, advance directives, even their wishes about funerals and other rituals. Yet the discussion suggests that this may create a paradoxical situation: older adults with an awareness of finitude may need to address the issues of their death, but their middle-aged children struggling with their own awareness of mortality may be deeply threatened by their parents' death and hence avoid such discussion. That same paradox may trouble adult children's end-of-life decision making as they confront the death of an older parent.

Conclusion

There may be, then, three overlapping and related processes that occur as humans struggle with death. In the first process, conceptualization, the child must cognitively comprehend the reality of death. The second process, beginning in late childhood and culminating in middle adulthood, is one of personalization. In this process, the person becomes aware of his or her own individual mortality. In the final process, the older adult concedes that death will occur soon, that life is near end.

The awareness of mortality and finitude may represent a significant process in adult life. While such awareness of mortality increases anxiety at first, as individuals learn to live with the specter of death in midlife, death becomes less foreboding as they near it. As Frank Herbert (1977) states in his epic novel *Children of Dune*:

> To suspect your own mortality is the beginning of terror; to learn irrefutably that you are mortal is to know the end of terror. (44, pp.133–134) ■

Kenneth J. Doka, PhD, MDiv, is Senior Consultant to the Hospice Foundation of America (HFA) and a Professor of Gerontology at the College of New Rochelle in New York. He is an ordained Lutheran Minister and a former President of the Association for Death Education and Counseling (ADEC) and recipient of ADEC's 1998 Death Educator Award. He is former Chairperson of the International Work Group on Death, Dying, and Bereavement. Dr. Doka has been a panelist on HFA's National Bereavement Teleconference since 1995. Dr. Doka serves as Editor of Omega *as well as* Journeys, *a newsletter for the bereaved published by the Hospice Foundation of America. He is the author of numerous books as well as more than 60 published articles and chapters.*

References

Alexander, I., Colby, R., & Alderstein, A. (1957). Is death a matter of indifference? *Journal of Psychology, 43*, 277-283.

Blenkner, M. (1965). Social work and family relationships in late life, with some thoughts on filial maturity. In E. Shanas and G. Streib (Eds.), *Social a structure and the family: Generations relations.* Englewood Cliffs, NJ: Prentice-Hall.

Bluebond-Langner, M. (1978). *The private worlds of dying children.* Princeton, NJ: Princeton University Press.

Brim, O. (1976). Theories of the male mid-life crisis. *Counseling Psychologist, 6*, 2-9.

Butler, R. (1963). The life review: An interpretation of reminiscence in the aged, *Psychiatry, 26*, 65-76.

Doka, K. (1988). The awareness of mortality in mid-life: Implications for later life. *Gerontology Review, 1*, 19-28.

Doka, K. (1995). The awareness of mortality in mid-life: Implications for later life (revised). In J. Kauffman (Ed). *The awareness of mortality.* Amityville, NY: Baywood.

Erikson, E. (1963). *Childhood and society.* New York: MacMillan.

Freud, S. (1925). Thoughts for the times on war and death, in *Collected papers,* (IV). London: Hogarth Press.

Herbert, F. (1977). *Children of dune.* New York: Berkeley Books.

Jacques, E. (1965). Death and the mid-life crisis, *International Journal of Psychoanalysis, 46,* 502-514.

Kalish, R., & D. Reynolds. (1976). *Death and ethnicity: A psycho-cultural study.* New York: Baywood.

Kastenbaum, R. (1965). Time and death in adolescence, in H. Feifel (Ed.) The meaning of death. New York: McGraw-Hill.

Kastenbaum, R., & R. Aisenberg. (1976). *The psychology of death.* New York: Springer.

Koestenbaum, P. (1971). The vitality of death, *Omega, 2,* 253-271.

Levinson, D.J. (1978). *The seasons of a man's life.* New York: Alfred A. Knopf.

Lifton, R.J. (1975). On death and the continuity of life: A psycho-historical perspective, *Omega, 6,* 143-159.

Lifton, R., & Olson, E. (1974). *Living and dying.* New York: Bantam Books.

Marshall, V. (1980). *Last chapters: A sociology of aging and dying.* Monterrey, CA: Brooks/Cole.

Middleton, W. (1963). Some reactions toward death among college students. *Journal of Abnormal and Social Psychology, 31,* 155-173.

Moss, M., & Moss, S. (1983). The impact of parental death on middle aged children, *Omega, 14,* 65-7.

Neimeyer, R.A. (1994). (Ed.) Death anxiety handbook: *Research, instrumentation and application.* Washington, DC: Taylor & Francis.

Newman, A. (1987). Planetary death, *Death Studies, 11,* 31-135.

Neugarten, B. (1972). Adaptation and the life cycle. *Counseling Psychologist, 6*, 16-20.

Neugarten, B. (1968). The awareness of middle age. In B. Neugarten (Ed.), *Middle age and aging*. Chicago: University of Chicago Press.

Rothstein, S.H. (1967). *Aging awareness and personalization of death in the young and middle adult years*, Ph.D. Dissertation, University of Chicago, 1967.

Speece, M., & Brent, S. (1996). The development of children's understanding of death. In C. Corr and D. Corr (Eds.). *The handbook of childhood death and bereavement*. New York: Springer.

Stephenson, J. (1985). *Death, grief and mourning: Individual and social realities*. New York: Free Press.

Tamir, L. (1982.) *Men in their forties: The transition to middle age*. New York: Springer.

Weisman, A. (1972). *On dying and denying: A psychiatric study of terminality*. New York: Behavioral Publications.

Zacks, H. (1980.) Self-actualization: A mid-life problem, *Social Casework, 61*, 233-233.

CHAPTER 4

Voices

Preparing for Departure, Rounded Corners and All*

Richard C. Wald

In the last year of her life, my mother had accumulated bladder cancer, emphysema, osteoporosis, macular degeneration, heart problems, and an apartment in North Miami Beach. But there was nothing wrong with her hearing.

During one of my last visits with her, when she was mostly confined to bed, I went to see my Uncle Sidney, a large, wonderful man who lived in a nearby condominium and always had something funny to say.

"You ought to plan for a funeral," he said. "Your mother is not going to live forever, and chances are you won't be here when she dies."

So a few days later, as I was sitting in her dining room with him, the doorbell rang and in came the man who had sold Uncle Sidney a funeral on a prepaid basis. Mother was in the bedroom, and I was extremely uncomfortable.

"Who's there?" she shouted.

"The guy who plans the funerals," Uncle Sidney said.

"I'm not dead yet."

"That's why we're only planning," he said.

"Hello, Forstate," the funeral planning man said.

"Tell him hello for me," Mother shouted.

I had just started to sweat when Aunt Flo walked in. She was slim, smart, intense and blunt. Also, she never knocked. She had a key.

"Who's this?" she asked Uncle Sidney. She meant the funeral planning man. She knew who I was.

"He's the funeral planning man," Uncle Sidney said.

"Great," she said, "I can get some ideas."

"Hey, Flo," my mother shouted from the bedroom. "Don't let him buy anything expensive."

"Don't worry, Lilly," she said.

The funeral planning man gave me a sheet of paper with boxes to check off. "Where will interment take place?" he asked.

"In New York," my mother shouted. "Ship me back."

The funeral planning man asked about cremation.

"What's the point of that?" Uncle Sidney asked.

"Well," said the funeral planning man, "if you are cremated and you have your ashes scattered, you can save about $1,500."

"I've always wanted to get out to Yellowstone National Park," Uncle Sidney said.

"You want your ashes scattered in Yellowstone Park?" Aunt Flo asked.

"No. But with the $1,500 extra I could have taken Frieda for a visit to Yellowstone."

"You wouldn't like it," my mother shouted. "It's empty."

The funeral planning man said the only real expense after cremation was a $150 urn.

"But if I'm going to be scattered, why do I need an urn?" Aunt Flo asked.

"You have to put the ashes in a nice receptacle," the funeral planning man said.

"But I'm going to be emptied out in a few days," she said. "How about a big two-pound coffee can?"

The funeral planning man turned to Uncle Sidney, who said, "Let's talk about caskets."

"Don't spend a fortune, Richard," my mother shouted. "A plain pine box. That's all."

"Would you like rounded corners?" the funeral man shouted at her.

"What are rounded corners?" I asked.

The funeral planning man turned to Uncle Sidney and said:

"Rounded corners are a little nicer. The pine has a little better finish. It looks better."

"Dead is dead." My mother shouted.

"I'll take the rounded corners," I said.

The funeral planning man smiled at Aunt Flo. She said, "Give him the rounded corners."

We got through the long list very slowly. By the time the evening was over, I felt like an infant with a splitting headache.

When I said goodbye, my mother was in bed, lion-hearted, but a much smaller figure than she had ever been. She smiled brightly at me and said, "Don't worry, Richard— I'll leave you my grandchildren."

And she did. ■

*Originally published in *The New York Times*, reprinted by permission from the author.

Richard C. Wald is a professor at the Columbia Graduate School of Journalism.

■ CHAPTER 5 ■

Stories of the Oldest-Old as They Face Death

Lin E. Noyes

INTRODUCTION

Ancient theories about aging held that old age was not a problem to solve but an expected consequence of living and that little by little aging people lose "heat" (vitality) until they eventually become cold and die. The aging process was "seen as a personal journey to self-knowledge and reconciliation with nature or God" (Cole, 1988, p. 48). Although this concept of *Homo viator* (man on a journey) was initiated and persists in spiritual writings about older adults (Sherman & Webb, 1994), life as a journey is not a theme discussed in the scientific literature on aging.

Instead, life has come to mean productive life, and aging has become a problem that needs to be fixed because society considers life's productive years to be finished by the time people reach old age. This positivistic approach to aging, dissecting it into its observable and measurable parts, has wedged itself between the process of aging and the meaning and significance of aging. Focusing on the losses and decrements that occur with physical aging is much easier than measuring the less tangible issues of growth in older adults.

Health policies developed for the oldest-old ought to take these factors into account. Public policy developed with a humanistic understanding of the aging process that takes into account growth and development will enlighten the social construct of aging. As long as aging is seen only as a period of decline, policies that support growth and independence will not be embraced (Minkler, 1999).

In addition to a limiting effect on public policy, dissecting old age into its component parts has not helped researchers discover the meaning of this period of life that ends in death. They have found it difficult to reconcile the decremental changes and losses of aging with the apparent increased life satisfaction and contentment of the oldest-old, who are developmentally closest to death. Erikson (1968) has said that one cannot understand the meaning of a developmental period of life unless one looks at it in the context of preparing for what comes next. Though humankind has not yet grasped what life after death may mean, the fact that the event of physical death ends physical life is universally accepted. In this last developmental period, then, what preparations are the oldest-old making? What gives life meaning at this stage?

Discovering that there is meaning to life for people age 85 and older, which overrides the view that aging is just an accumulation of losses, could have a profound effect on ethical decisions made for and about these older adults. We need to know more about the nature of human development before death before we can begin to decide when a person's life ought to end, who receives scarce health resources, and when and what kinds of treatments should be terminated.

If a process of development occurs before death that requires active participation, then perhaps ending this process prematurely affects or hinders future development of the person through the event of death. Discovering the developmental nature of preparing for death in older adults may also give insight into the process for any person who faces death prematurely from injury or illness.

This chapter is a summary of my research study of the oldest-old. The purpose of the study was to explore how people age 85 and older, who are developmentally close to death, understand their lives as they come to face death in a framework that anticipates continued human development.

An Optimistic Framework

Martha Rogers (1970, 1986), a nursing theorist, provided the framework for my own research. Rogers's theory of aging describes human development as an ongoing process that does not end with death. Rather, death is just an event in the continuous growth and development of a human being. Humans continue on into infinity even though the body dies.

According to Rogers's view, changes that are usually considered losses are really value-neutral and may even occur to prepare the person for what comes after death. For instance, no one mourns the loss of a sucking reflex in a child who has learned to drink and eat. In fact we consider the loss of the sucking reflex as a sign of growth. Rogers would ask us to hold off our judgment on whether the changes that occur in old age are good or bad because we don't know what follows death and therefore cannot say what kinds of attributes people will need after death. All we do know, if we accept this theory, is that when people experience the event of death, they do not take their bodies with them.

Most spiritual beliefs include some sort of afterlife and acknowledge that the spirit or soul goes on despite the death of the body. This perspective would dictate that people (or their souls) in heaven do not need their eyes or their ears or their other earthly senses. Common changes of diminished senses in older adults would not necessarily be a handicap but a preparation for future growth. This view of aging also permits the researchers to look for other changes that seem more positive and support the continuing development of the human being.

Research Methodology

The research consisted of 3 to 5 hours of in-depth interviews with people who fit the requirements of being 85 years old or older and in good health. None were facing death from acute illnesses. They were facing death only developmentally, as the event that would end their old age. The final research project contained four stories of people who were the best examples of continuing growth and development in the oldest-old. The answers to the following four research questions revealed the growth, development, and meaning of life that are very much a part of this period of adulthood:

1. What are the thoughts, feelings, sensations, dreams, and daily experiences of the oldest-old as they face death?
2. What meaning do they attach to these experiences?
3. How do the oldest-old view death and death anxiety?
4. What purpose in life do the oldest-old see and what meaning does it have for them?

I used a mixed qualitative methodology (Denzin & Lincoln, 1998) to conduct this research and analyzed the data using narrative analysis as described by several researchers (Bell, 1988; Lawless, 1993; Lieblich, Tuval-Mashiach, & Zilber, 1998; & Miller, 1988).

The Research Participants

Beyond meeting the criteria for the study—being 85 years old or older, living outside of a nursing home, and not suffering from a life-threatening illness—each of the four people had a faith background in Christianity, although this was not an intentional similarity. In addition, all hailed from east of the Mississippi. One person was Black and the other three were White. Two were women and two, men. Following are brief introductions to these four remarkable individuals. Their names have been changed to maintain their confidentiality.

Fr. David Larkin

His face, posture, and demeanor are strikingly reminiscent of Obi-Won Kenobi, the Jedi Knight who taught young Luke Skywalker the power of "the force." The ptosis of his eyelids is severe, making me wonder what he could see from underneath all the folds of gravity-laden skin. His body shows each one of his 94 years, very lean, no fat, and very little muscle mass remaining. His shoulders are slightly hunched and his arms seem too long for his diminutive frame. Folded close to his body, he extends his right hand and uses his long graceful fingers to emphasize his remarks.

Fr. David T. Larkin, Society of Jesus, is a holy man, a learned man, a brilliant man whose mind will not slow down, housed in a body that can no longer keep up with him. His eyes dance when he talks about his new book or his experiences of feeling the exhilaration of success as a teacher, a writer, an athlete, a priest, and a thinker. Otherwise they retreat into his sagging body.

When we met for his interviews, he humbly recognized his superior intelligence and was careful to make sure I kept up with him as he explained his ideas and related them to other concepts and experiences. His choice of meeting place for the interviews was a seating area on the third floor of the university's theological library where he works five days a week, when he is not leading retreats for college students. His work: writing his 17th book on modern rhetoric as it appears in Disney movies and science fiction epics such as Star Wars.

Mrs. Sarah Walters

At 103 years old, Mrs. Sarah Walters is a woman who has outlived her own expectations of a long life and still finds a way to face each day knowing that she is doing pretty well and feeling ambivalent about leaving her 82-year-old son alone when she dies. Mrs. Walters still cooks two meals a day for her son, Fred, cleans the house, and keeps Fred in line. When I came for the first interview, she smiled broadly and welcomed me into her home.

Sarah Walters is a tiny woman, straight boned, except for the beginning of kyphotic changes to her spine. She moves slowly, purposefully, and gracefully. Having known no other centenarians for comparison, I cannot say if Sarah looks old or not. Her skin is smooth but pulled over high large cheekbones, and dark age spots punctuate what was once most likely a flawless complexion. Her hairline is high off her forehead and her hair is silver white. She wears thick eyeglasses with hearing aids attached on both sides. Her eyes are bright and focused, and she looks like she might know a secret that she cannot wait to tell you.

Underneath her rather simple presentation, Sarah Walters has woven her own cosmic philosophy about life and dying and death from what she has learned over her long, long lifetime. Her philosophy weaves her life and her talents with the generations that have preceded her and those who will live on beyond her own physical death.

Mr. Tucker Caldwell

Mr. Caldwell was the first example of a renaissance man I have ever met. He is quite tall with lots of steel gray hair combed straight back from his face without a part. At 86, he holds his head high and his broad shoulders back. This grand, proud body was once an athlete's. It was not until he began to talk and move about that the multitude of medical assaults to this athlete's body became apparent. Even with these limitations, Mr. Caldwell is a tall southern gentleman who was once an athlete and who has maintained himself far better than many his same age.

His face is asymmetrical; on close inspection it pulls to the right when he talks because his left lower jaw and cheek are paralyzed from repeated surgeries to remove cancerous growths from his mouth and to reconstruct his jaw and face—a partial success. When he smiles, the hollow created in his left cheek becomes larger. The constant flow of saliva from his mouth is impossible to ignore, although more of a problem to the observer than to Mr. Caldwell himself. While he is aware of it and ministers to it vigilantly, his loss of sensation on that side of his mouth prevents him from always capturing it in a tissue before it finds its way to his clothing. His box of tissues is never far from his side, and his ritual of wiping is more like swatting away bothersome flies than concealing an embarrassing liquid.

Mr. Caldwell has residual motor loss on his right side that becomes apparent when he begins to walk. His gait is broad-based, slow, and deliberate. Climbing steps, of which there are many up to and inside his house, is a skilled, practiced maneuver, slow but flawless in execution. This learned precision is evident again when he signs informed consent forms in letter-perfect penmanship; using his left hand since his right and previously dominant hand has been rendered functionally useless since his stroke.

Mr. Caldwell was very attentive and eager to tell me about his life. His smile, his eyes and his attitude all pointed to the fact that his many medical problems are nuisances, but they would not stop him in his pursuit of learning and living his life. He is curious about what would happen to him, to others, and to the world.

Mrs. Harriet Chimes

Although short, Harriet Chimes stands tall and erect, with no dowager's hump on her back. A matronly bosom is outlined under her white shirt and navy blue jumper. At 89, her hair is naturally black with only wisps of white at her temples. Cut to her chin, her hair gently frames her face in soft waves, less well manicured in the back, perhaps because she cannot reach that part of her head. Her skin is smooth and the color of creamed coffee. She wears a four-diamond brooch on a chain around her neck, earrings, and her wedding ring.

She is a talker, and she talks with her mouth and hands and arms. She has a habit of punctuating her statements by lifting her right arm as high as she can and then dropping it down on the table. She often speaks quickly and quietly when she offers her own opinion on a subject. Harriet Chimes seems to have a hunger for talking, perhaps a symptom of her isolated lifestyle in a family dutifully taking care of mother. Our conversations were often interrupted by phone calls from her friends who, as she explained, were stuck in their houses like she was and trying to keep their friendships alive via telephone.

When I first met Harriet Chimes, she was sitting in her bedroom, which was down a ramped hallway from the kitchen and dining room. She stood up behind her wheeled walker, which is three fourths as tall as she is. Explaining that she had just awakened, her speech was slightly disjointed and difficult to understand. Quickly she regained herself and began giving me a tour of her room, as if she were fulfilling some unspoken need to orient me to her space. "This is my room, my bed, my desk. These are my things, my card table, and my windows. These are all my things from my house in Washington. There is my door to get to my car, isn't it all beautiful?" Then I realized she was not fulfilling my need but her own to let me know that even though she lived in her daughter's house, this room, this furniture, and this space were hers.

FINDINGS

Through the analysis of the research participants' stories (Baldwin, 1985; Labov & Waletzky, 1967) under the umbrella of Roger's optimistic framework, I found that growth and development do continue into the developmental period of the oldest-old and that the "losses" that these people experienced made life a little harder but no less exciting or meaningful to them. Following is a summary of my findings and as well as examples from the stories I listened to while interviewing the research participants (Noyes, 2001).

Each person's story is unique and supports the long-standing belief that older people become more heterogeneous as they age. There were some astounding similarities among the participants that support Roger's theory of aging that growth and development do continue with increasing age. Contrary to our myths of the uselessness of old age, all four people expressed a sense of purpose in their lives; they did not feel that they were just waiting to die.

Most of the participants had experienced changes in the roles and responsibilities they had at younger ages, but most felt they had taken on new roles and responsibilities of their own choosing. They all had a splendid sense of humor and were content with their own lives as they were living them, as evidenced by Fr. Larkin's chuckling at his doctor's comment about his health,

> One of our doctors said a consoling thing. He says, "Father, one thing, when you get to your age, most of the things that would be really, really bad things, you would have had by this time."

All of the research participants had future plans in their lives despite increasing physical frailties. Mr. Caldwell commented,

> So, I don't go out socially a hell of a lot anymore, but I look forward to life every day. Partially I want to know what's going on. And, I don't know if I can make it, but I hope to live to 2000. I want to see the 21st century coming in—I'm very grateful. I've had a very happy life.

Growth was mainly in the area of creativity and development of a more inclusive worldview of people and circumstances. Insight into their continued growth varied from person to person, but areas of growth in each person nonetheless occurred, as demonstrated in this comment by Fr. Larkin:

> Oh, I can say this much, that during the last half a dozen years, I have never felt myself—in my work of writing, creative writing—I've never felt myself so good at it and enjoying it as much as I did before...I love my work, because it's creative. I love to play with ideas and get new connections. I feel like more, much more now than I did before, and it has no connection with death. It's not that I'm saying I just have this much time left. It's just things are more fascinating to me.

Each participant had a different idea of what comes after death. Fr. Larkin believed, as he always had, that heaven and hell existed and that God would be waiting for him with open arms. When asked what he thought was going to happen after he died, he responded,

> Well, very simple. I'm in the 94th year. I know that 50 years from now I'm certainly not going to be here. I'll be gone sometime before that, and I have had to come to terms with it. And so many complex things are solved and can be made simple. I don't mind saying, and I don't say this as a boast, it's just simply a fact—it is what I tell these [college students in retreats]—I am passionately in love with Jesus. And I firmly believe, my faith [is] that death means going into His embrace. It's as simple as that. And while it's a little bit frightening, I'm following what good old Einstein said he believes. I believe, that as the Church says in the preface of the...funeral Mass, [the] Mass of Resurrection, speaking of the deceased, life has not ended, but changed. I believe that the life we're leaving here is just one life. The life we're living here is the first stage and the real living thing comes after what we call earthly death. So, I am scared every once in a while, being human, the thought's frightening. And then I go back, and I think of Christ, and that it simply means falling into His arms. This is theologically correct. And then I say, "I'm ready."

By contrast, Mr. Caldwell felt that he would live on in the minds and hearts of those who loved him:

> I think your immortality is certainly sure in the hearts and minds of people you've known and affected. I think in that sense, I don't think my children will forget me entirely, and I don't think friends [will] forget me entirely. I was...part of their life. And they in turn, when they die, they become a part of somebody else's life.

Mrs. Walters believed that she would be buried and would rise from the dead one day to be reunited with her husband, and she wanted to be buried in a specific dress so she would be ready to meet him:

> I read the Bible a lot, and that just tells you where you... see one another "but in the wink of the eye"...I'm being buried beside my husband, see? In the country at the church. And, I used to think, "Well, I'll get to see him by the wink of the eye someday."

Mrs. Chimes no longer held on to her earlier beliefs of heaven and hell. She did not know what would happen to her:

> All that kind of religion they used to talk about—hell and damnation and all that stuff—see, I don't do all that thinking about that. If there's a hereafter, I'll find out when I get there, I guess. I don't know about it. But, I know we're not going to stay here. Of course the church teaches [that the] soul goes to heaven, so, I have no idea. 'Cause wherever heaven is, wherever God is, I think that a lot of people make their own heaven and hell on earth. And I think [you have to try] to live as well as you can, [be] as happy as you can here, 'cause you don't know what's coming...That's part of my philosophy. Has been for a long, long time.

All of them have prepared for death in practical ways as well as coming to grips with the notion that death will come at some point. They have come to accept death as a reality in the future and they no longer fear it. They are ready for death but want to enjoy and live every minute of life that is left for them. Mr. Caldwell stated,

> So I began to absorb the idea that death was natural, just like birth...And there's no point in getting excited about it. It's coming to everybody. [N]obody wants it, except a few do who are mentally disturbed. So I take it as natural. The only cure I see is an interest in life. If you don't have that, I'd just as soon lie down and die now. The obsession of eating and sleeping and all that. You've got to have something to keep your mind and your soul going.

Mrs. Chimes, while not afraid of death, said that she prefers not to dwell on it:

> Well, I don't concentrate on dying. When I'm dead, I'll be dead. But just don't kill me before I'm dead. Otherwise, I don't worry about it. *Que sera sera.* 'Cause I try to live while I'm living. I'm not going to die anytime soon.

When I asked Mrs. Walters if she had ever thought of what the perfect death would be like for her, she responded,

> No, I never have really, to tell you the truth, 'cause I feel like I'm ready to go any time the Lord wants me. That's just the way I feel. The only time I ever felt like that I didn't, [that I] would hate to be buried [was] when I used to see them bury people in the ground, you know. I thought, "Gee willikers." But I was just a kid then. [I thought,] "When I get old, I'd hate to be going in the ground like that." But now I don't think anything about it anymore. Just don't seem to have to worry a bit. But I'm in good health. I think, well, I hate to go and leave Fred. And my children, you know.

All of them had dreams about people who were already dead or that were so real it was hard to distinguish reality and dream reality. Mrs. Chimes, for example, talked of a dream she had about her late husband:

> And [it's] only since I've been out [living in my daughter's house], very recently, [that] I even saw my husband in a dream. But I dream very little. Now I don't know what it was all about…[In the dream he didn't speak], it's just like maybe you saw an apparition.

When asked if the dream frightened her or made her uncomfortable, she responded,

> No, 'cause it came and went that quickly, and it just looked like Clarence, and that was it…It was near enough for me to know that it was he, you know. It was like I used to see him normally, with his suit and tie and everything on.

Fr. Larkin experienced a different kind of dream that reveals how thin the border is between waking reality and dream reality:

> It was one of these dreams where I'm in trouble. It was a dream, and I've used this as an example of how real things can be, and how sometimes the difference between reality and dreams is pretty darn thin. I can recall, I was somewhere, and I had a topcoat, and I left the topcoat somewhere. And I came back and it was gone. Somebody had stolen it. And then, the next morning, I found myself in my closet, reaching to assure myself that the topcoat was there. Now wasn't that interesting? What kind of a state of mind was I in? Or… which was reality? They were both realities, I think. I believe there are levels of reality.

Another interesting story about the "borders" between levels of realities came from Mrs. Walters, who told a story about her grandfather several times during the interview in which two people travel together until they come to a border where one person must go beyond the border and the other must stay behind. It reveals how she is trying to make sense of dying and leaving her son behind:

> My granddaddy, he was in the Civil War, you know. And he used to sit and tell me about how he did at the war, you know. Come home, and then go back to war, you see. That's about all I ever heard about olden times much, talking to my granddaddy...Well, just about going to the war, and that he was married three times, you know...[H]e didn't have no children by his first wife. And he used to say that she walked with him across the field when he'd come home on a furlough. And then he'd say, "Now you can't go any further. You'll have to go back." And I can always remember that.

When the study participants were asked what meaning life had for them and what they would tell younger people about it, all responded that "living by the golden rule" was very important and helping one another was a priority throughout life. Mrs. Chimes responded:

> You know, I have my own views, and I have views that were taught to me. I was raised Catholic, and we went to church, said the Lord made you—[this] is probably the basis. But my own theory is, as I was growing up and growing older, to be of service to other people, to do what I could for them, be kind to them, as well.

Each one recognized that he or she had special talents and that these talents should be used and "grown." Mrs. Walters spoke with pride of her ability to quickly learn new skills:

> Anything I saw somebody else do, I had to learn it, too. Didn't matter what it was. I would look at something and make it. That's what I did. Just look at something. Just look at something and do it. Look like I could just do it, I don't know why. Just seemed natural for me.

Fr. Larkin related the feelings of joy and transcendence he has had on occasion when speaking to a group of people and making a strong connection with them:

> It sounds a little bit boastful, but it's God that gives me whatever power I have. I may add it to my own power. Once, talking to the students up there...I was talking about Christ, our Lord, his personality and how they should be attached to him...and I was on a roll. I was kind of exalted! Oh, that's not the word. I was different. I knew I could do this audience, I could hold them. And I felt I had them in the palm of my hand, see. I couldn't repeat that right now. You get on a level of reality where you can do things that you can't do when you're not on a level reality. Does that make sense?

Most of all, they felt that life was given to them to be enjoyed, and, especially at their ages, they needed to find ways to stay connected to what was important to them and enjoy life.

Implications

All four subjects epitomized an optimistic view of aging: Perhaps believing that life over age 85 has positive aspects influences a person's resiliency and progress throughout this developmental period. As health care professionals, we should expect growth to continue and acknowledge this growth while caring for older adults.

We need to listen to the oldest-old tell us about what aging is like for them. With improvements in health care and medical treatments, the oldest-old who have no previous role models of great age are forging new territory in life. Health care professionals need to listen within an optimistic framework and learn from the oldest-old how they approach the border between life and death and how they prepare for it.

We can no longer limit the horizons of the oldest-old with an outdated social construct that holds that life in old age is only a downhill ride. Older people need the opportunity to talk about what death and dying will be like for them. Using an optimistic framework will help the oldest-old find growth in previously unexplored areas to balance the losses they may be experiencing.

Health care professionals also need to recognize that being developmentally near to death, as one is at age 85 or older, does not detract from the self-value of one's own life. My final exchange with Mrs. Walters shows how life and death can be viewed from the vantage point of the oldest-old, acknowledging both the losses and the growth. I told Mrs. Walters that she is a good role model and that when I reach 103 years old, I hope that I will remember her. She responded,

> Yeah, well I hope you live to be as old as I am and feel just as good as I do...[I hope you] don't suffer with no aches no more than I do. I don't suffer with any, just a little rheumatism in those two hands...Long as you can keep going and keep working and keep moving about, that's the best thing. Course if I am down too long, you know you get kind of stiff like. But I really can't complain about anything. I go to church with Fred every Sunday—Sunday School too. I love to go to church. I read my teacher's lips, and that means a lot, you know. I can look right at her face and... tell just what she's saying—read the words. Means a lot. [A] person never knows what they can do 'til they go through it once, ain't that right?

Lin E. Noyes, PhD, RN, is currently the Clinical Director of the Alzheimer's Family Day Center in Falls Church, Virginia. She is a founding member of the Alzheimer's Association, Northern Virginia Chapter, and was a member of the Public Policy Committee of the national Alzheimer's Association from 1989 to 1994. She also served on the Virginia Governor's Commission on Alzheimer's disease and Related Disorders from 1986 to 1994. She received her PhD in administration, health policy and ethics in Nursing at the College of Nursing and Health Sciences of George Mason University. She has developed holistic programs for people with Alzheimer's disease and their families from the early stages of their illness to end stage care.

REFERENCES

Baldwin, K. (1985). "Woof!" A Word on women's roles in family story telling. In R.A. Jordan & S.J. Kalcik (Eds.), *Women's folklore, women's culture* (pp. 146-163). Philadelphia: University of Pennsylvania Press.

Bell, S.E. (1988). Becoming a political woman: The reconstruction and interpretation of experience through stories. In A.D. Todd & S. Fisher (Eds.), *Gender and discourse* (pp. 97-123). Norwood, NJ: Ablex.

Cole, T.R. (1988). Aging, history and health: Progress and paradox. In J.F. Schroots, J.E. Birren, & A. Svanborg (Eds.), *Health and aging* (pp. 45-60). New York: Springer.

Denzin, N.K., & Lincoln, Y.S. (1998). Introduction: Entering the field of qualitative research. In N.K. Denzin & Y.S. Lincoln (Eds.). *The Landscape of qualitative research: Theories and issues*, (pp. 1-34). Thousand Oaks: Sage Publications, Inc.

Erikson, E.H. (1968). Life cycle. In D.L. Skills (Ed.), *International encyclopedia of the social sciences.* New York: Free Press & Macmillan.

Labov, W. & Waletsky, J. (1967). Narrative analysis: Oral versions of personal experience. In J. Helm (Ed.), *Essays on the visual and verbal arts* (pp. 12-44). Seattle: University of Washington Press.

Lawless, E.J. (1993). *Holy women, wholly women: sharing ministries of wholeness through life stories and reciprocal ethnography.* Philadelphia: University of Pennsylvania Press.

Lieblich, A., Tuval-Mashiach, R., & Zilber, T. (1998) *Narrative research: Reading, analysis, and interpretation* (pp. 62-63). Thousand Oaks, CA: Sage.

Miller, N. (1988). *Subject to change: Reading feminist writing.* New York: Columbia University Press.

Minkler, M. (1999). Introduction. In M. Minkler & C.L. Estes (Eds.), *Critical gerontology: Perspectives from political and moral economy.* Amnityville, NY: Baywood.

Noyes, L.E. (2001). Stories of the Oldest-Old as They Come to Face Death (Doctoral dissertation, George Mason University, 2001). Dissertation Abstracts International- B, 62/03.

Rogers, M.E. (1970). *An introduction to the theoretical basis of nursing.* Philadelphia: Davis.

Rogers, M.E. (1986). Science of unitary human beings. In V.M. Malinski (Ed.), *Explorations on Martha Rogers' science of unitary human beings* (pp. 3-8). Norwalk: Appleton-Century-Croft.

Sherman, E., & Webb, T.A. (1994). The self as process in late-life reminiscence: Spiritual attributes. *Aging and Society, 14*, 255-267.

PART II

Growing Old and Dying

This book recognizes that there is an anticipatory aspect to loss, particularly for older people. In her work, Therese Rando (2000) suggests that anticipatory mourning is a misnomer in referring to the mourning of an expected death. Rather, she sees anticipatory mourning as an ongoing adaptation to the losses experienced throughout the duration of an illness. This concept can be extended to a larger recognition, acknowledging that older persons may not only mourn illness-related losses but also developmental losses and the normal declines of senescence.

Part II of our book addresses the fundamental losses and realities of growing old and dying. It begins with another chapter from Lin Noyes, one that illustrates the losses that accompany Alzheimer's disease. This chapter discusses the evolution of Alzheimer's terminology, describes the psychological impact of the personal losses that occur with Alzheimer's, and offers strategies that caregivers can use to help those experiencing these losses.

Avery Weisman (1972) coined the term "middle knowledge" to refer to the fact that dying persons may move in and out of an awareness of impending death, sometimes acknowledging and discussing it, and other times denying and avoiding it. For health care professionals, this shifting awareness represents a challenge to communicating at the patient's pace while at the same time meeting the family's needs. In the next chapter, William Lamers focuses on the difficulty of communicating in the context of a life-threatening illness by identifying barriers and challenges to sensitive communication and offering suggestions for improvement.

Family dynamics can complicate effective communication, as illustrated by our first Voices piece in this section. Denise Jones's story of her mother's slow decline from a once-vibrant woman to one experiencing multiple illnesses reminds us of the myriad losses that stem from chronic illness and how family roles can complicate the experience.

Paul Irion's chapter addresses a very important aspect of the emotional and psychological experience of older individuals: the need to retain a sense of hope. This hope, which can be expressed in many ways, is the center of spiritual care.

Several chapters in this section provide the context for—and discuss the question of—where older persons die. William Novelli offers an overview of what he terms "the spectrum of care." Novelli's chapter affirms the need for early intervention and careful case management to help people live as fully as they can in later life. Novelli calls for policy re-evaluation and reform and discusses an initiative of the AARP in its advocacy on behalf of older persons.

Ashley Davis Prend's *Practical Suggestions* piece reminds us that programs do not always have to be institutionally based. Prend's account of arranging regular visits to a nursing home for her young children reinforces the value of volunteer efforts and reminds us of the mutual benefits of intergenerational programs.

Timothy Keay points out that many older individuals die in nursing homes, and he suggests developing hospice programs within nursing homes. This idea is touched on earlier in the Lamers chapter. It reinforces the idea that hospice, at its best, can serve as a model for end-of-life care and clear and sensitive communication. Hospice programs in nursing homes should be encouraged to develop bereavement services similar to those now offered by hospices to survivors. Within nursing homes, these services could be offered to nursing aides, fellow residents, and roommates, who are all affected by a resident's death.

Stephen Connor's chapter suggests that the hospice ideal—palliative, holistic, family-oriented care—offers a model for the care of older adults. The chapter that follows, by Mark Waymack, complements those by Connor and Keay. It focuses on the ethical issues that derive from the fact that the most common setting for hospice care is the patient's own home. Waymack points out that many of the issues we think of as administrative or organizational are, in fact, ethical issues. One example is the difficulty of disclosing the fact of impending death. This can present a barrier to family members who may want hospice services but at the same time want to insulate themselves, the patient, or other loved ones from the clear knowledge of impending death.

With the last *Practical Suggestions* piece in this section, we acknowledge that the end of life brings to light administrative concerns such as settling final arrangements. Making such arrangements can be therapeutic, providing individuals with the opportunity for at least a symbolic mastery of their deaths. Although people who are dying cannot control the reality of death, they do have some control over end-of-life decisions, including those about their funerals and the disbursement of their estates. Jane Dryden Louis offers specific advice to encourage such decision making; she suggests planning a Final Affairs Fair. The purpose of such an event is to provide information about the choices available to older individuals as they put their affairs in order.

The last chapter in this section, which I have written, addresses what I call disenfranchised grief. The chapter discusses the many losses and hidden sorrows experienced by older individuals—those encountered in the course of life and those caused by a death. ■

References

Rando, T.A. (2000). *Clinical dimensions of anticipatory mourning.* Champaign, IL: Research Press.

Weisman, A. (1972). *On dying and denying: A psychiatric study of terminality.* New York: Behavioral Publications.

CHAPTER 6

Loss and Alzheimer's Disease

Lin E. Noyes

INTRODUCTION

When I teach body mechanics to new staff members at the day center, we talk about what to do when someone starts to fall. The rule is: Protect the head and ease the person to the ground. It is counterproductive to try to stop the person from falling because both the caregiver and the person falling will get hurt.

When helping a person descending into Alzheimer's disease, we should follow similar advice: We should cradle the humanity of the person as he or she falls into Alzheimer's disease because, like cradling the head in a fall, the humanity is what is important to protect as the disease progresses. We can't stop the descent, but we can preserve a person's dignity and humanity throughout the ravages of the disease.

When the first ripples of awareness about Alzheimer's disease (AD) and other similar dementias crept into our sights 20 years ago, these diseases were thought to strip away a person's human essence, bit by bit, until there was nothing left. This concept is well described by Cohen and Eisdorfer (1986):

> Loss of sight, hearing, an arm, or a leg challenges a person to cope with significant change. However, the victim of Alzheimer's disease must eventually come to terms with a far more frightening prospect—the complete loss of self. (p. 22)

This view of "the Alzheimer's victim" predominated and is evidenced in the focus on caregiving and helping the *families* of AD patients in the early 80s because it was believed that nothing could be done for "the victim." Being an Alzheimer's patient was like being a passenger on a very bad journey, on which haloperidol and banishment to the nursing home were the only things that could be done to ease the descent of the victims into oblivion.

Our evolving understanding of the losses of AD mirrors the growth of research and knowledge about the disease over the last 20 years. It also reflects an increasing awareness of how the disease affects the person who is diagnosed with the illness and his or her family caregivers.

It has been said that if you know one person with AD, you know one person with AD. Keeping in mind that each person is very different and that symptoms may present differently from one person to the other, this chapter begins with a discussion of terminology and then turns to describing loss as it occurs to people in the early, middle, and later stages of AD. Finally, it offers health care professionals some suggestions to help people who are experiencing these losses.

From "Victim" to "Person"

Our language reflects our values and beliefs. The use of the term Alzheimer's victim in the early 80s reflected a lack of knowledge about the disease and about what could be done to help the person whose life had been sacrificed to AD. Later in the decade we used the terms *Alzheimer's patients* and *Alzheimer's residents*, which reflected a growing awareness that at least these people needed care even though the emphasis was on the disease rather than the person.

In the late 80s and early 90s, people diagnosed with AD began to describe what it's like to have this disease. We began to hear more about public figures who were diagnosed with or had died from AD. This knowledge made it harder to think about them as *victims* or *patients* and made us acknowledge that it is indeed a person who gets AD. Diana Friel McGowan's book, *Living in the Labyrinth: A Personal Journey Through the Maze of Alzheimer's* (1993), is a revelation of what people in the early stages of Alzheimer's experience. This passage from McGowan's book shows how her humanity, her "self," is affected by the disease:

> As I march—or am dragged—further into Alzheimer's disease, I am less ashamed of my more primal urges. Consequently, I am also far less judgmental of others for theirs. Perhaps it is a result of premature dementia but I think not. It is more likely the realization that I am probably coming toward my final stretch—that I have experienced many "last times" without understanding they were, indeed, the last time. This knowledge enables me to savor life more openly and ravenously. I appreciate all good things more, whether they be trusted friends, cherished memories, nature's beauty—or physical pleasures. (p. 87)

It was only in the middle to late 90s that the depth of losses brought by AD became apparent, as people were diagnosed earlier and earlier in the disease process, some with exquisite insight into what was happening to them. People much further into the disease process began to express their personal losses, and caregivers began to contemplate how their actions affected the person and his or her experience with Alzheimer's disease. The use of the term *person with AD* reflected the belief that it is a person of value who experiences AD. Accepting the reality that being a person is more than remembering and being able to use brain functions helped normalize our view of people with Alzheimer's disease.

This expanded view of people with Alzheimer's shed light on the dimensions of loss of the disease. There are three kinds of losses in AD. The first is caused by brain deterioration and results in decreased cognition and function. The second kind of loss arises from people's awareness of what the disease is doing to them as human beings. The third and greatest loss occurs when a person loses the recognition by others that he or she is a fellow human being.

In discussions of Alzheimer's disease, we often find it useful to speak of the three stages—early, middle, and late—that typify the progressive nature of the disease. While this can be helpful in discussing the disease in general, we need to recognize the individual nature of the illness. In any individual case, clear evidence of stages may be absent. Each person with AD will show a unique pattern of decline.

Losses in the Early Stages of Alzheimer's

Even before a person is diagnosed with AD, losses begin to appear. Sam, a fellow in our early stage support group, told me he could attribute many of his early symptoms of AD before diagnosis to stress or being overworked, but the day he could not fill out his time sheet, which he had been doing for 15 years, hit him like a hammer in the middle of his forehead. He could no longer deny that something was terribly wrong.

This initial awareness that something was very, very wrong still ranks as the greatest loss he had experienced in the three years he has had the disease. For it was in that moment that he realized that his life had changed and would never be the same. His loss of the memory of how to fill out the time sheet was miniscule compared to what the loss of that little memory would mean in his life. Today, even though his words are few and his thoughts are sketchy, he still tries to tell about the day he couldn't fill out his time sheet and shakes his head as if he were remembering the worst day of his life.

Paula lost her confidence in herself in the early days of her dementia even though her mini-mental scores remained normal for several years. Knowing that she was highly intelligent and experiencing trouble with the math needed to do simple bills made her very sad. She knew she was sliding into dementia, and while she was eager to fight it and advocate for herself and others who had Alzheimer's, she became overwhelmingly sad. Issues of continued independence in making business deals, driving the car, and even walking her daily four-mile course by herself were points of contention between her husband and herself. She would argue that she knew she was slipping but was not ready to give up these things that meant so much to her...not yet.

These arguments led to the loss of her husband as a confidant, a lover, and a friend because in her view, he was not helping her, just trying to take things away from her. The warmth and comfort they gave one another were lost to both. Her suspiciousness led to her alienating her friends over time as she accused them of siding with her husband. While she was aware on some level that she was doing this, she could not stop it and she mourned the losses.

The time before and after diagnosis, and into the first couple of years of the illness, people's lives revolve around themes of loss: loss of their roles and responsibilities, loss of their future, fear of loss of their past, and the inevitable loss of independence and purposefulness. Along the way, as people begin to lose cognitive functioning, many people are fully aware of their loss.

Losses in the Middle Stages

Jack had been attending our day center for two years as a member of our midstage group. He had to be shown to the bathroom each time he needed to use it, had to be reminded about eating, and needed some cueing to finish a meal. He had apraxia (loss of the ability to carry out familiar, purposeful movements), which complicated his ability to put on his coat or use his silverware. The one thing he still enjoyed was fitting various colored rubber pieces into a grid to make a doormat. He was quite proud of each doormat design he made and showed them to everyone who came into the room.

His ability to communicate was hampered by serious problems finding words. It could take five minutes to find out that he wanted to know when his wife was coming to pick him up. On the other hand, he laughed at jokes and groaned when they weren't particularly funny. He still maintained his awareness and general orientation; he knew when he was at the day center and recognized his wife and the center staff (not necessarily by name). For the most part, he found such satisfaction doing the doormats and felt so supported in his environment that he accepted our cues and redirections fairly easily.

One day he came out of the men's room crying, sobbing inconsolably. He kept saying over and over, "Now it's gone too!" It took me a while to figure out what the "it" was, but finally I discovered that he could no longer manipulate the zipper on his pants to urinate by himself. He was reluctant to accept help but didn't like the alternative any better.

Once again, while there was a loss of function due to Alzheimer's disease, the real loss occurred in Jack's perception of what the function meant to him as a man and as a person. Because we were all matter-of-fact in our approach and respected his privacy as much as we could, he was not embarrassed and was able to maintain his stature at the center.

Losses in the Later Stages

Marge was about 80 years old when she came into our late stage program and was fairly advanced in her illness. She continued to live at home with her daughter, son-in-law, and their nine children. She came to the center three days a week to give the daughter a chance to spend time alone with the younger children.

Marge could put finger food in her mouth and swallow but needed help with liquids and items requiring a spoon or fork. She was incontinent and didn't like taking help at changing times. She uttered the same words or phrases over and over again. She walked through the center, calling out what seemed to be nonsense to the staff. She would have walked out the door but for the staff keeping a close watch on her.

Marge's calling out behavior became increasingly difficult to manage and became disruptive to the rest of the participants at the center. It seemed to increase in the afternoon. I asked the daughter if she had this behavior at home. The daughter acknowledged that she did, but just for a short time in the afternoon right before the school bus arrived with the majority of the family's children. I asked the daughter what happened after the kids got home, and she said they all sat around the TV and ate dry cereal for a snack. The calling out behavior may well have stemmed from the loss of Marge's afternoon routine, the loss of TV companions, and the loss of her crunchy cereal. Most of all, her feelings of being safe and feeling connected to other human beings were missing from her center routine. Since she could no longer participate in many of the activities, she may have felt lost in the afternoons. Needless to say, when Marge began calling out, she was led to the couch, seated snugly between two other participants, and given her crunchy cereal.

Helping Strategies

Tom Kitwood's book, *Dementia Reconsidered: The Person Comes First* (1997), provides a framework and a challenge to the caregiver to see the person first and then acknowledge both the losses and the wellness of the person. He states that a person doesn't lose his personhood because he has dementia. He defines personhood as "a standing status that is bestowed upon one human being, by others, in the context of relationships and social being. It implies recognition, respect and trust." (p. 8)

A humanistic framework such as Kitwood's assumes that the disease affects brain cells and behavior but does not erode the personhood of an individual. It assumes that a person, regardless of the level of disability, has the right to be treated with dignity, respect, and caring. Finally it assumes that, at some level, all interactions and stimuli in the environment of a person with AD have some effect on that person even when we believe the person is beyond perceiving.

Early Interventions

People in the early stages need support, education, and help to plan for their future. They need to feel that although they stand at the edge of losing control, there are ways they can extend their wants and desires into the future by making decisions about what they want to happen as the disease progresses.

Support groups give people in the early stages of AD the opportunity to see others who are experiencing similar losses and thereby decrease their sense of isolation. Support group can be a place where people can say how angry it makes them when they can't find their cars in the parking lot and how stupid they feel when they can't open the locks on the doors. They talk about medications they have tried and research projects and news they have heard about AD. Group members provide a sounding board for each other to discuss situations that are going on at home. Because they are in the group, they give and receive support; they have roles and responsibilities within the group.

After the first early-stage support group we held, I asked the people attending the group if they thought it was useful. They all agreed that it was. One man responded that being at that group had given him hope—not hope that he would get better but hope that it wasn't going to be as hard as he had thought.

People in the early stages need education to clear up the myths about what Alzheimer's disease is like and what is likely to happen to them as the disease progresses. They need to hold onto their hope that they will not become "like their father was" and that they will have opportunities to learn about research and new treatments. They also need to learn what they can do to keep themselves as healthy as they can be and to keep their minds working for as long as possible. For example, physical exercise benefits their well-being not only by helping their physical condition but also by improving their mood. Cognitive exercises may improve cognitive functioning for a while (Quayhagen, Quayhagen, Corbeil, Roth, & Rogers, 1995). People with AD also get a psychological boost from knowing that they can actively do something to fight the effects of the disease. Staying connected to people and involved in life not only stimulates the brain but energizes the person.

Middle Stages

Keeping in mind that respect and dignity should be maintained regardless of the stage in the illness, caregivers are challenged by the middle stages of AD, when the person's daily living skills are evaporating.

The goal here is to encourage the person to do as much of a task as he or she can do and to step in only when necessary. Sometimes the caregiver acts as a coach, other times the caregiver is an assistant, and occasionally the caregiver has to do most of the task for the person. Unnecessary losses occur when the caregiver does what the person can still do—even if the caregiver can do it more rapidly. The person loses not only the ability to do the task but also his or her sense of satisfaction and usefulness.

Purposeful activity and routine replace the person's loss of initiative and ability to remember the sequence of events. Failure-free activities that also challenge the person promote feelings of industry and mastery. Art and music therapy can help a person tap into creativity and imagination. The sense of art and beauty does not seem to diminish as rapidly as words, memory, or problem solving. Humor also keeps the person connected to others.

People in the middle stages of AD may also begin to forget who they are and what has been important to them. Caregivers ought to know the person's background and be able to tell the person his or her own story. Saying something as simple as "Tom, you take your coffee black, right?" or "Yes, your wife, Susie, will be here at 4 o'clock" can help a person stay connected to his own life. When people and their stories are separated, they become patients or victims again; they are recognized only by their accumulation of losses.

Late Stage AD

People in the later stages of AD are increasingly dependent on their caregivers for all their activities of daily living. Their need to feel connected to other human beings and to interact with their environment has not diminished. When all meaningful speech is gone, people may relax or be comforted with singing, listening to music, or being in motion. Nonverbal communication (voice tone, eye contact, body language) becomes very important and can express care, concern, and respect. Smiling and using a soothing tone of voice help a person feel safe.

Sometimes the ability to understand lasts longer than a person's ability to speak. Since it is impossible to assess what a person understands, it is best to assume that he or she understands everything. Before beginning to help, tell the person what you are about to do. The words and the tone address the humanity, even if the words are not fully understood.

Physical touch and sensory stimulation help minimize the feeling of being disconnected from the environment. Exercise (even passive range of motion) diminishes the discomfort of stiff joints. Hand and leg massage can improve circulation and provide the human touch that everyone needs.

Even in the very late stages of AD, when people may have to be fed by the caregiver, meal times should be more than simply taking in nutrition. Telling the person what he or she is eating or whether a food is hot or cold can heighten the sensory experience of a meal.

Underneath it all, people with Alzheimer's have needs and desires common to every human. They feel scared in new surroundings, they long for something familiar. They want to do things well and be appreciated. They want to express their opinion and be able to make choices and have influence in their arena of companions. They want to understand and feel understood. They want others to know their story; they want to be reminded of their loved ones and the things that were important to them, even when they can no longer remember by themselves.

The greatest losses encountered by people with Alzheimer's are not necessarily caused by the disease. Often, they are caused by the failure of others to recognize the person's humanity. Recognizing a person's humanity, using strategies to minimize the losses caused by Alzheimer's disease, and helping the person live every moment with as much life as is possible should be the goal of all those who care for people with Alzheimer's disease.

Lin E. Noyes, PhD, RN, is currently the Clinical Director of the Alzheimer's Family Day Center in Falls Church, Virginia. She is a founding member of the Alzheimer's Association, Northern Virginia Chapter, and was a member of the Public Policy Committee of the national Alzheimer's Association from 1989 to 1994. She also served on the Virginia Governor's Commission on Alzheimer's disease and Related Disorders from 1986 to 1994. She received her PhD in administration, health policy and ethics in Nursing at the College of Nursing and Health Sciences of George Mason University. She has developed holistic programs for people with Alzheimer's disease and their families from the early stages of their illness to end stage care.

References

Cohen, D., & Eisdorfer, C. (1986). *The loss of self: A family resource for the care of Alzheimer's disease and related disorders.* New York: Penguin Books USA.

Kitwood, T. (1997). *Dementia reconsidered: The person comes first.* Philadelphia: Open University Press.

McGowan, D.F. (1993). *Living in the labyrinth: A personal journey through the maze of Alzheimer's.* San Francisco: Elderbooks.

Quayhagen, M.P., Quayhagen, M., Corbeil, R., Roth, P., & Rogers, J. (1995). A dyadic remediation program for care recipients with dementia. *Nursing Research, 44* (3), 153-159)

Additional Reading

Fazio, F., Seman, D., & Stansell, J. (1999). *Rethinking Alzheimer's care.* Baltimore: Health Professions Press.

Noyes, L.E., Daley, P., & French, K. (2000). Community-based services help people in the early stages of Alzheimer's disease and other cognitive impairments. *American Journal of Alzheimer's Disease,* September–October, 309-314.

Noyes, L.E., & Wexler, M. (2001). *Caregiving at a glance: for professionals assisting people with Alzheimer's disease and related illnesses.* Falls Church: Alzheimer's Family Day Center Publication.

Snyder, L. (1999). *Speaking our minds: Personal reflections from individuals with Alzheimer's.* New York: W.H. Freeman & Co.

Volicer, L., & Hurley, A. (1998). *Hospice care for patients with advanced progressive dementia.* New York: Springer Publishing Co.

CHAPTER 7

Communicating with Families during Advanced Illness

William M. Lamers, Jr.

INTRODUCTION

Most Americans are familiar with the oil painting from more than a century ago that shows a physician seated in a thoughtful pose at the bedside of a young patient. This memorable scene represents what many envision as the ideal: a physician present in the home, at the patient's bedside, observing, caring for, and supporting a seriously ill patient.

Since the advent of the hospice a quarter century ago, more people are being cared for at home during the final stages of life. Yet physicians rarely make home visits. This places increased emphasis on excellent communication between physicians and those caring for patients in the home (Lamers, 1990).

The rise of group medical practice and the wide application of managed care have changed the practice of medicine and further complicated patient-physician communication. Gatekeepers abound in medical offices to take messages, to enhance physician productivity, and to maintain reasonable separation between the tightly scheduled physician and callers seeking everything from prescription refills to questions about bothersome symptoms.

Today, cellular phones, pagers, answering machines, and the Internet offer multiple options for communication. Medical data and even live video can be transmitted via phone lines from a patient's home to the physician's office. Yet the basic difficulties in patient-physician communication have not diminished. This brief chapter examines some of the problems inherent in the specific area of patient-physician communication in the care and treatment of patients with advanced illness.

Communication

Communication, in simplest terms, is the transmission and reception of meaningful messages. Successful communication requires a clear message that is received and understood by the intended recipient. When we attempt to communicate through a third party or leave a message on an answering machine, we run the risk that the message may be mislaid, not forwarded, misunderstood, erased, or delayed. When we do not receive a reply in a reasonable period of time, we experience disappointment, frustration, and perhaps anger, depending on the urgency of the situation (Calland, 1972).

Communication between patient and physician is fairly easy when all goes well. In trying clinical situation, however, communication can deteriorate even when the physician provides clear, timely messages. There are a number of barriers that can impede the communication process.

Disordered Communication

Disordered communications occur when strong emotions such as fear impede even seemingly clear communications. Several years ago I observed an unusual example of disordered communication. A woman with advanced cancer complained to me that she was upset with her oncologist, who, she claimed did not answer her questions. I suggested transfer to the care of another oncologist and spoke with one noted for his skill at communicating with patients. I accompanied the woman to her first appointment with the new oncologist and sat in on the first half of their appointment. I observed that the new oncologist carefully listened to her history and thoughtfully answered one question after another in easily understandable language. I returned to my office where I was joined later by the patient. I expected her to thank me for arranging for the new oncologist. Instead, I was surprised when she began by saying, "Did you see that? He didn't answer my questions?" This otherwise credible woman was not able to process what the oncologist was saying, no doubt because of the implication of his answers to her direct questions. She had difficulty accepting what the new oncologist said and therefore was unable to process what he was saying. Fear got in the way. One way to counter this problem is to ask patients to repeat *in their own words* what the doctor has just said.

Many years ago a friend asked me to tell him what his chances were for survival from his recently diagnosed cancer of the pancreas. At the time we spoke, I did not know that his surgeon and oncologist had not told him his grim prognosis. Without inquiring further about what he knew and did not know, I thoughtlessly broke the news to my friend. He was shocked and abruptly withdrew from me. It has been said that good judgment comes from experience; that experience came from bad judgment. From that day forward, I have been more circumspect when answering patient's questions about their prognosis.

Children with advanced illness can be disarmingly straightforward. An adolescent girl with osteogenic sarcoma called me one night to say she had some questions and wanted to see me. I drove to her home. Her parents, who were still grieving the death of her only sibling a year earlier, were seated outside. Before the patient could ask her questions, I said, "I need to know what kind of answer you want. Do you want the truth…or do you want me to make up a story?" She said she wanted the truth. In brief, she wanted to know if her advancing symptoms meant she was dying. In as gentle a manner as possible, I let her know that her cancer was spreading and that there was little likelihood of its being cured. She responded to each answer with horrendous crying that lasted for several minutes. When she regained her composure, she said that if she was dying she wanted some chocolate cake. Her parents had told her she could not have any cake because a "healer" they had consulted in desperation had told them that if she refrained from eating sweets her cancer would be cured.

Nonverbal Communication

We generally think of communication in terms of verbal communication. Yet nonverbal communication is very important. Goffman (1967) reminds us that glances, gestures, positioning, and things such as tone and cadence communicate as loudly as words.

A patient of mine with a seriously disabling but not life-threatening illness flew to a distant city for a medical consultation. As she left the doctor's office he handed her a religious medal. She misinterpreted this gesture as an indication that she was going to die. The physician did not realize that his benevolent, nonverbal gesture would be misinterpreted as a death sentence.

A surgeon once told me that he experienced fear and discomfort when he had to deliver what he called a "death sentence" diagnosis. He never fully entered the patient's room, but stood near the door and talked steadily until he backed out of the room without letting the patient say a word. His greatest fear was that if he stopped talking, the patient might say something that would cause the surgeon to lose control and cry.

Conspiracy to Withhold Information

Occasionally a family requests that their relative not be told the diagnosis. They ask, in essence, for health care professionals to engage in a conspiracy to delude the patient. The doctrine of informed consent, now widely employed in the United States, undercuts the development of such informational conspiracies that were once quite common.

Challenges For Communication

Despite the myriad considerations and obstacles, the physicians must surmount these barriers if they are to effectively meet the challenges they face in communicating with patients and families. These challenges include communicating the diagnosis, communicating hope, and communicating death.

Challenge to Communicate the Diagnosis

What should a patient be told? Stewart Alsop in his memoir, *Stay of Execution (1973)*, wisely suggested that a patient should be told "the truth, and nothing but the truth—but not the whole truth." Diagnosis and prognosis should be conveyed in unambiguous language, free of euphemisms. The doctrine of informed consent, now the rule in the United States, mandates that patients be told their treatment options, possible side effects, and the anticipated outcomes of various treatment alternatives.

Patients and families need time to understand the implications of diagnosis, prognosis, and treatment alternatives in serious illness. Arthur Ablin, a pediatric oncologist at the University of California Medical Center in San Francisco, invites the entire family (including grandparents) to the diagnostic conference. After discussing the diagnosis, prognosis, and treatment alternatives, Dr. Ablin and his staff answer questions. The family is then given an audiotape of the entire session and told to replay it as needed to clarify what has been said.

Breaking the news about a difficult diagnosis is never easy. When it is done over the phone, as is sometimes the case, complications can develop. I received a call from a friend a while ago who told me that he had recently had an appointment for a complete annual physical. A week later the doctor called and said, "The lab tests are back, Tom, and you have cancer of the prostate." Tom asked what that meant and the doctor replied, "Well, Tom...we all have to die some day." Although this doctor was trying to break bad news in a gentle way, his awkwardness created confusion and fear in his patient. When communicating a diagnosis, physicians and other health professionals must find a balance of candor, clarity, and compassion.

Challenge to Communicate Hope

One of the major problems associated with informing patients about their diagnosis and prognosis is reducing their hope. Some patients tend to minimize the significance of their illness; others automatically fear the worst and leap to unreasonable conclusions. When I worked in a cancer center, local newspapers wrote about a sudden increase in deaths of young women from cervical cancer. After this article appeared, on the evening following biopsy of her cervical lesions, a young single mother made a successful suicide attempt. Later we learned that her lesion was not malignant. For whatever reason, fear of cancer supervened and she saw no reason to hope that she might survive.

Hope has been described as the chance greater than zero of a positive outcome. Hope is a fragile element in advanced illness. It can also be a powerful force in influencing the course of illness. Those of us in hospice who worked with her will always recall the lady who said repeatedly, "I am going to walk again, Praise the Lord." She had advanced breast cancer with metastases to her spine that caused paralysis from her waist to her toes. She was bedridden but filled with confidence. We did not dare confront the strong and obviously misplaced hope that was central to her being. We knew she would never walk again. Yet somehow before her death, she was able to boost herself up with both arms and took several faltering steps.

On the other hand, a physician I worked with many years ago told me how a fellow medical school professor was diagnosed with a brain tumor that was deemed to be malignant because of its characteristics. His fellow physicians gradually stopped visiting; he was transferred to a back room on the ward and his condition deteriorated. After he died, an autopsy revealed the presence of an encapsulated, nonmalignant brain tumor that could have been safely removed by surgery. The physician who died was described as "catching the diagnosis" (an incorrect diagnosis) from his medical colleagues (Aring, 1971).

Challenge to Communicate Death

When death is sudden and unanticipated, physicians are sometimes involved in informing the next of kin. It is essential that the person informing the survivor be unambiguous and that the message be conveyed in a timely manner. Several years ago a patient died unexpectedly during the night of a heart attack after being hospitalized for an unrelated illness. Her physician was called and told of the untimely death of his patient. The physician, in turn, telephoned the husband and said, "Your wife is no longer with us." The husband arrived at the hospital the next afternoon during regular visiting hours and inquired about his wife's present location. Shortly thereafter, I was called to help deal with the husband's justifiable rage, confusion and loss. He had no idea from what he had been told that his wife had died during the previous night.

While on active duty with the U.S. Navy Medical Corps during the Vietnam War, I observed the impact of announcing an unanticipated death to a seriously disturbed patient on a locked psychiatric unit. The hospital administrator received notice that the wife of a patient had died of an unanticipated heart attack. As the officer on call for the psychiatric unit, I was notified. I had the option of not informing the husband, who happened to be on a locked unit because of his violent physical outbursts, and deferring the situation until his own psychiatrist returned from a holiday weekend three days later. I believed that the man deserved to know that his wife had died. I made several phone calls to check on the accuracy of the information. Then I went to the man's ward, read his chart and asked a corpsman to wait outside the door of a conference room. After I introduced myself to the man, I told him I had some difficult news for him. I gradually told him that we had learned that his wife had experienced a heart attack. I next told him that his wife did not recover, that she had died. His initial reaction was one of disbelief followed by anger rising out of the paranoia that precipitated his psychiatric hospitalization. In time he came to sense that I was telling the truth, and his anger turned to tears and heavy sobbing with outbursts of guilt and self-recrimination. During the next hour he managed to put the difficult situation into reasonable focus, which prompted me to ask the commanding officer for permission to authorize emergency leave so the man could attend to his wife's death and organize her funeral. The man flew by commercial airline, behaved in a rational manner, and upon his return several days later was discharged from the hospital.

A different challenge developed for me several years ago, when I was working at a cancer center. A young woman was dying of cancer. Her parents, who lived several hundred miles away, were called and told that it was time for them to come to say goodbye. On their way to the city where their daughter was hospitalized they were both killed in an auto accident. The team treating the daughter debated about whether or not to tell her why her parents could not visit as promised. One faction said that the shock would surely kill her; the other side claimed she deserved to know. Reluctantly, her physician decided to tell the truth about what had happened. To everyone's surprise the young woman smiled and said, "I'll see them tomorrow." The next day she died.

How Hospice Can Help

Hospice has proven to be tremendous resource for dying persons, their families, and their physicians. Since its inception in the United States in the mid-1970s, hospice has expanded to more than 3,000 programs that provided care to some 700,000 patients last year. Excellent communication is at the center of hospice care at its best. Hospice facilitates communication between physician and caregiver, relays concise and clear reports on changes in patient condition to the treating physician, and coordinates the work of the interdisciplinary team with family and community caregivers. When indicated, hospice serves as an advocate for the patient and family. Hospice also serves to clarify physician orders, to implement strategies for pain and symptom management, and to prepare the patient, family, and caregivers for anticipated changes in the patient's condition.

All of this requires excellent, clear, and timely communication among hospice staff as well as between the attending physician and the patient and family. The ease of communication among hospice staff enables rapid response to calls for information or assistance, 24 hours a day, seven days a week. Hospice programs get some idea of the importance of availability through the way in which patients often make a night-time call within a few days of enrolling in hospice "just to see if someone is going to answer."

Summary and Conclusion

Communication is critically important during end-stage illness, especially when discussing matters related to dying and death. The clearer the message, the more likely it will be received, understood, and responded to. Euphemisms generally have no place in communications in advanced illness. Each physician has his or her own particular preferences in receiving and responding to messages. Patients and caregivers should ask for clarification on the best way to contact a physician when help is needed. Advance directives clearly communicate patient preferences for care at the end of life. Preparation of these documents can facilitate communication if and when the illness progresses. Hospice can be of great assistance in easing communication when patients experience increasing symptoms. Hospice personnel are available 24 hours a day, seven days a week. They know the patient, are expert in pain and symptom management, and will make visits to the home as needed (Lamers, 2001).

To conclude, I want to share an example of communication with a patient with advanced illness. The physician is Sir William Osler, the most famous practitioner in American medicine. The patient is a little girl with a fatal illness. This story was first told in a letter written by the girl's mother and published in Harvey Cushing's 1940 biography of Dr. Osler. It was retold more than three decades later in *The Understanding Physician* (Aring, 1971):

> He visited our little Janet twice every day from the middle of October until her death, a month later, and these visits she looked forward to with pathetic eagerness and joy....Instantly the sick room was turned into a fairyland, and in fairy language he would talk about the flowers, the birds and the dolls. In the course of this he would find out all he wanted to know about the little patient. The most exquisite moment came one cold, raw, November morning, when the end was near, and he brought out from his pocket a beautiful red rose, carefully wrapped in paper, and told how he had watched this last rose of summer growing in his garden and how the rose had called out to him as he passed by, that she wished to go with him to see his "little Lassie." That evening we all had a fairy tea party, at a tiny table near the bed, Sir William talking to the rose, his little lassie, and her mother in a most exquisite way. And the little girl understood that neither fairies nor people could always have the color of a red rose in their cheeks, or stay as long as they wanted in one place, but that they nevertheless would be happy in another home and must not let the people they left behind, particularly their parents, feel badly about it; and the little girl understood and was not unhappy. (p. 169) ■

William M. Lamers, Jr., MD, is one of the first physicians to develop a hospice program in the United States with the Hospice of Marin in northern California in the mid-1970s. He helped establish the first program to train people to develop hospices and served as the chair of the Standards and Accreditation Committee of the National Hospice and Palliative Care Organization. Dr. Lamers is the author of many books on hospice care, grief, and bereavement. He is currently Hospice Foundation of America's Medical Consultant.

References

Alsop, S. (1973). *Stay of execution.* New York: Lippincott.

Aring, C. (1971). *The understanding physician.* Detroit: Wayne State University Press.

Calland, C. (1972). Iatrogenic problems in end-stage renal failure. *New England Journal of Medicine 287*(7):334-336.

Cushing, H. (1940). *The life of Sir William Osler.* London: Oxford University Press.

Goffman, E. (1967). *Interaction ritual.* New York: Anchor-Doubleday.

Lamers, W. (1990). Hospice: Enhancing the quality of life. *Oncology 4* (5):121-126.

Lamers, W. (2001). *What caregivers need from doctors.* Washington, DC: Hospice Foundation of America.

CHAPTER 8

Voices

My Maggie Memories

Denise C. Jones

As I listened to the family reunion audiotapes from 1987, and I hear my mother, Maggie, debating the political scene of World War II with her brother-in-law, Levi, and his brother Frank, I thought, my God! Listen to this very opinionated, authoritative, extremely knowledgeable woman. Storytelling and political analysis have always been captivating to me, and I know the same was true for Momma.

Because we were the children of working parents, we learned to be independent at a young age (cooking, cleaning, knowing how to lock up the house, etc.) In spite of the fact that Momma seemed to work constantly, there was never a day that we didn't eat a hearty breakfast and have huge lunches and dinners because my mother always had food cooked and ready to be heated up at a moment's notice. Sure, McDonald's and the corner stores were around, and as kids we were itching for the moment that my parents allowed us to buy burgers and fries at the Red Barn, but Momma, being the southern-bred woman that she is, believed children should always have a warm breakfast before leaving the house each day, preceded by a good dose of cod liver oil. She was never big on eating any meal out, believing that no restaurant could feed her or her children as well as she could. She was right. Throughout our childhood, we were healthy children—never a broken bone or major illness outside of the typical measles and chicken pox. After being raised so painstakingly, it is heartbreaking to watch her battle with illness now as a 76-year-old woman.

One of the most profound pains is to see a loved one grapple with chronic pain and illness. We—my siblings and I—have watched our mother transform from a vibrant, independent, very opinionated woman to a person who has grown almost too weary in the battle. It's like an unrelenting fog that has moved in and is sucking the lifeblood from her, and in many ways, from us. Each of us struggles quietly, in our heads and hearts, to find answers.

On a recent Saturday evening we sat in the hospital emergency room, waiting and hoping for answers. Momma had spent five months of this year withstanding severe pain from kidney stones, and I felt there was more to the problem. My siblings and I had spent countless hours arguing, even negotiating with doctors in an effort to get them to look more aggressively to find the source of her pain. The carelessness of the managed care industry strikes a chord in me because I'm already skeptical about the quality of care. It seems to be a never-ending battle trying to navigate the health care system. It took the doctors four months to abandon medicines to melt the kidney stones and schedule the lithotripsy surgery. It felt as though we were going in circles trying to figure out the source of her severe stomach pain. Above the recommendations of the managed care insurance carrier, the hospital physician who took exceptional care of Momma following a stroke two years ago, on this day admitted her to the hospital. Although she had fainted in her bathroom that morning, Momma arrived at the hospital weary from pain, but alert.

With each passing week, I watched as my mother lost more and more weight, rapidly developing the frailness of cancer patients. I knew that lymphoma, which she had kept at bay for the past three years, was the demon stifling her breath, robbing her of that typical feisty spirit. A battery of tests was run during the week she stayed in the hospital, ultimately finding that the lymphoma was in her bone marrow and that she had gallstones.

After we heard the diagnosis, I recalled my brother Daryl's long struggle and death from AIDS seven years ago. I remember how he struggled to maintain his independence, securing a small sunny apartment in West Philadelphia. In those last months, he was back and forth to the hospital—dialysis, diarrhea, vomiting, constant pain, and an attempted suicide. In the final weeks, he was admitted to a hospice facility.

As Daryl's primary caregiver, I experienced unimaginable exhaustion, both mental and physical. Although my family came almost every weekend to help me care for Daryl, I felt a deep and abiding sadness, even though I masked my pain through smiles at my job and public settings. It was impossible to focus on my studies, so I took a leave of absence from graduate school. I didn't believe that I could ever repair the hole in my heart when I lost Daryl. Each of us grappled with the pain of losing him, but it was very much an internal dialogue. Although we're a close family, we didn't know how to reach out to each other emotionally to deal with our loss.

Six months after Daryl passed, my mother had a heart attack. Although she had suffered from hypertension for approximately 20 years at that point, Daryl's death was a turning point in my mother's health. It was the beginning of a long line of illnesses: diabetes, non-Hodgkins lymphoma, a double stroke, and pneumonia.

For the past 16 years, my mother has lived with my older sister in a beautiful, spacious and comfortable home. Although Dottie is 17 years older than I am, she is only 16 years younger than Momma, which makes them seem more like sisters than mother and daughter. Born under the same astrological sign, my mother and older sister are more alike than different. It's amazing to see how each of my siblings and I have a different relationship with our mother and with each other. Dottie is a warm, loving, very accommodating person who subsumes her needs to others. Ricky is equally warm and loving, a utilitarian guy who has made many road trips from his family and home in Detroit to spend time with Momma and help with her care, taking care of different household repairs for each of us. Debbie, the youngest of my siblings, has an incredible ability to get Momma to do just about anything, including taking medicine that she really can't stand. Although she's a bit controlling, Debbie has an irresistible charm, and I think Momma enjoys the attention. I am the pragmatic one, never leaving out details, always focused on the matters at hand, but not as affectionate as my siblings, at least not outwardly.

This year has been an anguishing challenge for each of us as we've juggled our lives between weekly doctor's appointments or diagnostic tests. I have never seen my mother deal with the level of physical pain as she has for the better part of this year. Over the past two years, I've had to really look at the face of mortality. Before therapy, I felt at times an unspeakable fear of losing my mother.

It is a blessing to have an audio record of our 1987 family reunion as I listen to Momma, my Aunt Bea, her husband Levi, several elder cousins, my older brother and sister, and myself laughing and carrying on about the tall tales and musings of my extended family. In many ways, my mother is the oral historian of her generation. As a youngster, she listened intently to the stories told to her by my grandfather, and my grand aunts and uncles. I always get a good laugh when Momma shares these stories. I am always overjoyed to hear the wonderfully creative and imaginative stories found in African-American folk culture, reminiscent of one of my favorite writers, Zora Neale Hurston.

Now, in the most recent months and weeks, my mother has been so ill and weak that I've not heard her tell stories in her unique style. This is the Momma that I've missed. Although she's not as spry mentally or physically, she is blessed to remember an incredible amount of the family's history. I know my mother has asked herself and God why she was the last in her generation to remain on the planet. Perhaps the Creator in its infinite wisdom endowed her with the keys to the kingdom because she's always had just the right mix of common sense, intellect, intuition, and motivation. Momma has always had great leadership qualities. She can be very charismatic, yet somewhat shy. A woman of high integrity, she's never tolerated lying or gossip. My mother has strength of spirit and mind that is incomparable to that of any human that I know.

Countless times this year, my family wondered if she would make it through this battle. But even now as she wages war with lymphoma, I can see her vibrancy shining through. Recently, she underwent two rounds of chemotherapy, after refusing it for three years.

My mother is not an incredibly religious woman, although she believes in God and the power of prayer. I, we, have invoked the spirits to heal her. Now as we wait to see her oncologist to hear the results of the latest diagnostic tests, I believe the answer is already here. There are two primary barometers of physical wellness for my mother—cooking her favorite meals and making her opinion known about any given subject, especially politics. In the last week, I've seen both: her favorite foods that would make any mouth water and her total fixation with CNN. I smile to myself, as she provides insightful political commentary that would draw circles around the news anchor. In that moment, my heart says, that's my Maggie! ■

Denise C. Jones is a freelance writer based in Washington, DC. She has worked as an award-winning radio news and public affairs producer. She has also produced independent videos for Montgomery Community Television in Maryland. She is currently tracing her maternal family's genealogy.

CHAPTER 9

Spiritual Care as Death Approaches Late in Life

Paul E. Irion

The essential spiritual task in the later years of life is to have hope. The satisfactions of an increasingly productive career, of a growing family, of travel, and of a widening circle of social relationships gradually begin to diminish as the later years of life unfold. The excitement and expanding possibilities of retirement fade as walkers and canes replace golf clubs, and bridge clubs become bereavement support groups. Family homes are left behind in favor of the one-last-move to the home of a daughter or son, or to the life-care retirement community with its apartments, personal care section, and skilled nursing facility. Eventually, for everyone lucky enough to have reached old age, life becomes a series of declines, diminutions, disappearances, separations.

The declines of later years accumulate and accelerate. Creaky joints and reduced energy gradually blend into chronic illness. More and more things start going wrong in one's body. Hearing and sight are diminished. Eating is less for pleasure than for keeping going. Ailments multiply and become more serious. Finally such illness or the sheer running out of time bring about the ultimate element of decline: death. If we reflect that dying is a process rather than a single event of the final breath, we must acknowledge that the late years of life are a process of dying and that the hope we are thinking about here is hope in the face of mortality.

How can one be hopeful in the face of such accelerating cumulative losses? That is the spiritual quest in the later years of life. Of course, it is easier to have hope when all is going well. But obstacles to the achievement of goals, hindrances to moving forward, disappointments, and defeats can make hope more difficult. If such limitations are severe, a person in the later years may have periods of hopelessness.

To begin, we must understand something of the nature of hope. So often it is confused with magical thinking, as if by wishing for something we could bring it into being. Dobihal and Stewart (1984) clarify the nature of hope. "Hope...may be seen as different from wishing. To wish for something to be different is a passive emotion and tends to lead toward wanting someone to effect a magical solution. Hope, on the other hand, is a goal-directed vision that enables one to live effectively in the present and move trustingly toward future possibilities."

Erik Erikson (1963) speaks of the final stage of life as maturity. Successful maturity, in Erikson's terms, involves finding integrity in one's life, or put in the vernacular, "getting it all together." The person who in the late years of life can look back over the years and say sincerely, "It's been a pretty good life," finds that the pieces of his or her life experience fit together like a picture emerging in a jigsaw puzzle. The person with integrity feels "connected" to that which gives life meaning. Such integrity forms the basis of hope when all else is diminishing.

For each of life's stages Erikson poses a tension between the positive developmental achievement and the consequences of failing to achieve that goal. For the old-age stage, Erikson sees people struggling between integrity and despair. Since the opposite of despair is hope, it is clear that integrity, connectedness, is the foundation for hope.

Although there are people who are so disadvantaged by social injustice that they tragically live most of their lives without hope, most of us accumulate some experiences of hope throughout our lifetimes. Hope pulls one into the future, drawing us on with the possibility of reaching or approximating goals. Usually these hopes occur when some new phase of life begins: marriage, changing to a new job, moving to a new home. In young adulthood people are motivated by their hopes, drawing them into a promising future. There are seemingly unlimited possibilities, goals to be achieved. Sometimes these hopes become realities; sometimes they deflate as impossible dreams.

As people reach middle age, there is often the realization: I am not going to accomplish everything I set out to do, I am not going to be able to be everything I wanted to be. This detonates what many have called the midlife crisis. Some make feverish attempts to regain youthful momentum, others adjust realistically to what they have been able to accomplish.

In the later years of life we can draw on the reservoir of these experiences of hope, even though they may be in the distant past. The problem is that there may not be in the present situation the same kind of challenges, the same energy, the same possibilities that fueled these earlier hopes. The enthusiasm of youth, the ambition of early adulthood, the job satisfactions of middle years have faded away. The world of present reality has become increasingly limited, making the content of earlier hopes increasingly irrelevant. The choice is to scale back, to learn to live in hope with illness, weakness, loss and mortality, or to retreat into apathy, compulsive nostalgia, or despair. In the later years of life it is the form of hope that must be revived and filled with new, and appropriate, content.

What, then, are appropriate hopes for older persons? They should be able to find hope in connectedness, the courage found in not being alone, and the support that comes through the loving care of others.

Connectedness can have so many dimensions. In its simplest form it is being connected to other people. We have grown up in a family network, a web of relationships. But parents have died, spouses may no longer be with us, children may live far, far away. In the time of our grandparents, old people were looked after and supported by friends and neighbors when family members were not available. In our time we have developed a mechanism of surrogate families, people who are employed to care for people in retirement communities and frail older persons in nursing homes and hospitals. Even those who no longer have family can find hope in the connectedness to their caregivers. They can have hope because they are not alone.

Or an older person may find hope in the connectedness that goes beyond personal relationships. Some would interpret this theologically and draw hope from their sense of being connected with God. Facing a dark and unknown future, they find hope in the sense of not being alone. They draw upon their religious faith and its promise of a life to come, which surpasses their present existence with all its difficulties.

Robert Lifton (1970) has noted five ways in which people who are dying or grieving express hope for the future. Some hope in terms of biological immortality: living on after death through one's children and thus continuing to participate in the genetic pool. Others frame their hope in the form of social immortality, in which the creativity of one's life endures in contributions that have been made to the lives of others. Still others interpret their hope for the future as the continuity of the natural process. One's life may end, but the process of which one has been a part lives on. Yet another way of portraying hope is to think of dying as an experience of ecstasy, or absorption into a transcendental reality. Finally, there is the theological view expressed in Judeo-Christian imagery as life after death, in which personal existence continues or is restored in a spiritual life beyond death. Note that all these involve connectedness in real but differing dimensions.

What a person thinks or believes is only a personal reflection, not the substance of truth. Just by thinking something, we do not make it true. In a sense, any of the five ways in which Lifton describes hope for overcoming death can be a viable interpretation. One selects from them the way that is most personally meaningful and helpful, to shape one's perception of the future.

Older people hope in many different ways, ranging from the articulation of hope in their religious tradition to highly personal aspirations. To hope is to reach beyond the present, desiring something better than the present situation.

Most religious traditions offer the hope of somehow transcending death, the ultimate loss, in the hope of heaven or its equivalent peace and blessedness. For some this is a literal belief in heaven. For others heaven is not a literal place but a new quality of existence they cannot know but nevertheless believe awaits them. It is variously described as life with God, everlasting peace, eternity. Clearly some people hope for an existence that is free from all the pains, privations, and limitations of present life.

Belief in some ideal existence beyond death is not the only hope. Some, without positing a life after death, may simply hope for release from existence, which has become painful or debilitated. And there are those who hope for strength to confront their growing losses. A good friend, unexpectedly diagnosed with terminal cancer, told those who were concerned for him, "Don't pray for a miracle to make the cancer go away. That is not going to happen. Pray that I will have the strength to confront this crisis." They did and he did.

Again and again we see hospice patients express hope in the peace they find in living out their days in the company of family and friends. Hospice care makes it possible for people to be hopeful that they will not suffer, that they will not be alone in the hour of their death, that their family will be supported. These are very tangible, immediate hopes, but they are also powerful aids in living with the ultimate limitation, in dying with dignity and poise. Hope really accomplishes a great deal more in changing the attitudes and responses of the person than it does in changing external circumstances.

These forms of hope are not mutually exclusive. Older persons, depending on their accumulated experience, their belief system, their values, their character, can find hope in any or all of these ways. This is no simple either/or; it is quite possible for people to hope simultaneously in several dimensions.

While there are many useful dimensions of hope, we need to be reminded that there are also counterproductive hopes. Some would hope to avoid aging and make pathetic attempts to clutch at fading youth. Others hope to avoid any signs of approaching decline by refusing to think about or plan for diminished years. Still others hope to avoid death by clinging to our culture's pervasive denial of death, refusing to admit the possibility of mortality until it is inexorably forced upon them.

Hope that denies the reality of one's situation, hiding from limitation and decline, is bound to be counterproductive. Such hopes usually are either naive optimism or useless distractions. Unrealistic optimism fails because it is based on illusions rather than the way things really are. Distraction, simply refusing to think about what is actually happening by paying attention only to superficial matters, focuses on the irrelevant.

These hopes are counterproductive for two reasons. First, they are doomed to fail because unfolding circumstances will prove them false hopes. The person who has pursued these will-o'-the-wisps must face the unavoidable decline with a sense of defeat, which easily becomes despair. Secondly, such unrealistic hopes for too long are substituted for realistic hopes, leaving the person hopeless as he or she confronts significant diminishment and the need somehow to live through it.

Each person throughout life seeks his or her own forms of hope. In the early and middle stages of life we can risk exuberant hopes and recover fairly readily if they cannot be achieved. But in the late stage of life hope must be tempered by realism. The options present in earlier experience are drastically narrowed and there is less and less time for recovering from the consequences of a misplaced hope.

Expressing hope is a creative way of adapting to one's perception of the future. For the person late in life, the immediate future is foreshortened; five- or 10-year plans are irrelevant. So the person often seeks meaning by positing a future beyond the experience of death and expresses that hope in ways that are personally meaningful. The hopeful aged person does not stay fixated on the past to slow down the passage of time, but, by engaging the future with courage, lives out the remaining time positively.

The radical termination of life as we know it is difficult, if not impossible, to accept fully. So it is very common to think in terms of some ongoing existence after death. Such concepts of afterlife cannot be empirically based but are articles of personal faith. Because the life-death continuum is not directly known, it is only natural that people have many questions about life after death.

These questions take two general forms: What is the nature of life after death? and will I live after death? The nature of life after death has to be described metaphorically. Some of the metaphors are used to describe hoped-for continuity with present life. Personal identity and relationships are thought of as continuing on, described in terms of recognition and reunion. Metaphors of completion and fulfillment describe ways in which life after death continues this life in a perfected state: life with God, relief from pain, peace, purification, reward, release, rest. Still other metaphors describe discontinuity with present life. The life after death is characterized by freedom from finite limitation, by being no longer subject to time and space, by entering a new realm of existence, by being accepted into the whole.

Answers to the other question—Will I live after death?—depends in part on how judgment figures in a person's view. For those who think in Platonic terms, immortality of the soul is a standard human endowment; it is for everyone. But for those who think of life after death as a gift from God, as in the Christian concept of resurrection, immortality may or may not be given. The thought of judgment impinges here and a person may wonder: Will I be found worthy? Will I be forgiven? Will I find grace? Christian thought ranges along a continuum from those who propose a universalism in which everyone is given new life by the love of God to those who hold to a process of election by which new life is given only to some.

Those facing death and their family members will be in one of two modes as they talk about life after death. In the affirming mode, they have either accepted the teaching of others or have worked out their own responses to their questions about this mystery, so they are able to state their belief affirmatively. Those in a questioning mode probe what life after death might mean for them. They may find that earlier conceptualizations are no longer satisfying. They struggle to state their hope in new ways.

In either mode the spiritual caregiver supports whatever affirmations individuals can make. The concern is not so much for people to have a "correct" understanding as it is that they have an understanding that satisfies their personal quest; if we *knew* the truth, it would be different. We need to acknowledge with intellectual humility that we deal here with a mystery.

A second crucial step is to help the person facing death or the family member to reflect on what that particular understanding does for him or her. This is not done in an effort to discount or devalue a particular interpretation, but to help the person understand why that interpretation is helpful in dealing with the situation of terminality.

How does this happen? How do we help persons late in life have hope? We might begin by recognizing that we do not give a person hope. Hope is not a commodity that is handed from one person to another. At best, our desire to be helpful takes the form of enabling hope to emerge from within the person.

It is understandable that people cling very hard to their own expressions of hope for the future beyond death. The need to somehow overcome death is very strong, as is the need to control the future. So people are heavily invested in whatever form their hope is expressed and assume that their way is true. They tend to be very defensive of that interpretation, which is part of their way of controlling the future.

A helpful caregiving attitude is to permit the person to express hope in his or her own way rather than to force a particular interpretation on the individual. While the caregiver is free to share the expression of hope that he or she has found most personally meaningful, it must not be presented as normative: the only good hope. The very nature of hope makes such an absolute a contradiction.

When the hopes that have sustained and energized in the past are no longer possible, one is faced with two choices: abandon hope or refocus it. Even in serious illness we struggle with the rightness of giving up hope for a cure. The words, "All hope abandon, ye who enter here," inscribed over the gates of Dante's hell, convey the ultimate in despair.

Such hopelessness is linked with the symbolization, deeply rooted in Western culture, of ultimate evil.

Facing up to approaching death means careful assessment of the future. It involves defining one's most precious hopes; it requires a reshaping of attitudes and behaviors. There is a difference between giving up hope and giving up a particular hope. It is a great cruelty to deprive a person of hope altogether. The crucial question is: For what is the person hoping? The task of families or other caregivers often involves helping people to work through a transfer of hope from one wish to another, from a hope that is becoming unrealistic to one that has more promise for sustaining the person through the crisis of approaching death.

Sometimes this transfer of hope is from this life to a life to come. In this instance one person might give up hope for extending life in the present world and express hope in terms of being in a world beyond death. Others might give up hope for cure through further medical treatment and find hope instead in the profound caring of others who will not abandon them to die alone. Hope is transferred from one kind of response to life-threatening illness to another, from medical technology to high-level caring.

The spiritual caregiver has a function in helping people understand the feelings they have about giving up hope for extending life. While there is great value in understanding the transfer of hope, an astute caregiver will not assume that the transfer is made easily. In the abstract a person may talk about giving up one hope and finding strength in another, but in actual situations giving up a hope may be a wrenching experience, even when another form of hope is available.

The inner, personal response to giving up a hope that is no longer realistic is grief. We have long recognized that it is possible to grieve in anticipation of death. We recognize that anticipatory grief (although very real) is not the same as grief, which takes place following a death, because it does not have the strong sense of finality. There is still some life remaining in the anticipatory situation. It is the same with grieving for a hope no longer possible, because there is still the possibility of a new, more realistic hope.

Abandonment of hope for extending life does not mean that everything else is abandoned. Part of the caregiving function is to help the patient and family to discuss what is being abandoned and what is not being given up. For example, when a person enters hospice care active therapy and the hope for extending life indefinitely are being abandoned; however, the support of family and hospice personnel is not lost. The pain control measures brought by hospice are not abandoned. Spiritual care is not abandoned. Persons struggling with their ultimate decline are helped to experience that they belong, that they are connected—to other people who love them, to the whole world in which they live, to God. ■

Paul E. Irion is Emeritus Professor of Pastoral Theology at Lancaster Theological Seminary of the United Church of Christ in Lancaster, Pennsylvania. Prior to his teaching career, he was a parish pastor and a hospital chaplain. Specializing in pastoral counseling, he is the author of six books and numerous professional articles. He was the Founding President of Hospice of Lancaster County in Pennsylvania.

References

Dobihal, E.F., Jr., & Stewart, C.W. (1984). *When a friend is dying.* Nashville: Abingdon Press, 84.

Erikson, E.H. *Childhood and society.* (1963). New York: Norton, pp. 268-269.

Lifton, Robert Jay. (1970, November). The politics of immortality. *Psychology Today*, 70ff.

■ CHAPTER 10 ■

The Senior Population and the Spectrum of Care

William D. Novelli

THE CONTEXT

Of all the great accomplishments of the 20th century, perhaps the most significant and least recognized is increased life expectancy. We added more years to average life expectancy in the last century than throughout all the rest of history. A person turning 65 today can expect to live another 18 years, nearly five years longer than a person age 65 in 1900, and life expectancy of persons who live to age 85 today is about seven years for women and six years for men. (Administration on Aging [AoA], 1999)

As a society, we are not only living longer, there are a lot more of us. Consider these facts (AoA, 1999):

- Since 1900, the number of people 65+ has increased 11-fold (from 3.1 million to 34.4 million).
- By 2030, the 65+ population will double to more than 70 million people.

- More than half of all people who have ever lived to be 65 are alive today (Rowe & Kahn, 1998).

All of this has been the result of remarkable advances in medicine and public health throughout the 20th century and public policies that contributed to greatly improved health across all generations. We made it a priority to reduce death rates for children and young adults. We created a system for providing adequate medical care to older persons and persons with disabilities through Medicare and to the poor and disadvantaged through Medicaid. We have made tremendous advances in public health measures, including sewer construction, management of the water supply, and widespread vaccination programs. Many discoveries of basic and clinical medical research have produced new medications and other therapies for the prevention, treatment, and sometimes cure for many diseases and disorders. This combined, intensive effort has given us a population living better, healthier, and *longer* than any in history.

It is important to understand that we are at the forefront of this global aging revolution, not at the end. Among industrialized nations, the population of the United States is still relatively young. We can begin to define and understand the American context of an aging population by looking at census numbers (Census Bureau). As a benchmark, consider figures from 1950. The total population of the United States was 151 million, and the number of men and women over 65 was 12 million, or 8%. The population today is slightly more than 280 million, and 35 million are 65 or older; that is, 12.5% or one person in eight. The projected figures for 2016 are 315 million total and 47 million over 65 (15%); for 2025, 338 million total and 63 million at least 65 years old (19%). Thus, within a generation, almost one person in five will be at least 65 years old. And in 2075, three generations from now, it will approach one person in four, about 22%. This is not a trend that will end with the baby boomers, and it is a critical part of the context for any present and future discussion of care and older people.

Another factor to consider is the growth of the population that is age 85 and older, currently, the fastest growing segment of the older population. In 2000, this segment accounted for approximately 2% of the population, but by 2050 almost 5% of the population will be 85 and older.

The increasing number of older people in the American population is not itself a problem. We have long since abandoned the outlook expressed 2,000 years ago by the Roman poet Seneca that "Old age is sickness itself." We have too much happy evidence to the contrary. More and more older people enjoy longer lives in good health than ever before. There is no reason to believe, or to fear, that today one person in eight—and in a few generations one person in five—will be a hopeless invalid and nothing but a drag on our resources just because they are older.

Yet older people do tend to need more care and their demands for care, once they begin, tend to increase and often become long term. Given the progress of medical research and clinical treatment, we have good reason to be optimistic that techniques to prevent many illnesses, to treat many diseases and disorders, and to delay the onset of others may be available in the future, but when and at what costs is of course unknown. Therefore, any current analysis and planning must depend on knowledge and not simply on hope.

Care is not just medicine, and long-term care may be anything from limited help around the house to full-time nursing assistance to palliative care at the end of life. In fact, we think and talk about a *continuum of care* that in schematic form usually looks something like this:

independent life at home → home care → informal care → formal care → assisted living → nursing home → hospice

This schema may have different forms and may include hospitalization(s), urgent care, and other events or interventions; but these other elements are neither predictable nor even placeable along the continuum.

The odds that any one person would move step by step along this continuum (or any other version of it) are small. Some people may go directly from independent living at home to hospice care. Most avoid being in a nursing home altogether. Not many people in nursing homes go to hospice care; they either die in the nursing home or in a hospital. Although the arrows all point to the right, most of us probably know someone who has moved along to the right and then abruptly back to the left. A friend told me about an uncle who was at home, diagnosed with a terminal disease in a hospital, sent to a nursing home to live out his remaining time, and went back home three months later, able to resume his normal routine.

Rather than a continuum of care, it is more useful to look at a *spectrum of care*. This discards the notion of inexorable (and downward) slide in the health of older people and replaces it with a range of choices. The concept of a spectrum of choices in health care, along with our understanding of the growth of the older population, establishes the context for this discussion of long-term care and end-of-life issues.

Completing the context is a discussion of the costs of long-term care. A few examples will suffice here since more statistics appear later in the chapter. Over the last decade, the real costs of nursing homes have increased more steeply and rapidly than has general inflation. According to the General Accounting Office (GAO), a year in a nursing home costs on average $55,000 (2001); for perspective, the median household income in the United States is around $40,000 and the average household income is virtually the same as a year in a nursing home, just under $55,000 (Bureau of Labor Statistics, 2000). According to the Centers for Medicare and Medicaid Services (CMS), formerly the Health Care Financing Administration, the total public and private spending on long-term care services in 1999 was $133 billion, about 11% of total national health expenditures (2000). The public and private dollar costs are measurable and enormous; the human costs to caregivers may not be priced in dollars, but are no less overwhelming.

The Facts

This context of long-term care gives us the perspective to examine the facts as they are today. These facts can be categorized as follows: coordination, financing, access, and quality. It is important to keep in mind that these categories are neither exclusive nor exhaustive. Moreover, they do not have sharp boundaries so that a question of financing, for example, may pose another question about the delivery of care.

Coordination

We talk about our *system* of long-term care, but, like our broader system of health care, it is not systematic. It is more accurately described as ad hoc or a patchwork. It is composed of publicly funded and privately paid services and of the care provided privately by family and friends. The "system" is extremely difficult for most persons to navigate.

Publicly funded services and funding are divided among various state agencies and the federal government. Using or attempting to use private services makes the lack of coordination even more daunting. Information about what is available, from whom, and at what price is not transparent or easily obtainable. Few individuals and families have the ability to find the services they need from those competent to provide them, and few employers provide assistance in arranging and paying for long-term care. There is little coordination among physicians and other health and long-term care providers.

Financing

Nursing-home care is very expensive. Home care, which for many is more desirable and appropriate than institutional care, can cost around $65 for a home health aide visit, meaning that a daily visit would total nearly $24,000 a year (CMS, 1999). Such visits usually last about four hours. There are no provisions for catastrophic long-term care costs as there are for standard health care, and less than 10% of people over 65 have private insurance coverage, which is expensive and not usually available through a group policy.

Medicare pays for limited nursing home care and home health care. Medicare does, however, fully cover hospice care. Medicaid pays for long-term care only for the poor, including those who have *become* poor by exhausting their resources paying for private care. The federal government discourages family caregiving by reducing supplemental security income (SSI) payments to persons who live with their families.

Access

The term *access* usually refers to the place where care is needed and given. AARP surveys have consistently shown that some 90% of older people want to stay in their homes and communities as they age, but the care they need to remain there is often unavailable or beyond their means. For many people with severe disabilities, some level of home care would enable them to stay at home; however, nearly three quarters of Medicaid's long-term care budget is spent on institutional care, and state-funded programs that might serve middle-income people have limited funding and scope. This is clearly at odds with the desires of those who need care at home and is an expensive way to deliver an imperfect solution to a difficult problem.

Nearly two thirds of people 65 and older who need assistance with daily activities get this help from relatives, usually women who have families and jobs of their own. Lack of access to affordable supportive services in the community and Medicaid's bias towards institutional care clearly contribute to family burdens, as does the scarcity of qualified and competent home care aides. Thus, even in a well-to-do family for whom the high costs of care might be affordable, the weight of care may still fall to a relative for want of reliable workers.

Quality

Reliable facilities with reliable employees can be hard to find and just as hard to evaluate. There is no federal regulation of assisted living facilities, and state regulation is often meager. Home care regulation is most often done by a review of records, without a visit to the facility itself. Despite federal law and regulations establishing quality standards, in nursing homes, year after year, studies reveal serious and sometimes horrifying failures of quality. For example, according to the General Accounting Office (GAO), between 1997 and 1998, a quarter of nursing homes caused residents actual harm or put them at risk of severe injury or death; and half of all nursing homes did not provide the staffing time necessary to prevent actual harm to their residents (GAO, 1999). Terminally ill patients and their families consistently report a chasm between the care they need—especially in pain management and communication with physicians about the choices available to them—and what they actually receive.

To find solutions to these problems, we must approach them from three different angles. The underlying issue is not only long-term care, but long-term health and quality of life. Thus, we must address (1) independent living; (2) coordination, financing, access, and quality in long-term care; and (3) end-of-life issues, all in a complementary way.

Independent Living

The first priority should be to avoid or postpone for as long as possible any need for long-term care or other interventions. This is desirable in terms of quality of life and from an economic standpoint. In many cases, simply providing help with some daily activities, such as cooking and dressing, can enable many older people to avoid institutions. Fostering independent living has a double benefit: it reduces strain on public and private facilities and provides a richer emotional and social life for those receiving assistance. This second benefit has real health consequences, since people who continue to feel part of the world around them are less inclined to suffer from depression, a gateway to many other disorders.

Two other important factors can contribute greatly to living at home. The first is home modification, such as ramps, better lighting, and first-floor bathrooms, which increase mobility and decrease the risk of injury. The second factor is a public matter—community planning of transportation with the particular needs of older persons, especially those who no longer drive, to help people retain some independence and mobility.

Ideally, architects and home builders will employ universal design in residential construction. This is a way to accommodate the changes aging people may require at minimal cost and with minimal disruption. Built-in safety and mobility features ultimately cost less than later modifications to maintain independence. Both original and modified designs cost less than the high fees of a nursing home.

Promotion of healthy living, especially good diet and regular exercise for people of all ages, but especially middle aged and older, will produce a healthier and fitter population. Recent data show (Manton & Gu, 2001) a 2% annual reduction in the rate of disability among people 65 and older over the last six years, attributable in large part to growing awareness and practice of healthy lifestyles.

Some of this reduction is also due to medical breakthroughs, such as in the treatment and delay of the onset of osteoporosis. Drug therapy is now available to treat many disorders of older people, and prescription drug coverage in Medicare would support treatment at home rather than in hospitals and institutions. In addition, research in disorders usually associated with age, such as Parkinson's and Alzheimer's diseases, is a critical need and deserves increased public funding. Just as the possibility of delaying entry into a nursing home is obviously beneficial, so too are the benefits of delaying the onset, or slowing the advance, of progressive, degenerative diseases such as Alzheimer's or arthritis.

Thus, the responsibility for maintaining independence lies both with individuals, who must try to maintain their good health, and with the public and elected officials, who must implement policy changes and provide funding. Through public and private sharing of responsibilities, we can reduce the need for institutional long-term care, extend active and healthier living, and bring down the costs of care.

Components of Long-term Care

Should we accomplish all this tomorrow, there still would be a population, though happily much smaller, in need of formal and informal long-term care. There are several ways to improve this situation. One critical improvement would be a single point of entry into the system of long-term care services. This important first step would begin to change the current patchwork of care into a better functioning, well-coordinated system. A point of entry that leads to the current situation is of little value, but, a single point of entry that presents those who seek long-term care—or simply information about long-term care—with the tools to navigate the array of programs, services, and agencies would be invaluable.

A single point of entry must provide two things: an assessment of an individual's needs for care and a range of care services and care management options suitable for that individual. The range of possibilities in the spectrum of care is often bewildering. Without full information and guidance, it is nearly impossible to make a reasonable choice to obtain the most suitable care. We need a user-friendly environment for understanding and choosing appropriate care and then an equally humane environment for delivering care.

Just as responsibility for good health is shared between private individuals and public agencies, the financing of long-term care also should be shared. First, we must look at long-term care coverage as a social insurance program like Social Security and Medicare. Such a program would be the core of long-term care coverage and would be publicly financed, with individuals paying into the program and receiving benefits, including a cash payment option, when needed.

Second, we must find ways to improve private long-term care insurance. Since most people who buy this insurance pay premiums for many years before they receive benefits, the premiums must be predictable, stable and affordable, and the policies must provide good quality coverage for purchasers.

Third, we should offer tax deductions for premiums on qualifying long-term care insurance policies and change policies to help individuals finance their care. Two current proposals before Congress are to enact a proposed $3,000 tax credit for caregivers and to provide full SSI payments to those in need of care who live with their families.

Fourth, we can improve information for low-income older people about public programs for which they may be eligible, such as Medicaid, QMB (Qualified Medicare Beneficiary), SLMB (Specified Low-income Medicare Beneficiary), QI-1 (Qualifying Individuals), and Supplemental Security Income. In addition, we can fund these safety-net mechanisms for those without the means to pay for their own care.

These various mechanisms for financing both public and private long-term care insurance programs require a long-term commitment. A successful program will not grow out of a single burst of energy nor a one-time cash infusion from Congress, the states, or individuals. It must be a permanent and manageable cost, just as Social Security and Medicare have proven themselves to be permanent and manageable.

In recent years, the percentage of people paying privately for care in a nursing home has dropped from 42% in 1985 to 24% in 1999 (National Center for Health Statistics). This reflects the desire to stay at home, suspicions about (and experience with) poor quality of care in many nursing homes, and the increasing costs of these institutions. To meet both the health care needs and the desire to remain at home of this growing population, we can promote expanding Medicaid and state programs that offer more choices at home or in the community, such as assisted living, adult day services, and personal care. At the same time, we must also make sure that more qualified long-term care personnel are available. This is about staff quality and financing. Currently, the pay for such workers is low, the work is hard, and turnover in many institutions and agencies is close to 100% a year. Financing mechanisms must ensure a good wage with benefits and good working conditions. Without a sufficient number of trained staff, no approach—at home or in an institution or anywhere—will work. Without qualified workers, the affluent and the poor alike will have fewer choices and many needs will be unmet.

Quality assurance is essential. It must be a matter of thoughtful regulation with stringent enforcement. The standards of enforcement must be strengthened and performance must be consistently monitored in all nursing homes and in all home and community services as well. No single setting or kind of care should be either singled out for greater scrutiny nor exempt from serious examination.

Adequate staffing levels must be determined for each setting, and maintenance of those levels monitored and enforced. Data about staffing and all other factors that affect the quality of care should be readily available public information. The Center for Medicare and Medicaid Services is already providing this information about nursing homes that receive federal money and is launching a new effort to make this information, which is so essential to quality, more user-friendly. Its website (at www.medicare.gov) makes such information widely available, current, and inexpensive to update.

End-of-life Concerns

All of this inevitably raises the issue of end-of-life planning and care. Ideally, by age 50, everyone should have made plans by preparing clear advance health-care directives, including a will, a living will, and, in those states that recognize it, a health-care power of attorney. This last item is important because it creates a designated agent or advocate who speaks with the voice of the patient. These are important personal responsibilities for all of us. Unfortunately, most people are either unaware of the need for planning or for other reasons have not done this critical planning for end of life.

Good end-of-life care in America today is sadly lacking. Although Medicare has a good hospice benefit, there are barriers to using it. Public action can help remove these impediments and also help remove other barriers, notably to medically appropriate pain management for the seriously ill. We must work to improve reimbursement for palliative care. Medical schools and hospitals must do more to train physicians in recognizing the need for palliative care and in providing it in a timely way. Quality of life for the seriously or terminally ill and their families is very important, and institutionalizing palliation through hospitals, health systems, and the entire health care system must be part of our spectrum of care. Medical schools and hospitals can also do a better job of teaching physicians how to communicate with seriously ill patients and their families, in particular, how to explain treatment and pain management options.

Conclusion

America's older population is healthier and living with less disability than ever before, but we will continue to need long-term care services of one kind or another simply because the sheer numbers of older people are growing. Comforting though the notion may be, we will not any time soon outgrow our need for long-term care by living in perfect health, then dying peacefully, painlessly, and quickly in our beds at home. How and where we provide the care, how we pay for it, and how we manage the spectrum of health care choices are critical questions. In 20 years, the oldest baby boomers will be 75. The demographic trends are inexorable, and improvements must be in place well before then. The obvious and important connections among independent living, long-term care, and end-of-life decisions and care call for wide-ranging and integrated approaches.

The ideas suggested here represent one blueprint for a newly designed and built system of care. There may be others, but it is clear that we must create a real *system* out of the present patchwork—and that the new system we design and build must have choices to serve the needs of those who need the least care *and* of those who need the most. ■

William Novelli serves as Executive Director and CEO of AARP. He has been the President of the Campaign for Tobacco-Free Kids and Executive Vice President of CARE, the world's largest private relief and development organization. Earlier, Mr. Novelli co-founded and headed Porter-Novelli, now one of the world's largest public relations agencies. Mr. Novelli is a recognized leader in international social marketing. He has managed programs in cancer control, diet and nutrition, cardiovascular health, reproductive health, infant survival, charitable giving and other programs in the United States and the developing world. Mr. Novelli holds a master's degree from the University of Pennsylvania's Annenberg School of Communication and pursued doctoral studies at New York University. He taught marketing management and health communications for 10 years at the University of Maryland.

References

Manton, K.G. and Gu, X.L. (2001). Changes in the prevalence of chronic disability in the United States Black and non-Black population above age 65 from 1982 to 1999. *Proceedings of the National Academy of Sciences, 98*, 11, 6354-6359.

Rowe, J.W., & Kahn, R.L. (1998). *Successful aging.* New York: Pantheon Books.

U.S. Department of Commerce, Census Bureau [On-line]. Available: www.census.gov

U.S. Department of Health and Human Services, Administration on Aging. (2000). A Profile of Older Americans: 2000 [On-line]. Available: www.aoa.dhhs.gov

U.S. Department of Health and Human Services, Centers for Medicare and Medicaid Services. (1999). A Profile of Medicare Home Health, August.

U.S. Department of Health and Human Services, Centers for Medicare and Medicaid Services. (1999). National Health Expenditures 1999.

U.S. Department of Health and Human Services, National Center for Health Statistics. National Nursing Home Survey 1985 and 1999.

U.S. Department of Labor, Bureau of Labor Statistics. (2000). Current Population Survey, March Supplement. Detailed Household Income Tables: 1999 P60 Package [On-line]. Available: www.bls.census.gov/cps/

U.S. General Accounting Office. (2001). Long-Term Care: Baby Boom Generation Increases Challenge of Financing Needed Services. GAO-01-563T, March.

U.S. General Accounting Office. (1999). Nursing Homes: Additional Steps Needed to Strengthen Enforcement of Federal Quality Standards. HEHS-99-46, March.

Chapter 11

Practical Suggestions

Linking the Generations

Ashley Davis Prend

The good news about living in a geographically fluid society is that I didn't have to remain trapped in Texas (my childhood state but not my adult home of choice). The bad news about this mobility is that by choosing to relocate north, I am raising my three children far, far away from their grandparents and great grandparents. Certainly my children and I talk to our far-flung relatives on a regular basis and have multiple visits each year, but there are no consistent Sunday dinners with grandma and grandpa, no weekly rituals to connect the generations.

Feeling this void and knowing that my children would benefit by knowing and having regular contact with older generations, I decided to enlist my children's help in volunteering at our local "retirement village." We began our visits several years ago when my children were five, three, and one.

The first time we went for a visit, I had my baby daughter in a stroller while the two older children tagged along beside me. I wasn't quite sure what to expect, but I knew that we were going to play a game with the residents during their activity hour. We entered the lounge, a kind of large, old-fashioned parlor with green floral couches, wooden card tables, and a baby grand piano in the corner. Before me I saw about 10 to 15 residents assembled in a circle in the center of the room. Some were sitting in chairs while others rested in wheelchairs. As we entered the room, I began to wonder "What are we doing here?" and "What if the children misbehave?" and "What will we talk about?"

The four of us crept into the room, somewhat tentatively. We began by walking around the circle and saying hello, introducing ourselves, and learning their names. When the residents gazed upon us, especially upon the children, their faces lit up like the spring sun that was cascading through the French doors. Many reached out to touch the baby's hand and I immediately was overcome by a profound sense of respect for the cycle of life. I was watching representatives from opposite ends of life's spectrum meet, literally touching each other, connecting.

My other two children were initially shy and fairly quiet, but when the activity director brought out a large balloon and catching net, they quickly got into the spirit of the game. One child would hold the net while the other threw the balloon to a resident who would then attempt to bounce it into the net. The children began to laugh and giggle, chasing after the balloon, cheering when it went into the net. The residents clearly were delighted to tap the balloon and watch the children dash about with the net, all the while squealing with glee.

Then came snack. My children were thrilled to be able to help pass out the snack and the juice. I watched my five-year-old carefully carry a piece of cake to a woman in a wheelchair. And when the children got to partake in the snack as well, I knew it wouldn't be difficult to convince them to return.

We've been going regularly ever since. Now my children are nine, seven, and five and they still love to go visit the "old" people. Through these years we have continued to play the balloon and net game. We've also sung around the piano during sing-a-longs. We've paraded around in costumes during the Halloween party. We've danced and done the hokey-pokey during dance time. We've listened to stories during story time. We've attended the annual summer lawn party and volunteer appreciation tea. Once we even brought our golden retriever dog with us who got so excited that he jumped up on the couch (which fortunately had no people on it at the time). He happens to be terrified of balloons, however, so when the kids started playing the balloon game with the residents, he ended up under the couch.

After each visit I always tell the children how much their visit meant to the residents. I'll comment, "Did you see how they smiled when you were playing with them? Did you notice how happy they were to watch you and sing with you? You really brightened up their day." It's not just the game or the song or the snack that lures the children to the visits; they actually enjoy the feeling that volunteering brings. I'm reminded of the expression, "Those who bring sunshine to others cannot keep it from themselves."

One particular visit stands out in my memory. For some reason, the activity director and I got our signals crossed. When we arrived at the appointed hour, the lounge was completely empty. I found a nurse in the hall and I asked, "Where is everybody?" She informed me that the regular activity group had gone on a picnic that had been rained out earlier in the week. She told me that we could walk around and visit people in their rooms if we wanted. I wasn't sure what to do. We had never actually gone door to door and I wasn't sure if the children would be patient without an organized activity to focus the visit, but I thought we might as well try since we were already there.

What happened next was amazing. We visited briefly with only three people, but the visits were more intimate than our usual group gatherings. First, we found a man painting in his room. We came in and admired his considerable talent. He was a retired dentist, he told us, and took up painting when he was 75. "How old are you now?" I asked. "Ninety-five," he replied. Wow! The children were impressed.

Next, we talked to a man in a wheelchair outside his room who was one of our regulars from the activity group. But during this visit we learned that he was a retired pro baseball player, that he had lived for many years in California, and that he had lost a grown daughter to cancer. We also learned that he was 90. Amazing, I thought. We'd been playing group games with him for almost five years and I didn't know any of this.

Finally, we went into the room of a woman who gave the children Hershey's chocolate kisses and let them play with her walker. She told us that she had been a teacher for 60 years and had been written up in the newspaper—she showed us the clipping. Then she announced that she was 97. We left that visit pleased with the friendships newly forged, but in the end, whether we connect with the residents individually or as a group, I know that the children have fun and are deeply touched by each encounter.

Our volunteer experience is teaching us all of the beauty of life and its natural cycles. I do not want my children to be afraid—not of older people, nursing homes, or death itself. Yet this kind of experience may not be right for all children. Their parents have to be comfortable with it, first of all. Children, too, need to be able to behave and understand ground rules. They cannot be overly rambunctious on a visit, screaming or running through halls, nor can they be disrespectful to a resident. On any given day, if the child is in a withdrawn, tearful, or overwhelmed mood, it is probably not the best day for a visit. Finally, you should "debrief" the children after each visit, conversing on the ride home about their experiences and questions, and reflecting on the value of volunteering.

There is a richness in linking the generations that truly transcends any age barrier. I know my children are gaining a broader perspective on life as well as a familiarity with and respect for older people. This was confirmed for me one day when our grandma from Texas came to visit. She was complaining about some aspect of the aging process when my son asked her, "How old are you again grandma?"

She replied, "Seventy-four."

He retorted, "That's not so old. I know a bunch of people who are in their 90s and they're in great shape."

I just smiled. ■

Ashley Davis Prend, ACSW, is a psychotherapist and supervisor at the Center for Marital and Family Therapy in New York City. She is affiliated with St. Vincent's Hospital where she leads AIDS-related bereavement support groups in the Supportive Care Program. Ms. Prend is the author of Transcending Loss: Understanding the Lifelong Impact of Grief and How to Make It Meaningful. *She is a frequent lecturer on bereavement, regularly offers workshops on various aspects of grief, and has trained student social workers in bereavement counseling. Ms. Prend earned her master's degree in clinical social work from Columbia University and her Bachelor of Arts in psychology from Smith College. Ms. Prend has also completed an advanced training program in psychoanalytic psychotherapy at the National Institute for Psychotherapies in New York City.*

CHAPTER 12

Issues of Loss and Grief in Long-Term Care Facilities

Timothy J. Keay

INTRODUCTION

One and a half million older Americans now live in nursing homes. Although nursing facilities have seen increased medical acuity and decreased lengths of stay among their residents in recent years due to relentless health care cost containment and long-term care reform, for many older residents the nursing home is their home—their final home. Currently, more than one fifth of all deaths in the United States take place in nursing facilities.

Because of this concentration of terminally ill residents, issues of dying, grief, and loss take on tremendous importance in nursing facilities. However, due to heavy government regulation and a mandated focus on rehabilitation, financial pressures, staffing demands, and the lack of specialized training in end-of-life care, nursing facilities often are not the ideal environment for responding to the loss-related issues experienced by residents, their families, their neighbors in the facility, and even staff.

In fact, the laws and regulations governing nursing home care and current financial pressures on facilities can be significant impediments to achieving peaceful life closure. In the current environment, staffing levels are low and the fiscal incentives for providing appropriate end-of-life care are minimal. On top of that, many nursing home staff and physicians have limited education and experience in modern methods of caring for dying patients, also known as *palliative care.* Palliative care is the careful, attentive, and appropriate management of the full range of care needs experienced by terminally ill residents, delivered in a timely manner using specialized medical expertise.

Good end-of-life care can be provided in the long-term care setting. But it will happen only if rational care planning processes are brought to bear in order to ensure an ethically safe, comfortable, self-determined, and fitting final phase of life. It also requires overcoming widespread antipathy to nursing homes. In a recent survey, 30% of seriously ill hospitalized patients said that they would "rather die" than be placed in a nursing home. Such attitudes, reflecting the public's concerns over the quality of nursing home care, need to be taken seriously.

No doubt the dilemmas of end-of-life care in the nursing facility leave many family survivors feeling guilty that their loved ones did not receive better care as they were dying. Families of facility residents who died while receiving less-than-optimal care often feel that they must complain to their legislators, regulators, and anyone else who will listen, trying to achieve some measure of justice as a way of making their loved one's death mean something.

One obvious solution to those dilemmas is *hospice*—an intensive form of palliative care focused on the relief of suffering, life-transition issues, and bereavement follow-up for survivors. Hospice care today has a small but growing role in nursing facilities as specialized hospice teams come into the facilities to coordinate, supplement, and enhance the end-of-life care given to eligible, hospice-enrolled residents. Despite these advances, regulatory demands on nursing facilities and legal requirements shaping their contracts with hospices challenge both partners to develop an effective working relationship in order to expand access to appropriate hospice and end-of-life care.

The Long-Term Care Continuum

In our society, with its large and growing population of older persons, how to provide humane yet cost-effective long-term care looms as an ever greater challenge. Yet there are also myths about nursing homes that don't necessarily reflect current realities. Dramatic shifts have occurred in health care over the past 30 years, especially in the sites where it is delivered. Patients who used to be cared for in nursing homes now live primarily in assisted living facilities or else receive home care. Patients who used to be in hospitals are now in nursing homes. Patients who used to be in intensive care units are now maintained on regular hospital wards. And patients whose illnesses used to be fatal are now in the intensive care unit. Medical care has become much more adept at prolonging life while dealing with constant fiscal pressures to deliver the care in the environment that is least expensive to health care payers.

According to the American Health Care Association (AHCA), a trade group representing nursing facilities, "Long-term care now includes a broad spectrum of care, from subacute medical care, ongoing skilled nursing care, care for the developmentally disabled and special populations as well as adult day care, residential care, assisted living, and home and community-based care. Facilities providing this range of services are increasingly diversified and include nursing facilities, subacute care centers, rehabilitation centers, intermediate care facilities, residential care facilities, and assisted living facilities" (AHCA, 2001; Executive Summary, p. vii).

Currently there are more than 17,000 certified nursing facilities in the United States with approximately 1.8 million beds. Another 800,000 seniors reside in assisted living facilities and 600,000 live in continuing care retirement centers.

In the past, nursing homes focused on providing long-term custodial services to older people, including basic medical and residential services, AHCA notes. The current trend, however, is for nursing facilities to seek Medicare or Medicaid certification in order to provide services to a patient population with a significantly higher medical acuity with an increased emphasis on rehabilitation therapies. Subacute care is a newer piece of the long-term care continuum, merging some of the sophisticated technology of the hospital with the skilled operations of the nursing facility and providing high-tech, hospital-like care to seriously ill patients at a lower cost.

Assisted living facilities, by contrast, offer supervision, assistance, protective oversight, meals, and limited health care services to relatively independent seniors in a homelike atmosphere. Assisted living facilities vary widely from state to state in terms of their licensing requirements and even what they are called. Such care is also known as residential care, board-and-care, congregate care, or personal care. While the nursing home industry is highly regulated, assisted living facilities have not received comparable standards or regulatory oversight.

Trends in the Regulation of Long-Term Care

The two major priorities for health care payers are cost and quality. Understandably, payers want to get the most value for their money, especially as the baby boom generation ages. The United States already pays more than 14% of its gross domestic product on health care—more than any other developed country—and could wind up spending much more if escalating health care costs are not moderated. One way to control costs is through the regulatory structure that governs reimbursement under the Medicare and Medicaid programs.

In recent years the government has tried to aggressively legislate the quality of care in nursing facilities by developing detailed rules about care processes and outcomes, all tied to regulatory scrutiny and enforcement efforts. The regulations do not favor comfort measures; they reinforce rehabilitation or aggressive medical interventions in response to all identified declines in function.

A major federal legislative initiative, the Nursing Home Reform Act (1987), was passed in an effort to prevent the warehousing of older residents. The act requires that all residents receive care designed to "maintain or improve function." Detailed assessment, reassessment, care plans, and processes are now required of all nursing homes, with regular transmission of the data by electronic means to the government. Facilities that do not comply are subject to withholding of payment, fines, bans on admissions, closure, and even threats of criminal prosecution. The consensus has been that while this law has improved overall care for many nursing home residents, it has also led to new problems.

Since the passage of the Nursing Home Reform Act, nursing homes have become larger, more often corporately owned, more aggressive in rehabilitation efforts, and much more aware of their own costs. Issues not addressed clearly and specifically in the act, however, including terminal care and pain control, have not received the same attention. In one well-known study of nursing home patients with cancer, it was found that 29% of them had daily pain, while 26% of those with daily cancer pain had no analgesics ordered—not even aspirin (Bernabei, Gambassi, Lapane, et al., 1998).

The recent introduction of an HMO-style, capitated reimbursement mechanism called Resource Utilization Groups to the nursing home industry has accelerated the pace of change in nursing facilities by dramatically cutting their reimbursement at an even faster rate than what was envisioned by cost-cutting legislators. The six largest nursing home chains, as well as many smaller companies and nursing homes, are now in bankruptcy. Many facilities are struggling to find adequate nursing staff in the face of an acute nursing shortage just to meet the legal minimum staffing requirements, much less the optimal staffing required to address all of the specialized needs of residents, including those at the end of life. In Maryland, for example, the minimum staffing requirement is 2.0 hours per resident per day (which includes all charting as well as patient care), despite a consensus by experts that doing all of the required tasks demands at least 3.5 hours of staffing per resident per day (Harrington, Kovner, Mezey, et al., 2000).

If the nursing home has additional funding beyond the usual government reimbursement, it may be able to provide some extra services. One way of gaining additional funding is to ask residents to pay privately for the costs of adequate and appropriate end-of-life care. For residents of assisted living facilities, that is often what is attempted. Older individuals pay a considerable sum—in many cases their entire life savings—to enter an assisted living facility that promises to care for them for the rest of their lives. What actually transpires routinely in those facilities is not yet clear.

Some nursing homes get additional funds, beyond the $30,000 per year in reimbursement that is the industry's average, by charging private-pay residents $60,000 or more per year for their care. Other nursing homes receive support from religious or charitable organizations. But simply paying more for nursing home care does not ensure that the special needs of dying residents will be addressed. Too often, those who are dying in long-term care get the "standard of care" only in the minimal sense of "this is what happens to most people."

Perverse fiscal incentives may also delay the application of appropriate and needed palliative therapies to dying patients. To counter that danger, the quality of end-of-life care should be factored into any discussion of the costs of long-term care, or else the value of the care is without meaning. For too many terminally ill nursing home residents, the evidence shows that they are dying in pain, with uncomfortable symptoms and marginal hygiene and without their families' bereavement issues being addressed—or they are sent off to a hospital for aggressive, unwanted, and usually futile attempts at prolonging their lives.

The Hospice Solution

In the context of such financial, regulatory, and human-resource challenges to optimal end-of-life care in the long-term care setting, hospice emerges as a more appealing solution for some dying residents of both nursing homes and assisted living facilities. Hospice is a specialized philosophy of care for the terminally ill and their families emphasizing comfort and symptom management; life-closure issues; attention to psychosocial, spiritual, and bereavement needs; and treatment of the patient and family together as the unit of care. Hospice is a medically directed, multidisciplinary approach that provides or coordinates all of the services needed to manage the care of terminally ill patients, regardless of the setting for their care. The hallmarks of hospice care, as articulated by the National Hospice and Palliative Care Organization (NHPCO), include achieving self-determined life closure, a safe and comfortable dying process, and effective grieving by family survivors.

Hospice care was introduced to the United States from England in the 1970s, and then codified as a Medicare benefit by an act of Congress in 1982. Subsequently, the federal government clarified that terminally ill residents of nursing facilities were just as entitled to hospice as those residing in their own homes. The actual funding mechanism for such care is complicated and requires a contractually defined relationship between the nursing facility and the Medicare-certified hospice program, addressing such issues as development and oversight of the hospice plan of care, coordination between staff of the hospice and facility, payment, and specified services.

When the nursing facility and the hospice program are able to work together, they can collaborate in ensuring the provision of appropriate end-of-life services to the facility's terminally ill residents. Such collaboration offers residents access to hospice's specialized expertise in the needs of the dying, additional nursing and other professional care that otherwise would not be available, the support of volunteers and spiritual care professionals, and attention to issues of loss and grief. Bereavement services, which are required from all Medicare-certified hospice programs, include professional assessment, counseling, and other support. Such services simply are not part of the mandate for nursing home care, nor are they covered by standard reimbursement for either nursing homes or assisted living facilities except under contract with hospices.

Hospice services are regulated and monitored to ensure that the hospice program provides all of the services that it promises. That assurance can provide a level of comfort to residents of long-term care facilities when they are diagnosed as terminally ill. Residents who receive hospice care experience less pain, have their hygiene needs attended to, and are assured that their loved ones will be comforted after their deaths.

Unfortunately, the same voluminous regulations designed to ensure quality of care when hospice services are delivered in patients' homes may tend to discourage access to those same services in nursing facilities. In 1997, only 1% of nursing home residents who died actually received hospice services, while 70% of nursing homes did not have a single person who died while receiving hospice services. Thus, there is a considerable gap between what is theoretically possible by adding hospice services to long-term care and the actual realities of dying in that setting.

Hospices operate under federal Title 18 regulations, whereas nursing homes operate under Title 19 rules, so a carefully structured contract is required that allows each entity to meet its own regulatory requirements without jeopardizing the other's compliance. Model contracts have been developed by the national trade associations but are not widely in place, primarily due to lack of interaction between the cultures of the two provider models and to the nursing homes' fundamental mandate to "maintain or improve function."

Beyond the issue of access is the matter of what services are provided. NHPCO impaneled a Nursing Home Task Force (NHPCO, 1998), whose final report identified a number of tasks that need to be performed in order to provide adequate care to dying nursing home residents—whether they are receiving hospice services or not. A plan of care should be developed that is personalized for the resident and addresses pain control, dyspnea, activities, incontinence, skin breakdown, mental status changes (including mood, delirium, seizures, agitation, and coma), nutrition and fluid maintenance, life-sustaining medical interventions (CPR, antibiotic use, other medications), anticipatory grief, and other pertinent issues. The nursing home is required to develop such a plan of care and to keep it up-to-date, but ensuring that the plan actually addresses the needs of the dying person in a timely manner with the latest methods of palliative care may require persistent advocacy by residents or their families, as well as by professional staff of both the nursing facility and hospice.

What Can Residents and Their Families Do?

The need for advocacy is even greater when there is no hospice program involved, either because of the lack of a contract or because the resident doesn't meet eligibility criteria for the Medicare Hospice Benefit. Caring for a terminally ill resident requires a tremendous amount of work and significant expertise. It is often the task of the resident or family to advocate and monitor care in order to ensure that the dying person gets the services he or she needs.

On a practical basis, the resident and his or her family, when faced with the challenge of end-of-life care in the long-term care setting, need to be aggressive in insisting that hospice services are engaged or that the facility provides equivalent care. Many assisted living facilities are happy to get hospice services involved, since hospice provides high-quality care that is charged directly to Medicare. Nursing homes, however, vary widely in their willingness to consider relationships with hospices. Residents and their families may have a role in urging the facility to establish a contractual relationship with a hospice program that could allow the resident to enjoy the support of hospice care.

It is no longer automatic for a nursing home resident to be transferred to a hospital when death nears. For both patients and their families, a death that comes shortly after an ambulance transfer to the intensive care unit or another acute hospital ward introduces an unfortunate and unnecessary instability and emotional turmoil at a time when calm and familiar surroundings are especially important. By contrast, the presence of other residents who may have gotten to know the patient over time, the lack of pressure to move the patient yet again to a different setting when the allotted hospital stay is finished, and the more homelike surroundings of the long-term care setting that still retain adequate medical supervision and professional support are all reasons why remaining in the nursing facility might be desirable at the very end of life.

Nursing homes have been caring for dying people for many years, and assisted living facilities have an additional opportunity to deal with end-of-life care without some of the regulatory burdens that nursing homes bear. If combined with the expertise and supplemental services of hospice care, the long-term care setting may be the very best place to die for many older patients. Having a vision of what needs to be done and how it can be accomplished can guide the resident, his or her family, and professional caregivers towards appropriate life-closure tasks. That is of paramount importance in learning to live with grief and in taking advantage of opportunities for personal growth at the end of life.

Nursing home staff and residents are well acquainted with death; on average, one out of every three people admitted to a nursing home dies within the first year after admission. Thus, there is a tremendous amount of grief already present in most nursing homes, as well as in assisted living facilities. Perhaps one of the greatest benefits that hospices can provide is to address the grief of the facility's staff and the surviving residents, who become in effect the patient's extended family. That broadly disseminated grief support could provide a real service to the professional care providers, friends, and acquaintances of those who die, bringing a new dimension of meaning.

It is fitting that the lives of those who die be appropriately remembered and honored and from their death a new sense of purpose can emerge. That renewed sense of purpose will benefit everyone involved in long-term care, as well as society at large. ■

Timothy J. Keay, MD, has taught geriatrics, ethics, and family medicine at the University of Maryland School of Medicine since 1988. He has a medical degree from the Medical College of Wisconsin, a master's in theological ethics from Pacific Lutheran Theological Seminary, and has received fellowship training at the University of California, San Francisco. He is the first Faculty Scholar of the Project on Death in America, a project of the Open Society Institute, that focuses on improving end of life care in nursing homes. He is currently the medical quality consultant to Baltimore's Medicare waiver program, a teacher on hospice and palliative care at the University of Maryland School of Medicine, and medical director of a large Baltimore nursing facility.

REFERENCES

American Health Care Association, Washington, DC. The nursing facility sourcebook 2001. Accessed via AHCA website: www.ahca.org, 2001.

Bernabei, R., Gambassi, G., Lapane, K.L., et al. (1998). Management of pain in patients with cancer. *Journal of the American Medical Association, 279,* 1877-1882.

Harrington, C., Kovner, C., Mezey, M., et al. (2000). Experts recommend minimum nurse staffing standards for nursing facilities in the United States. *Gerontologist, 40,* 1:5-16.

Keay, T.J., & Schonwetter, R.S. (2000). The case for hospice care in long-term care environments. *Clinics in Geriatric Medicine, 16,* 2:211-223.

National Hospice and Palliative Care Organization. (1998). *Nursing Home Task Force report.* Alexandria, VA.

Nursing Home Reform Act of 1987, 42 C.F.R., Part 483.

CHAPTER 13

Lessons for an Aging Population from the Hospice Model

Stephen R. Connor

INTRODUCTION

Death happens primarily to older persons. Fully three fourths of those who died in this country in 2000 were 65 years of age or older (National Vital Statistics Reports, 2001). Death rates for major cardiovascular diseases and cancer—the two largest killers of Americans—have recently begun to post small declines, while deaths from kidney failure, infections, Alzheimer's, Parkinson's, primary hypertension, and other nonspecific conditions are rising. As new medical treatments and interventions are devised to manage such conditions, even diseases once considered death sentences, such as cancer and AIDS, are becoming chronic, long-lasting conditions.

That trend in the evolution of life-limiting illnesses, coupled with the gradual aging of the population as a whole, suggests that the U.S. health care system of the future will need *not* more hospital operating and emergency rooms, but more home- and community-based services offering monitoring and interventions to help prevent exacerbations of chronic illnesses that otherwise could lead to avoidable hospitalizations.

We will need interdisciplinary care that addresses the multifaceted physical, psychosocial, spiritual, and practical needs of older, chronically ill patients, their caregivers, and their families. In other words: hospice care.

Hospice care in the United States has found its niche primarily in caring for older adults with terminal illnesses such as cancer. It has grown from a small-scale health care experiment introduced from England in the mid-1970s to a nationwide community of providers that together serves one fourth of all dying Americans. Hospice care and its community of providers offer some valuable lessons for a health care system that needs to transition from an acute medical orientation to one that can more effectively answer the chronic care needs of an aging population. Because hospice care has often been misunderstood by the public and potential consumers as well as by other health professionals it is worth exploring in some depth.

Hospice Philosophy

An operational definition of hospice care can be found in the recently revised Standards of Practice for Hospice Care, set by the National Hospice and Palliative Care Organization (NHPCO):

> Hospice provides support and care for persons in the last phases of an incurable disease so that they may live as fully and comfortably as possible. Hospice recognizes that the dying process is part of the normal process of living and focuses on enhancing the quality of remaining life. Hospice affirms life and neither hastens nor postpones death. Hospice exists in the hope and belief that through appropriate care, and the promotion of a caring community, sensitive to their needs that individuals and their families may be free to attain a degree of satisfaction in preparation for death. Hospice recognizes that human growth and development can be a lifelong process. Hospice seeks to preserve and promote the inherent potential for growth within individuals and families during the last phase of life. (NHPCO, 2001a)

According to the NHPCO standards, hospice programs provide palliative care, which is defined as "treatment that enhances comfort and improves the quality of an individual's life during the last phase of life." NHPCO's definition of hospice care is consistent with the philosophy of care first promulgated at St. Christopher's Hospice, the first modern hospice, by Dame Cicely Saunders in England in 1967. The following tenets of hospice care developed at St. Christopher's have served as touchstones for American hospices (Connor, 1998):

1. *The patient* and *family is the unit of care.* Hospices don't just admit patients, they serve the whole family and address the family's needs as well as the patient's.

2. *Symptom management is the focus of treatment.* Rather than continuing attempts to cure the disease, hospice care focuses on control of symptoms of the illness through effective palliative care.

3. *Care is provided in the home and at inpatient facilities.* Although most hospice care is provided in patients' own homes, hospices have arrangements to deliver care in inpatient settings when patients are unable to remain in their homes.

4. *Hospice care is for the whole person, including social, psychological, physical, spiritual, and practical needs.* Rather than just focusing on physical care, the hospice approach recognizes that social, psychological, spiritual, and practical needs often are critical to good quality of life at life's end.

5. *Services are available 24 hours a day, seven days a week.* Dying patients have problems at all hours of the day or night, and hospices need to be able to respond promptly to those needs.

6. *Hospice care is interdisciplinary, involving carers who can respond to all of the patient and family's needs.* Interdisciplinary care requires collaboration between all team members, who have specialized expertise in the care of the terminally ill.

7. *Hospice care is physician directed.* All patients are under the care of a physician who can order all needed care. Hospice physicians work with the patient's attending physician to achieve optimal medical management.

8. *Volunteers are an integral part of hospice care.* They contribute a special quality of compassionate caring and support for the family.

9. *Services are provided without regard to ability to pay.* Hospices have always believed that financial limitations should never prevent access to needed care at the end of life.

10. *Bereavement services are provided based on need.* The provision of bereavement support to families before and after their loved one's death is a hallmark of hospice care.

Hospice Facts

In short, hospice programs provide a comprehensive set of services to meet the diverse needs of patients and their families at the end of life. Those services include nursing, social work, spiritual support, physicians, counseling, personal care, homemakers, medications, medical supplies, and durable medical equipment. Each patient is assigned to an interdisciplinary team, who develops a plan of care with direction from the patient and family. Staff members visit intermittently to provide the care, with special attention to preventing and controlling pain and other symptoms. The hospice team also assesses and responds to psychosocial and spiritual concerns and attends to the patient and family's emotional coping.

In 2001, NHPCO identified more than 3,000 hospice program offices in the United States and its territories (NHPCO, 2001b), representing 2,505 hospice agencies, some of which have multiple locations. Since hospice care is provided primarily in the patient's home, hospice teams need to be located in the communities they serve, able to respond to patients' needs without having to travel long distances.

In 2001, 20% of U.S. hospices were for-profit corporations, some of which provide operations across wide regions. The majority of hospice agencies continued to comprise not-for-profit organizations (73%). The remaining 7% are government entities. According to NHPCO membership data, 43% of hospices are freestanding entities (not corporately affiliated with another health care provider), while 33% are affiliated with hospitals, 22% with home health agencies, 9% with managed care providers, and 8% under other organizational auspices. According to 2001 Medicare data, 2,280 hospice programs are certified to provide and be reimbursed for the Medicare hospice benefit (described below). NHPCO estimates that 9% of hospices are volunteer programs, not certified to participate in Medicare.

Nearly 2.4 million Americans died in 2000. NHPCO estimates that hospices enrolled 700,000 terminally ill patients that year, and more than 600,000 of them died while receiving hospice care. That figure represents one out of every four people who died from any cause in the United States in 2000. Among those patients, 1% were 17 years of age or younger and another 1% were aged 18 to 34. Eighteen percent were aged 35 to 64, 26% were 65 to 74, 32% were 75 to 84, and 22% were 85 or older. Thus, patients aged 65 and above account four fifths of the hospice population. In 2000, 82% of the patients served by hospices were white or Caucasian, 8% were black or African American, 2% were Hispanic or Latino, 2% were other and 6% were not classified by race.

In its early days, the U.S. hospice industry served primarily patients with cancer, but in recent years, the proportion of patients with diseases other than cancer has been growing. In 1999, 64% of hospice patients were diagnosed with cancer while 36% had other diseases including end-stage heart disease (8%), end-stage lung disease (6%), dementias (5%), end-stage kidney disease (2%), end-stage liver disease (1%), HIV/AIDS (1%), and stroke or coma (3%). Diabetes and ALS patients accounted for less than 1% each, and 8% had other diagnoses.

Of all deaths in the United States, slightly less than 50% currently occur in a hospital, about 25% occur at home and another 25% in a nursing facility. For those patients who died under the care of hospices,

56% died at home, 19% died in a nursing facility, 4% died in a hospice unit, 8% died in a hospital, 11% died in a freestanding inpatient facility operated by the hospice, and 2% died in a residential care setting. Thus, hospices have shown considerable success in their goal of offering patients the option of dying at home.

Funding

When the hospice movement began in the United States, there was little or no funding for the care of dying patients. Contributions, grants, donations, and limited reimbursement under home health agency licenses paid for essential costs, while volunteers delivered most of the services. Because of the financial constraints, the number of people that hospices were able to care for was small.

The pioneers of hospice recognized that in order to have a significant impact on care of the dying in America, they would need a payment mechanism. Since most people who die are over 65, the obvious choice was to seek Medicare reimbursement. In 1982, Congress created the Medicare Hospice Benefit, which is reimbursed under Medicare Part A (hospital insurance). In order to be eligible for this benefit, beneficiaries must be entitled to Medicare Part A and certified by both their primary physician and the hospice medical director as having a terminal condition with a prognosis of six months or less to live—if the illness were to run its normal course.

The regulations established benefit periods for eligibility for Medicare hospice coverage, currently two initial 90-day benefit periods followed by an unlimited number of 60-day periods. At the start of each new benefit period, a physician (usually the hospice medical director) must recertify that a patient still has a medical prognosis of six months or less to live. At enrollment, the patient must sign a consent for admission acknowledging his or her understanding that hospice care is palliative in nature and that he or she has chosen to forgo regular Medicare services for the terminal illness by opting for hospice care. Patients cannot receive both curative medical treatment and palliative hospice care simultaneously. Under the Medicare benefit, the hospice program must directly provide or else arrange for essentially all services needed to manage the terminally ill patient's care and finance those services out of an all-inclusive daily payment.

Eighty-two percent of hospice patients had their care covered by Medicare, while 5% reported Medicaid, 10% had private insurance, 1% were self-pay, and 2% cited alternative sources. Other payment sources may include, but are not limited to, Worker's Compensation, home health agency benefits, or donations. In addition, hospices received, on average, 12% of their total revenues from charitable contributions in 2000.

A 1995 Lewin-VHI study, commissioned by NHPCO, showed that for every dollar Medicare spent on hospice, it saved $1.52 in Medicare Part A expenditures. The 1995 study also demonstrated that in their last year of life, hospice patients incurred $2,737 less in costs than those not enrolled in hospice care, as home-based hospice care substituted for more expensive hospitalizations and futile, cure-oriented treatments. A 1988 study conducted by the Health Care Financing Administration (now the Centers for Medicare and Medicaid Services) identified savings of $1.26 for every Medicare dollar spent on hospice care (NHPCO, 1995).

Length of Service and Other Challenges

America's hospices are now approaching 20 years under the Medicare system. The Medicare benefit has fueled remarkable growth for the movement, but reimbursement has also brought about some unintended problems. One of those is length of service. The regulations specify that the patient must have a medical prognosis of six months or less to live in order to qualify for hospice coverage under Medicare. Since it is impossible to know in advance how an individual patient's disease will progress, some patients with a prognosis of six months or less may reasonably end up living far longer.

Still, hospice organizations are very concerned about length-of-service statistics, for two reasons. First, very short stays (i.e., the final few days or hours leading up to the patient's death) typically mean that the hospice team provides crisis management only, with little opportunity to facilitate meaningful farewells or peaceful life closure for the patient. On the other hand, the federal government has been scrutinizing hospice programs in recent years to make certain that they are not enrolling—and billing Medicare for—patients who could be expected to live longer than six months.

NHPCO data indicate that the average length of service in hospice in 2000 was 48 days and the median (a more accurate marker of actual experience, since it represents the midpoint at which half of patients were on service for either shorter or longer periods) was 25 days. Both of those numbers have dropped significantly over the past decade (NHPCO, 2001b).

As medical advancements bring more and more disease-modifying treatments, most people with advanced illnesses want to be cured of their disease and will opt to continue such treatments if possible. Because hospice care was designed (and funded) as a palliative alternative to high-intensity, disease-modifying or cure-oriented medical treatments, the recent advances in medicine have presented hospice agencies with a serious dilemma.

Each hospice program has to decide which treatments are curative and which are palliative (and thus potentially an appropriate part of the hospice plan of care). Many new disease-modifying treatments are not curative but are aimed at life-prolongation—and they can be quite expensive. As such, they cannot feasibly be provided within the financial constraints of hospice's all-inclusive daily reimbursement, which was not intended to cover such treatments.

Another dilemma is that patients often are reluctant to give up such treatments if they have even a slight hope of benefit, a situation that results in delays in accessing hospice care and the short lengths of service described above. It also forces patients into a terrible choice between disease-modifying treatments and the palliative care that could relieve their suffering. While no one wants a system that encourages futile treatment, the hospice community wants to ensure that comprehensive comfort care is available to those with advanced illnesses throughout the course of their care.

Hospices now serve one of every four people who die in the United States, but to reach a larger proportion of those who need end-of-life care, it is essential to test and explore new ways of delivering hospice and palliative care. Two possible changes that could significantly improve the current system are (1) a payment mechanism that allows for interdisciplinary palliative care consultations to be provided by hospice teams in hospitals, homes, and nursing facilities prior to hospice enrollment and (2) a health benefit for patients with advanced chronic illness to receive care management services focused on education, advanced care planning, conversations about life-closure issues, and enhanced connections to existing health services. Increased payments or "carve-outs" to cover emerging new medical treatments would also help improve access to hospice's professional expertise in end-of-life care.

Discussion

The older we live the closer death comes. People of all ages want to be assured that reliable care will be available to them as death approaches and that such care will be effective in assuring them a comfortable passage. Hospice care is the most widely used and comprehensive system for care at the end of life and currently provides the gold standard for such care, designed to meet all of the needs that can be expected to arise as death approaches.

NHPCO has defined three essential outcomes from optimal end-of-life care: (1) safe and comfortable dying, (2) self-determined life closure, and (3) effective grieving (NHPCO, 1996). The dimensions of care important to patients and families at the end of life include treatment of problems, prevention of problems, and realization of opportunities for growth.

Unless a patient feels safe and has troubling symptoms controlled, there is not much opportunity for personal growth at life's end. Similarly, each person ends life in his or her own, highly individual way. It is important to attend to the unique needs, preferences, and priorities of each dying person so that life can end with as few unresolved issues as possible. Grief and mourning permeate the time surrounding a person's death. Most of us manage to live through our losses with the help of friends and supporters, but for some, more intensive assistance is needed. Hospices provide needed grief support and serve as a bridge to competent mental health practitioners for those whose grief is more difficult and complicated.

Staff from hospitals, nursing facilities, assisted living environments, and other health programs and care settings need to acknowledge that death is part of the continuum of care for older persons. Since experiences of loss tend to accumulate in older individuals, we can learn from hospice professionals about what is most useful in helping the bereaved find their way through this process. As one experiences more and more losses, attention must be paid to the fact that the emotional impact from such losses can add up if they are not fully acknowledged and worked through. Hospice staff have learned, as part of their assessment process, to take a loss history. Expression of thoughts and feelings about previous loss is encouraged, as is acknowledgement of current and anticipated loss. Social support and prevention of isolation are other key ingredients to prevention and treatment for those at high risk of a poor outcome.

The hospice movement originated as a consumer-driven response to the depersonalization of conventional medical care for the dying. In response, hospice has emphasized care in the home over institutionalization; simple but effective interventions over intrusive high-tech therapies; and whole-person care over fragmented, specialist-driven treatments.

What can be learned from this successful health care experiment? We know that there are tremendous vested interests in the financing of health care. Hospitals, physicians, and health facilities want to continue to receive the lion's share of health care resources. Hospices, likewise, have nurtured their position as a distinct sector of the health care system. What is starting to emerge within that complex of competing interests is a true partnership between acute and long-term care institutions and hospice providers.

No sea change in health care policy and payment is likely to occur in the current political climate. Still, hospices must challenge themselves to become more integrated into health care institutions while acute facilities must retool their services and facilities to better meet the needs of the chronically ill. Those of us who work in the health care field need to realize that the changes we make today will have a direct impact on the quality of end-of-life care that we will receive in coming decades, as we come to face our own deaths. ■

Stephen R. Connor, PhD, is Vice President for Research and Professional Development at the National Hospice and Palliative Care Organization (NHPCO) in Alexandria, Virginia. He has worked in the hospice movement since 1975 as the CEO of four different hospice programs. In addition to being a hospice executive, he is a licensed clinical psychologist with private practice experience and a researcher. He is a former JCAHO hospice surveyor and a member of the International Work Group on Death, Dying, & Bereavement. Dr. Connor has chaired the NHPCO Standards and Accreditation, and Research Committees as well as the NHPCO Medical Guidelines Task Force. He is the author of Hospice: Practice, Pitfalls, and Promise *and has published a large number of journal articles, reviews, and book chapters on issues related to the hospice movement and care of dying patients and their families.*

References

Centers for Disease Control and Prevention. (October 9, 2001). National vital statistics reports. *Deaths: Preliminary data for 2000, 49* (12). Retrieved October 10, 2001, from http://www.cdc.gov/nchs/data/nvsr/nvsr49/nvsr49_12.pdf.

Connor, S. (1998). *Hospice: Practice, pitfalls, and promise.* New York: Taylor & Francis.

National Hospice and Palliative Care Organization. (1995). *An analyses of the cost savings of the medicare hospice benefit.* (Item 702901). Alexandria, VA. Author.

National Hospice and Palliative Care Organization. (1996). *A pathway for patients and families facing terminal illness* (Item No. 713800). Alexandria, VA: Author.

National Hospice and Palliative Care Organization. (2001a). *Standards of practice for hospice programs* (Item No. 711077). Alexandria, VA: Author.

National Hospice and Palliative Care Organization. (2001b). *Facts and Figures.* Retrieved October 6, 2001, from http://www.nhpco.org/.

CHAPTER 14

Ethical Issues in Hospice Care

Mark H. Waymack

INTRODUCTION

From the very beginning, the hospice movement in the United States has focused on allowing and encouraging most patient care to take place in the dying patient's home whenever possible. In 2000, the majority of patients who died in the care of hospice died in their own homes (NHPCO, 2001b). From the start, this focus on the home setting has raised a variety of ethical questions. These ethical questions are informed by the dominant demographic in hospice care—the age of the typical hospice patient. More than 80% of patients served by hospice programs in 2000 were 65 or older (NHPCO, 2001b). The ethical issues involved in providing care in the home, combined with the fact that the patients being cared for are older and facing the end of life, become particularly relevant for those working with an older population. Both the mission and the setting of hospice care place certain kinds of ethical concerns and worries foremost on the table.

The Winding Road of Bioethics

Bioethics, as a contemporary discipline, began in earnest in the 1970s. The antiauthoritarian streak of the 1960s had chipped away at the moral power of physicians to make decisions unilaterally. Additionally, the rapid change in medical technology served to raise many questions on the part of patients and families concerning the appropriate goals and methods of contemporary, advanced medical technology. In 1976, the New Jersey State Supreme Court was asked to decide the fate of Karen Ann Quinlan, a permanently comatose young woman whose parents wanted to have her ventilator removed and whose physicians refused to withdraw the breathing apparatus. Cases such as Quinlan's began to emerge, where questions arose concerning both what the proper use of technology might be as well as who ought to be making the decision to use it. Should we pull the plug? Should we allow death to come? Unsure of their new role, physicians and hospitals turned to philosophers and theologians for assistance in working their way through this ethical quagmire.

What first emerged was the product of interaction between acute care physicians and academic philosophers. Not surprisingly, the literature focused almost exclusively upon the dramatic life and death questions and the answers, enthusiastically offered by the academicians, were cast in the abstract mode of the moral principles and universal moral truths that were the bread and butter of academic philosophers. *Principles of Biomedical Ethics (1979)*, a textbook by Tom Beauchamp and James Childress, was a stunning success. The book's four principles quickly became the mantra of biomedical ethics: autonomy, beneficence, non-malfeasance, and justice. In its popular application, the principle of respect for patient autonomy became the heavily predominant, ruling principle.

In a way, this was fortuitous. Many of the unsettling, ethically difficult questions that arise in the acute care setting deal with life and death decisions. Furthermore, the traditional structure of the hospital, emphasizing physician power combined with intimidating technology, an alienating environment, and the very fact of acute illness, conspires to erode patient autonomy. Hence, an ethics that strongly asserts patient autonomy was a well-needed corrective to the power imbalances in the acute care setting.

The long-term care industry soon decided that it, too, needed to sharpen its ethics. This was partly a matter of high technology working its way into the nursing home setting and partly a wish to adopt a more medical model. Hence, nursing homes began to have ethics committees that worked diligently on policies for such things as Do Not Resuscitate orders, withdrawal of feeding tubes, and provisions for advance directives to promote patient autonomy (e.g., the living will and the durable power of attorney for health care decision making). After many years, thanks to the challenging work of Rosalie Kane and Arthur Caplan (1990), it became evident that the decisions that worried nursing home residents themselves were different from the issues that had absorbed the interest of the academics doing nursing home ethics. Instead of being focused upon high-technology issues of medical life and death, the residents of nursing homes were far more concerned with the issues of everyday life: Who gets the chair by the window? Why can't I have personal money? Why can't I have some privacy? Why can't I use the telephone?

These are issues that rarely come up in the acute care setting. This is because the issues of long-term care are different (they are about living with chronic conditions) and because the residents really *live* in the long-term setting. They are not just visiting for a few days. Whereas the hospital is almost never home to the patients, the nursing home very often becomes home for the resident.

Contemporary trends in nursing home ethics are seeking to go even further, to focus less on autonomy of the individual in this abstract sense and more on autonomy in a social, communal context, with other residents, paid staff, and family all in the picture.

What we have learned is that at the practical level where we actually experience ethical and moral conflict or obscurity, the particular context can make a great deal of difference in the issues, questions, and strategies that arise. It should be no surprise, then, that the questions and principles that might have served relatively well in the acute care setting do not satisfy the ethical needs in the hospice setting.

The Mission of Hospice

While there may be some discussion over the finer points of what constitutes the mission of hospice, it is inarguably very different from that of acute care. The acute care setting, de facto though not de jure, focuses upon saving life. The hospice mission, on the other hand, is to care for those who acknowledge that they are in the process of dying. Contemporary, high technology medical care in Western countries, perhaps especially in the United States, emphasizes preserving life through the use of its technology. There can come a time, however, when the use of such technologies (surgeries, chemotherapy, radiation, etc.) actually cause great suffering in themselves, but their use will not save the patient from dying. At this juncture, many patients might choose a course of care that emphasizes comfort, palliation, and dignity rather than pursuing invasive, futile interventions that cause even greater suffering. Hospice, then, focuses upon support of the dying patient so that he or she might benefit from humane, comfort-centered, person-centered care through the course of the dying process.

Issue of Setting

An important facet of hospice ethics is how the physical setting of care dramatically affects ethical issues. In particular, the setting shapes our ethical obligations and relations to the patients, but it also affects our moral relations to hospice workers as well as to patients' families. All of these parties are involved in complex caregiving relationships. What one does for one party is likely to have an affect on other parties as well. While it is true that some hospice care is delivered in the institutional setting, most hospice care is delivered at home. Patients are living (and dying) in their own homes, in their own beds, and often with their own families participating in the care process.

Family members and friends play an important role in providing care during this process. The hospice team includes physicians, nurses, social workers, clergy, and physical and occupational therapists. A good deal of care is delivered by certified nursing assistants and home health aides, and many hospices have a strong base of trained volunteers who provide respite and support. These last two categories of hospice workers are often significant part of hospice care. The complexities of where the patient receives care, who is giving it, and who is supervising the caregivers all affect the ethical texture of hospice care.

Lack of Direct Supervision

Each individual has an ethical obligation to act morally towards others, but in organizations, including hospice agencies, supervisors are shouldered with the added responsibility of ensuring that others in the group behave in an ethically appropriate manner. As in many organizations, managers and supervisors may talk a fine talk about maintaining a high standard of ethics in the delivery of care, yet it falls to the "front line" workers to actually deliver care. So, managers and supervisors have a moral responsibility to effectively supervise their workers to ensure that high standards of care—in technical and in ethical terms—are maintained.

In a nursing home or hospital, the work area is limited. It is quite feasible to have supervisors literally monitoring how care is delivered. Supervisors can readily see if care is not being delivered. They can also see when care is being delivered in an inappropriate manner that places the worker at risk. Thus, supervisors at many levels may monitor care delivery to ensure quality care, ethical care, care that is appropriate for the patient and that also protects the worker. Based upon direct observation, they can remonstrate when necessary, educate when appropriate, and reward whenever it is deserved. Although the manner in which such supervision is exercised may vary depending upon whether the worker is a physician, a nurse, a social worker, or a nursing assistant, there is still the opportunity for effective oversight and education.

In the home setting favored by hospice, however, this all becomes highly problematic. Direct supervision is either cursory, sporadic, or nonexistent. The patient has a moral right to the care that is being paid for. The patient has a moral right to our respect, consideration, and compassion. But how do we know if the worker showed up on time? How do we know if the worker did the chores, delivered the care in a caring, humane, compassionate manner? Often, we rely upon the worker's own integrity and upon the reporting of the patient or family. But, given the shortage of willing and qualified hospice care workers and thus how difficult it can be to find willing workers, how eager will patients or families be to report a worker who sloughs off or perhaps even abuses the patient? Additionally, hospice patients may feel vulnerable. They are not able to care for themselves adequately. They *depend* upon others to help, and they may well be reluctant to jeopardize the relationship with the person they depend upon by reporting them for showing up late, leaving early, or slighting some tasks.

Home is the Patient's Turf

In the acute care setting, it is the medical establishment that has the upper hand. Acute illness brings its own assault upon our ability to exert autonomy, a diminishment that is exacerbated by the difference in knowledge between patient and physician. Hence, in the acute care setting, medical ethics has been keen to redress that imbalance. In the home setting of hospice, it is the paid caregiver who is a guest, a visitor, not the patient. The patient is in his or her own home, on his or her own "turf."

One way that this affects the ethic of the patient-caregiver relationship is that it effectively becomes much more of a "do for" relationship than a "do to" one. What happens, then, when the care the patient wishes for differs from what the professional deems appropriate, even requisite? The patient may refuse care that the professional thinks his or her standard of professionalism requires. Alternately, the patient's demands may go far beyond what the professional thinks is medically required or appropriate. While certified nursing assistants may not have the equivalent of a Code of Ethics to which they are ethically obliged as physicians and nurses are, such workers will have clearly articulated responsibilities as dictated by their agency. These workers may find that those obligations, as defined by the agency, may well differ from what the patient wishes. This concern is heightened when the patient lives in conditions that the worker may deem unsafe, yet the patient refuses any suggestion of admission to any kind of facility. Perhaps the dwelling is not geared for the patient's increasing physical frailty. Perhaps living in that particular dwelling exposes the patient to risk of violence. If the patient refuses to move to a more appropriate setting, there is little the health care worker can do to change the situation.

Second, since the worker becomes more like a guest, the patient may come to perceive the worker as more like a friend or companion than as a paid caregiver. Confusing this relationship as one of friendship rather than one of worker-patient can work in both directions. Perhaps the patient is keener on having a pleasant, intense, or diverting conversation rather than being bathed or having her medications and equipment checked. This leaves paid workers (and especially nonprofessional workers) in an awkward conflict. Should the worker do what the care plan directs (even requires), or should the worker do what the patient would like him or her to do, even if it means that the officially prescribed care plan cannot be fully performed in the allotted time?

Additionally, workers may come to see themselves more as their patients see them, as something of a guest and friend. While a paid worker generally has limited, fairly well-defined obligations, the obligations of friendship are much more difficult to delimit. Seeing themselves as more than just paid professionals, workers may find themselves staying many extra hours, coming in extra days, calling after hours to check on their charge. All of these are noble things to do, but if taken too far and for too long, the job becomes abusive to the worker. Workers become burned out or feel like they can never do enough. The ever-escalating demands upon the workers' time and energy become detrimental. In addition, since this is hospice care and all of their clients die, workers can become hardened, cynical, and may well leave the hospice work force. Once again, an ethic of strict rules may seems too harsh here, never allowing for the particularities of context, the idiosyncratic needs of the individual patient, but an ethic of working case by case leaves the worker open to abuse and burnout, neither of which is ethically desirable.

Obligations to Workers

While much of what has been said thus far relates most directly to the organization's obligations to its patients, we must also consider the organization's obligations to its employees. In the hospital or the nursing home, as noted above, management may be able to have a large measure of control over the work environment. They can ensure that the proper equipment is available and is being used and that there are other workers to assist when necessary. They can, in many ways, protect the safety of their employees in the course of their duties.

Where the agency has no real control, however, is in the home environment. The house may be in what the worker perceives as an unsafe neighborhood. The dwelling itself might be in unsafe condition; it might be structurally unsound. It might not be the dwelling or neighborhood that threatens the safety or well-being of the worker, it might be the patient. Anger and resentment are very common emotions felt by dying individuals, and caregivers certainly need to understand this, but anger, resentment, and prejudice can also be turned upon a caregiver in ways that constitute abuse of the worker. This can also happen in the nursing home, particularly since dementia is now so endemic in that setting, but in the nursing home it may be easier to control, defuse, and minimize the problem. Furthermore, there are other staff and supervisors to lend support to the worker on the receiving end of abuse. The mere presence of colleagues can serve to lighten the burden. But in the hospice (home) setting, where such emotions may run high, the visiting worker rarely has colleagues nearby for immediate support or to help defuse the situation. Hence, the wounds of abuse—physical or emotional—can cut much deeper.

Finally, as noted above, since this is hospice care, all of our patients are dying. Each patient we care for dies. Because our worker-patient relationships tend to be more personal than those in the hospital, the death of each patient may affect the worker far more deeply and personally than is typical in the acute care setting. Hospice workers engage in care that can be both physically and emotionally demanding. If employers are required to provide safe workplaces for their employees, then organizations must actively provide moral and emotional support to our workers as they regularly confront the deaths of those for whom they care. Most hospices have developed rituals and other means of support to help their employees cope. These rituals should also include contract employees, who may also become extremely close to their dying patients.

FAMILY

Family members typically play a significant role in hospice care. In an acute care setting, families may visit in the hospital, they may participate in discussion with the medical team and patient, but they are almost never involved in direct caregiving. Yet in the hospice setting, family may be asked to take on a significant caregiving role. We often encourage such participation and may even request it, because the family's participation benefits the patient. Thus, we often expect and request more from family members in hospice, not because the patient is dying, but because the care is being delivered in the home setting. Under ideal circumstances, everyone benefits from this arrangement. Unfortunately, reality is not always so ideal.

When crafting home hospice care plans, it is important to bear in mind the moral obligation toward the family. While we may expect families to play a role in caregiving and think it ethically incumbent upon them to do so, we should also understand that taking on that role constitutes a burden. Some family members may willingly, even gladly, accept such a burden. Others may shy away or outright refuse. But even in cases where the family members readily agree, the caregiving still remains a time- and energy-consuming burden. This gives rise to the question: What is morally *fair* to expect of families?

Regrettably, some family members may even take advantage of the dying patient. Is the patient valued by the family as a loved one, or is he or she valued as a source of income? There actually have been instances in which family members have stolen the patient's pain medications to sell on the streets or use for themselves. "Blood runs thicker than water," as the old saying goes, and the patient, even though dying, may feel an unconditional love and obligation to his or her family members in spite of the abuse that they suffer at the hands of their family. Thus, the patient may discount his or her own well being for the sake of family members. If hospice workers become aware of this, what are they to do? They are caught between what they perceive to be in the patient's best interests as opposed to what the patient sees as of greatest importance.

While such problems may arise in the acute care or long-term care setting, the home setting that is common in hospice greatly exacerbates the ethical difficulties here. There is at least a presumption that the home setting *belongs* to the patient and family in ways that the acute care setting certainly does not belong to them. Even in the long-term setting, though the room and bed may become a kind of substitute for home, there is not the kind of connection to the nursing home room that a family may often have to a dying person's home. The nursing home room still very much *belongs* to the nursing home.

In some cases, then, the worker and agency may be have to protect the family from the patient. In other cases they might have to consider protecting the patient from the family. In still other circumstances, they might have to worry about protecting the worker from the family. While the ethical tensions and stakes are real and may be high, each case must be dealt with on an individual basis, using the principles that have guided the hospice movement since its inception.

Conclusion

The mission of hospice—the humane, compassionate care of the dying person—inevitably provides a framework for ongoing ethical questions. In addition, hospice care's usual home setting accentuates numerous moral issues. The fact of this setting colors and complicates the ethics of relationship between worker and patient, patient and family, worker and family, as well as between the supervisor or agency and each of those three: worker, patient and family. Because of the individual nature of each case, and the focus on the patient as the center of care, it can be difficult to specify overarching ethical principles. Yet, as more older persons continue to be served by hospice, it is vital to continually re-examine and reconsider these important issues, while preparing to face those the future holds. ■

Mark H. Waymack, PhD, is Associate Professor of Philosophy and Co-Director of Graduate Programs in Health Care Ethics at Loyola University Chicago. He is also an adjunct Assistant Professor of Medicine (Medical Ethics and Humanities) at Northwestern University Medical School. Professor Waymack has been active in the areas of ethics and aging for many years.

References

Beauchamp, T., & Childress, J. (1977). *Principles of biomedical ethics,* (1st ed.). New York: Oxford University Press.

Kane, R., & Caplan, A., (Eds.). (1990). *Everyday ethics: Resolving dilemmas in nursing home life.* New York: Springer Publishing.

National Hospice and Palliative Care Organization. (2001b). "Facts and Figures." Updated November 8, 2001.

■ CHAPTER 15 ■

Practical Suggestions

A Final Affairs Fair

Jane Dryden Louis

Death can and does unfold at an alarming pace. At the core of the process rests the reality that human life has both a beginning and an end. Great attention is devoted in our culture to planning for the beginning of life, but for most, planning for the end of life gets short shrift. There are, however, numerous ways for professionals to help plan for the end of life with the same attention and care that we devote to the sacred time preceding it. One way is by hosting a Final Affairs Fair.

Saint David's Episcopal Church in Austin, Texas, is one faith community that has hosted a Final Affairs Fair. The fair, a day-long, end-of-life planning workshop, was a collaborative effort between the ministries of education, pastoral care, and stewardship. One goal was to bring end-of-life issues into active dialogue within the context of faith. Following are some tips for hosting a Final Affairs Fair, an illustrative look at how Saint David's fair helped one member, and a look at that fair.

Refashioned after a model used by another church, Saint David's day-long agenda included presentations by an attorney, a hospital chaplain, a financial planner, a planned giving professional, a funeral home director, and clergy staff. Participants learned how legal documents and services could bring beliefs, values, and priorities to light during health care decisions, distribution of assets, and designation of advocacy. The complex realities of industry-regulated health care; the ethical challenges lurking in the shadow of medicine's abundant treatment choices; and the importance of open and ongoing dialogue among health care professionals, family members, and support systems were all discussed. Also addressed were options for disposition of the body, issues of state and local laws affecting such choices, and the overall funeral service.

Participants received workbooks that included articles, resource information, and sample legal documents. During the fair, people could execute Advanced Medical Directives, designate powers of attorney, and explore Medicare benefits. They left the event knowing that their community of faith was willing to be an active partner as they faced the end of life. Every item on the agenda could have been addressed individually and elsewhere, but the fact that all aspects of concern came together on the familiar ground of their faith made the subject matter not only palatable, but also approachable and manageable.

One member who attended the fair, Allen, updated his will; executed Advanced Medical Directives; filled in the blanks on the planning form; and picked scripture readings and music for his funeral service. He was a 68-year-old divorced father with grown children in distant parts of the country. He shared his plans with his children, significant friends, and clergy and placed a copy of his plans on file at the church. As time passed, Allen's chronic health problems took a downward turn. Days after a biopsy, he went to his physician to hear of his advanced malignancy. On a Tuesday, a minister from the church accompanied Allen to the doctor's office. He left with no recommendation for treatment, a prognosis of six weeks, and a hospice referral. The hospice intake visit occurred on Wednesday and a consultative visit with an oncologist followed on Thursday. Friday, he visited with his priest and got a haircut. By Saturday afternoon, he was semicomatose and at midnight was transported to the hospital. A minister rode in the ambulance with him to the hospital, directives in hand, while two church friends followed in the car. Allen died on Sunday afternoon in the company of people he loved and who loved him, both through life—and all its glories and challenges, and through death—and all its mystery and hope.

A Final Affairs Fair can provide individuals with valuable information and tangible advice. During the fair, an opportunity exists for a free exchange of information and ample opportunity to question and seek clarification. In the process, fears can be addressed, misconceptions clarified, and doubts and confusion taken seriously and met with respect.

■

Planning a Final Affairs Fair is similar to planning any event. Organizers should identify planning and committee needs, date, location, costs, budget, and publicity. Every fair will have specific needs tailored to your individual organization or community. The following information is a general outline that can be used to create an end-of-life planning workbook for your participants.

END-OF-LIFE PLANNING WORKBOOK

- Death certificate information sheet
  - General information such as name, address, date of birth
  - Social Security, military, VA information
  - Spousal information
  - Parental information

- Communication and contact information sheet
  - Next of kin information
  - Names of children
  - Who should be contacted

- Legal matters information sheet
  - Attorney information
  - Insurance information
  - Accountant information
  - Employer, executor, power of attorney
  - Safe deposit box information
  - Location of policies and important documents

- Final arrangements
  - Burial benefits
  - Funeral home preferences
  - Prearrangements made
  - Obituary information
  - Cemetery plots
- Treatment of the body
  - Casket and burial
  - Alternatives
  - Organ donations
- Other comments and instructions
- Recommended resources ■

Jane Dryden Louis serves as the Assistant for Pastoral Care at St. David's Episcopal Church, a large congregation in downtown Austin, Texas. Her undergraduate education in biological science was followed by a career in medical research. After a second career in child-raising and community volunteerism, she returned to formal education, earning a Master of Arts in religion from the Episcopal Theological Seminary of the Southwest in 1995. Since that time Ms. Dryden Louis has combined her background in medical science with her faith and theological education to serve people in crisis.

CHAPTER 16

Disenfranchised Grief

Kenneth J. Doka

INTRODUCTION

Ed is in the early stages of Alzheimer's; he still recognizes the loss of his cognitive abilities. He is very aware of the sympathy people have for his wife when they see them together, but he is fearful of his own decline and deeply grieves his loss.

Nakeisha's best friend, a woman she had known for almost 80 of her 88 years, recently died. There were many signs that her grief was not recognized by others. No one sent her flowers. Even her children, when they took her to the funeral, commented on how difficult it would be for the children and grandchildren. It was difficult for Nakeisha, as well.

Jim's last fall, with an accompanying painful and big bruise, convinced him that he should give up skiing. A man of 79 years of age, living alone, cannot afford a broken bone. So last year, he gave away his equipment. This year, at the opening of the ski season, he was depressed.

Lisa's mom died at 96 years of age after a brief illness. Everyone told Lisa it was such a blessing. Lisa did not feel she was blessed at all. She misses her mom greatly.

All of these people have experienced a significant loss—of an activity, an ability, or a person. Each loss has engendered a sense of grief, but such grief is disenfranchised, meaning that, although these people have experienced a loss, those around them feel that they have no right to grieve, that their grief isn't valid. Disenfranchised grief is not uncommon in older persons. Senescence, or the process of aging, brings a host of developmental losses. In addition, as individuals continue to survive, it is inevitable that they will experience the loss of significant others.

This chapter explores the phenomenon of disenfranchised grief in the older population, beginning with a definition of disenfranchised grief and a list of the factors of disenfranchised grief. The second section features a sample of contexts where grief may be disenfranchised. The final section offers suggestions for counselors and other professionals on how to assist older persons in dealing with their many losses and recognize and legitimate their grief.

THE NATURE OF DISENFRANCHISED GRIEF

In earlier work (Doka, 1989), I first defined disenfranchised grief as "grief that is experienced when a loss cannot be openly acknowledged, socially sanctioned, or publicly mourned." In short, while a person has experienced a loss, the person does not have a "right" to grieve that loss since no one else recognizes a legitimate cause of grief.

Grief can be disenfranchised in a number of contexts, including relationships that are not recognized and losses that are unacknowledged. It can also be disenfranchised when the person experiencing the loss is not believed to be capable of grief. This can occur in cases where the person grieving a loss is developmentally or cognitively impaired or mentally ill. It can also be seen in situations when the very old or the very young are involved; others try to protect the person from the loss, feeling he or she is incapable or either understanding or processing grief. Grief also can be disenfranchised when the circumstances of the loss are such that sympathy is dismissed or the stigma of the loss inhibits the grieving person from seeking or receiving support. Finally, grief can be disenfranchised when the way the person grieves is not perceived by others as appropriate.

There are many factors that underlie disenfranchised grief. In some cases, those around the grieving person do not recognize the severity or meaning of the loss. In our society, the primacy of family ties is often stressed, leaving other relationships, however significant, ignored. Ritual, too, establishes in many people's minds a right to grieve. The reduced role of a non-family member in a funeral diminishes a claim to social support. Grief can also be disenfranchised when a loss is devalued. Here, the ageism of our society that makes the lives of older persons less valuable can be a significant factor in disenfranchisement.

The point is that disenfranchised grief is a concept that works on many levels. On a social level, it acknowledges that every society has "grieving rules" and norms that determine who may legitimately grieve what losses in which ways. There are other levels as well. Kauffman (2002) addresses the intrapsychic dimension of disenfranchised grief, that is, that the grieving people may disenfranchise themselves. Out of fear or shame, those experiencing the loss believe that they are incapable or unworthy of support or refuse to acknowledge and share the loss. For example, a person like Ed, the opening case, may be ashamed and fearful of his loss or cognitive abilities, unwilling to share that grief and anxiety with others.

Elder abuse is another example. Along with the abuse, the person feels a strong sense of loss—a loss of safety and a disappointment in a relationship. Yet the person may be ashamed to report it because of fear of appearing frail and of judgments about his or her abilities, support, or family. In such contexts not only is the abuse unreported, the consequent grief is disenfranchised.

Beyond guilt, fear, or shame, another reason for self-disenfranchisement may be the multiplicity of losses. Multiple losses over time may inhibit individuals from acknowledging all the losses that have been experienced. Neimeyer and Jordan (2002) suggest that the core of disenfranchised grief rests in "empathic failure." By that they mean that something—whether social, psychological, or relational—inhibits social support. Understanding the nature of that empathic failure can allow interventions than enfranchise grief.

Types of Disenfranchised Grief

Older persons experience a range of issues that can be disenfranchised. While this section cannot address all of these losses, I will discuss some representative examples of disenfranchised grief common in later life. Such a discussion is meant to stimulate consideration of other examples of disenfranchised grief. It is not meant to be an exhaustive or exclusive list.

Unrecognized Losses

One of the most significant losses in later life may be that of a sibling. Sibling relationships are unique in that they are kin ties, yet more equal than vertical relationships. Siblings are also part of one's intimate identity. A person may be "Dot's kid brother" or "Tommy's older sister"—an identity that becomes core early in life. Moreover, siblings share experiences they can recall and validate early family-related events and share perceptions. Beyond these psychological factors, siblings are often a significant source of social support, security, and assistance (Bengston, Rosenthal, & Burton, 1996). It is little wonder that the death of a sibling in later life, while little studied, seems to have a significant effect on siblings (Moss, Moss, & Hansson, 2001). Yet sibling loss may be largely ignored as sympathy is primarily extended to surviving spouses or children.

There are other relationships too, both within and outside of the family, that may engender significant grief reaction but remain unrecognized by others. There may be other kin who are significant in the lives of older individuals: kin-friends, that is, particular relatives with whom there is a very special and unique relationship, such as a favorite cousin, uncle, or niece. Friends and neighbors may assume significant and supportive relationships in an older person's life as well. Older persons may continue to enter into companionship relationships. Such relationships can include homosexual or heterosexual lovers. These relationships can occur regardless of marital status. Because of ageism, the sexuality and sexual/intimate relationships of adults may be largely overlooked. In addition, those residing in nursing homes or other assisted living facilities may forge strong bonds with other residents, roommates, or staff. There is some research that indicates, as individuals get older, they may limit their social network, focusing on a smaller group of emotionally rewarding ties (Carstensen, Gross, & Fung, 1997), but this does not preclude the fact that they do retain significant attachments. The impact of losing such attachments needs to be assessed. Moreover, even in clearly recognized ties such as with children, grandchildren, or great-grandchildren, the needs of the older family members can be ignored as others focus on surviving spouses or children.

Unacknowledged Losses

Another cause of disenfranchised grief is unacknowledged losses. These can be quite extensive in later life. Older persons, for example, can mourn developmental losses. In an ageist society, the very loss of youth can be grieved. Moreover, there are losses associated with aging such as the losses of various roles, including work and leisure roles. Older individuals may lose their abilities and independence, resulting in secondary losses such as the loss of home, neighbors, and community. As people age, they are likely to experience the cumulative and often subtle effects of social change. They may experience the loss of their native culture as they see their descendants assimilate into a newer culture and, for example, are unable to speak their ancestral language. They may mourn changes in their own communities such as the loss of favorite places.

A severe loss is the cognitive and relational losses associated with the onset of dementia. For the spouse and significant others, this can be a severe psychosocial loss, an experience in which the persona is so changed that the loved one as previously existed is perceived as dead even though that individual remains physically alive (Doka & Aber, 1989). There is a paradox in such cases; care demands may make surviving spouses or others more involved in the life of the individual with dementia, even as they mourn the passing of the person they once knew. In effect, the surviving spouse becomes a “crypto” or hidden widower, experiencing a range of losses, including companionship, independence, and intimacy. Since many causes of dementia such as

Alzheimer's disease are slow, progressive illnesses, the afflicted individual may experience a deep sense of loss as well, mourning the loss of cognitive abilities, connection, and memory.

This loss is typical of anticipatory grief or mourning. Anticipatory mourning refers broadly to the range of responses individuals have to an impending loss. As Rando (2000) reminds us, these responses are not only toward the anticipated future loss but rather the range of losses previously and presently experienced in the course of the illness. In the treatment of the disease, the psychosocial recognition of this loss—especially to the survivors—are often neglected.

There may be other losses that are unacknowledged. Animal companions can be significant to older persons (Meyers, 2002). They can be sources of companionship, stimulation, motivation, and protection. They may provide opportunities for interaction and socialization as, for example, when walking a pet dog. Animals may offer connection, linking the individual to earlier losses. For example, if a cat belonged to one's late husband, the loss of that pet can be significant (Meyers, 2002).

Not all unacknowledged losses are contemporary. The developmental processes of life review may bring to the fore earlier unacknowledged losses. For example, in earlier eras abortion and miscarriage were rarely addressed, recognized, or mourned. Grief over these events may reemerge in later life. In one case, I had a client who mourned an earlier abortion. He had insisted his wife have the abortion because he believed that their young family could not support another child. In his 90s, he had outlived one son and witnessed his only daughter caring for her only child who had severe developmental disabilities. He mourned the unborn child that he had fantasized now could run the business he had so laboriously built.

Other Types of Disenfranchised Grief

In other works (Doka, 1989, 2002), I discuss a series of factors that might disenfranchise grief. In addition to unacknowledged losses and unrecognized relationships, an individual's grief can be disenfranchised because the circumstances of the death or the way the individual grieves may inhibit empathic support. There are two situations that deserve special comment. In many cases, very old persons are considered frail and in need of protection. In such situations, even if they are cognitively aware, they may not be informed of the loss of others because others may not wish to upset or trouble them. Yet, in such cases, their right to grieve is denied, and they are disenfranchised. This is exacerbated when older persons show signs of confusion or dementia. Here, too, the fact that they are experiencing such symptoms may be a disincentive to involve them in any way with the loss. They may be deprived of knowledge or denied opportunity to attend any ritual. Careful assessment should be made of their ability to understand and participate when a loss occurs.

There is another circumstance of disenfranchisement. This is the disenfranchisement of the loss of older persons (Moss and Moss, 1989). Because of ageism, the death of an older person is seen as less noteworthy than that of a younger person. Survivors are often offered comfort that calls the death a "blessing" or comments on how long the person lived. Yet the grief over the loss of such a significant presence and person is discounted. When a child of 12 years loses a parent, there is recognition of catastrophic loss. But when that child is 62 years old, and the parent near 90, there is little recognition of the grief incurred.

Assisting Disenfranchised Grievers

It is critical to remember that disenfranchised grief is grief and should be treated as any other grief situation. But there are a few strategies that can be useful in helping older persons deal with disenfranchised grief. First, grief counselors should be sensitive to the range of losses that persons experience, particularly in later life. Remember, too, that loss is always individually perceived and evaluated. A role loss such as retirement may be a welcome respite to some but a grievous loss to others.

The key to counseling disenfranchised grievers is in analyzing empathic failure (Neimeyer & Jordan, 2002). This means that the counselor needs to assist the client in understanding what factors may be disenfranchising that grief. These sources can be many and complementary. In some cases, it may be intrapsychic. The individual's own sense of shame or guilt can inhibit both the acknowledgement of grief and the solicitation of social support. In other cases, the cause may be interpersonal. Others may not acknowledge the grief. There may be societal factors as well. As mentioned earlier, the lack of an inclusive ritual may inhibit recognition or support, or others may lack the social awareness of the effects of the loss.

Throughout this process, the counselor can validate grief. Once the factors leading to empathic failure are assessed, counselors can assist clients in developing effective interventions. These interventions can include individual therapy, bibliotherapy, support and self-help groups, and the therapeutic use of ritual. The last two suggestions may be especially useful. Support groups can offer a sense of shared validation, normalizing grief within a supportive community. Therapeutic rituals also can be validating by affirming either publicly or privately the legitimacy of grief. Such rituals can be conducted in a variety of places where older persons frequent and reside, including nursing homes and senior centers.

Conclusion

In an ageist society, feelings of grief can be easily discounted and devalued by others. While older persons experience the frequency of death and other losses more than their younger counterparts, there is as yet little research on the interrelationships between health, frailty, and grief (Moss, Moss & Hanssen, 2001). Nevertheless the effect of cumulative and often disenfranchised losses that older persons encounter in later life suggests the needs for sensitivity and support from the professionals who assist them. This support should encompass all relationships and all the losses that older persons experience. Professionals have a responsibility to educate others that older persons need not be protected from loss but rather should be offered opportunities to express grief in their own way and to offer support to others. The mandate is to empower the disenfranchised. ■

Kenneth J. Doka, PhD, MDiv, is Senior Consultant to the Hospice Foundation of America (HFA) and a Professor of Gerontology at the College of New Rochelle in New York. He is an ordained Lutheran Minister and a former President of the Association for Death Education and Counseling (ADEC) and recipient of ADEC's 1998 Death Educator Award. He is former Chairperson of the International Work Group on Death, Dying, and Bereavement. Dr. Doka has been a panelist on HFA's National Bereavement Teleconference since 1995. Dr. Doka serves as Editor of Omega *as well as* Journeys, *a newsletter for the bereaved published by the Hospice Foundation of America. He is the author of numerous books as well as more than 60 published articles and chapters.*

References

Bengston, V.L., Rosenthal, C., & Burton, L. (1996). Families and aging: Diversity and homogeneity. In J.E. Birren & K.W. Schaie (Eds.), *Handbook of the psychology of aging,* (2nd ed.), (pp. 263-287). New York: Van Nostrand Reinhold.

Carstensen, I.L., Gross, J.J., & Fung, H. (1997). The social context of functional experience. *Annual Review of Gerontology and Geriatrics, 17,* 325-352.

Doka, K.J. (1989). *Disenfranchised grief: Recognizing hidden sorrow.* Lexington, MA: Lexington Press.

Doka, K.J. (2002). *Disenfranchised grief: New directions, challenges and strategies for practice.* Champaign, IL: Research Press.

Doka, K.J., & Aber, R. (1989). Psychosocial loss and grief. In K.J. Doka (Ed.), *Disenfranchised grief: Recognizing hidden sorrow* (pp. 187-197). Lexington, MA: Lexington Press.

Kauffman, J. (2002). The Psychology of disenfranchised grief: Liberation, shame and self-disenfranchisement. In K.J. Doka, (Ed.), *Disenfranchised grief: New Directions, challenges and strategies.* Champaign, IL: Research Press.

Meyers, B. (2002). Disenfranchised grief and the loss of an animal companion. In K.J. Doka, (Ed.), *Disenfranchised grief: New directions, challenges and strategies for practice.* Champaign, IL: Research Press.

Moss, M., & Moss, S. (1989). Death of the very old. In K.J. Doka (Ed.), *Disenfranchised grief: Recognizing hidden sorrow* (pp. 213-228). Lexington, MA: Lexington Press.

Moss, M., Moss, S., & Hansson, R. (2001). Bereavement and old age. In M.S. Stroebe, R.O. Hansson, W. Stroebe, & H. Schut (Eds.), *Handbook of bereavement research: Consequences, coping and care* (pp. 241-260). Washington, DC: American Psychological Association.

Neimeyer, R.P., & Jordan, J. (2002). Disenfranchisement and comparative failure: Grief therapy and the co-construction of meaning. In K.J. Doka, (Ed.), *Disenfranchised grief: New directives, challenges and strategies for practice.* Champaign, IL: Research Press.

Rando, T.A. (Ed.) (2000). *Clinical dimensions of anticipatory mourning: Theory and practice in working with the dying, their loved ones and their caregivers.* Champaign, IL: Research Press.

Part III

Loss and Grief in Later Life

This section of the book addresses the many and particular losses experienced by older persons. We begin with Phyllis Silverman's chapter on transition and loss in later life. Silverman offers insights on the value of continuing bonds and the role of mutual support. A central tenet of her work is her emphasis on grief as a normal transitional experience and her belief in the resilience of bereaved individuals of any age to use their inherent strengths to assist themselves and others.

The chapter by J. Richard Williams adds a cautionary note and reminds us of the toll that the death of a spouse can take on the physical health of the bereaved widow or widower. These effects can be particularly significant for very old individuals whose frail health already limits their activities and social supports. These individuals may be less able to withstand the stress and disruption caused by a significant loss.

Both chapters offer a challenge to professionals to foster the natural support systems of older persons and to create new models of support for older individuals, particularly those who are frail. Williams reminds us that support can come in many ways and from a variety of sources.

The chapter by Dale Lund and Michael Caserta and the chapter by Brian de Vries, Rosemary Blieszner, and John Blando recall the intimate relationships that older persons share. These chapters sensitize us to the many losses that may be experienced in later life and reaffirm the power of individuals of all ages to craft and nurture significant ties that will need to be acknowledged and mourned when a loved one dies.

Two back-to-back *Voices* pieces offer reflections about such losses. First, Jack Gordon addresses the loss of a parent in middle and late life. Second, Judy Mann reflects on the loss of a beloved grandson. Both kinds of losses can be disenfranchised. The first may be dismissed because few acknowledge the grief of a 60-year-old orphan. The second loss may be devalued because most people will attend first to the grief of the parents. Mann's personal experience addresses the particular anguish of what is termed an out-of-order death. We expect that in the natural order of things, younger generations will bury older generations.

The way we die often engenders specific grief reactions. This is no less true for older persons but may often be ignored. Patrick Arbore considers the problem of suicide among older individuals. Arbore's chapter reinforces Williams's caution about the insidious effects of untreated depression in older adults. It also offers sound suggestions for prevention, intervention, and therapeutic support for survivors, who may have a difficult time reconciling themselves to a loved one's suicide.

Myra MacPherson's *Voices* piece considers traumatic loss, a critical concern in the aftermath of the September 11 terrorist attacks. MacPherson's experiences—both professional and personal—offer a caution about the delayed and cumulative effects of traumatic losses, especially for older adults. Clinicians need to be alert for manifestations of post-traumatic stress disorder (PTSD) in their older clients and the potential role for desensitization therapy to help relieve such symptoms.

Significant trauma such as that of September 11 raises another issue for gerontologists. While some individuals are directly confronting the devastating loss of adult children who died in the attacks, the impact has been felt more broadly among older adults, often triggering memories of past traumas accumulated over a lifetime and new feelings of anxiety, depression, and helplessness.

In a country that is growing ever more culturally diverse, health care professionals will face generations of older people whose cultural beliefs differ from their own. This is one reason why the chapter by Hosam Kamel, Charles Mouton, and Deborah McKee is significant. This chapter sensitizes us to the ways that culture influences end-of-life decisions, post-death rituals, and grief—as well as the heightened impact of culture on end-of-life views and practices. In their review, the authors address cultural differences due to ethnicity and spirituality, but implicit in the work is the understanding that culture is a way of life. We could identify other cultural groups based on shared lifestyle (such as the gay subculture), social class, or any of the other ways that individuals choose to identify themselves.

At the same time, the authors also acknowledge important differences within cultural groups and between individuals—requiring health care practitioners and providers to be on guard against cultural stereotyping.

The final chapters in this section offer counseling strategies and approaches for working with older bereaved clients. Robert Neimeyer reviews the narrative approach, an emerging therapy based in the movements of psychological reconstructivism and symbolic interaction. It seeks to have clients reconstruct meaning in the face of loss. Janice Winchester Nadeau applies this model to her work with families. Both Virginia Lynn Fry and Elaine Tiller offer variations of expressive approaches that can be used with older clients.

Taken together, these chapters offer a caution, a challenge, and a promise. The caution is to be eclectic and prescriptive in therapeutic approaches, which should be tailored to individual needs and strengths. The challenge is to reach out to persons in later life, realizing that they may be unfamiliar with counseling services and therefore reluctant to take advantage of them. The promise is that older persons remain capable of great growth and creativity. ■

CHAPTER 17

Loss and Transition in Later Life

Phyllis R. Silverman

INTRODUCTION

People dealing with the loss of a loved one often have the notion that grief is something they will "get over," as they might an illness. Yet, particularly in later life, bereavement is a normal transition in the life cycle, and, it is hoped, one from which the grieving person can grow. Critical to making the transition in a healthy way are three factors: how the bereaved change the way they relate to themselves and to others, how their relationship with the deceased changes, and, finally, what sort of support they have from family, friends, and the community.

During the grieving process, the bereaved must come to grasp that what is lost is not only the loved one, but also the relationship and the bereaved person's sense of self in that relationship. As bereaved persons adapt to their loss, they often develop a new relationship to the deceased that grows and changes as they do. In order for them to work through these changes, it is important that they have a network of friends and family who will provide both emotional and practical support as needed. Few people can prevail without help from family, friends, and others in the community.

Grief as a Process of Change

Grief is often characterized in terms of the pain and angst that bereaved persons experience as they cope with the death of a loved one. But there is more to grieving than dealing with these emotions; it is a transitional process. Rarely can the bereaved live their lives as they did before. Moss, Moss, and Hansson (2001) list the many losses that older people experience: spouse, siblings, friends, and members of the extended family. The current generation of older people is so long-lived that they may bury their adult children. This is a new population of bereaved parents. Some may also be raising their bereaved grandchildren. For each of these losses, there will be similarities in the experience of the bereaved as well as real differences. In dealing with a loss, there are several key questions to answer: What did the mourner lose? What part did the deceased play in his or her life? In the community's life? What did he or she contribute? What will be missing?

When grief is characterized as something people will get over, that time will heal, the choice of language implies that grief is an illness and with the proper treatment its consequences can be expunged. This rarely parallels the experience of the bereaved and they often feel disenfranchised when they cannot find "closure" and "get better" in a limited period of time. Grief is not an illness from which people recover, although it would make life much simpler if this were so. Realistically, the pain cannot be taken away. Instead, the bereaved learn how to deal with it. They learn to acknowledge the bumps, the derailments, the disappointments, the stressors, the bad moments of life that cannot always be avoided. How to manage adversity and deal with change is part of any effort to alleviate the pain and help people move forward.

Another way of characterizing what mourners experience after a death is to talk about grief as an expected life-cycle transition. The concept of transition provides a dynamic way of mapping the disruption, the stress, and the changes that the bereaved experience (Bowlby, 1961; Silverman, 1966, 1986; Parkes, 1996). It is a time of transition because it involves a turning point for the mourner, a change in status, and a shift in roles. A new sense of self begins to emerge as the bereaved person learns to live in a changed world. Neimeyer (1998) talks about the transformation of how people make meaning. As people age, they gain experience in coping with death. They build on this experience, and yet each new death can seem as if it is the first.

Gallagher-Thompson and colleagues (1993) report that, in terms of general distress and depression, there appears to be little difference between the grief of older persons and that of younger persons. Each death is unique, and bereaved persons continue to negotiate and renegotiate the meaning of a critical loss for the rest of their lives. This transition takes place on several levels. It begins with the awareness that it is no longer possible to live as before. The bereaved person's way of ordering and making meaning out of the world is changing. Often, the coping strategies that applied in other situations no longer work, and they must learn new coping skills. Thus, how people learn needs to be considered (Belenky, Clinchy, Goldberger, & Tarule, 1996). Lund (1989) identified the diversity of reactions found in older widowed people. Some were able to learn new skills and experienced personal growth; others had lingering despondency. The ability to adapt over a period of time is critical to a healthy transition.

Change over Time

With time, people mobilize and utilize their inner resources and the resources in the world around them. Since change occurs over time, it can be divided into phases during which people do the "work" of the transition. While it is impossible to say when one phase ends and another begins, noting these phases is helpful in recognizing that as time passes, the bereaved experience the loss differently and face different issues. The line of these phases is not straight or clear, however; people move back and forth, and may be in more than one place at a time. Usually, they follow a helix-like movement toward a place where they can look ahead with new interest and excitement. Even then, there will still be sadness that the deceased person no longer is living. It is difficult to capture this process in words. Words can help define experiences along the way that become part of each bereaved person's story, but it is important to bear in mind that each bereaved person's experience is unique.

Initial Responses

The initial period after a death brings with it numbness, disbelief, a sense of moving on automatic pilot, a clouding or veiling of the mind that allows the bereaved to get through the rituals of burial and the early period of mourning. It is almost as if the body is protecting the mourner from the full emotional impact of the death. Because of their numbness and almost reflexive behavior, mourners are able to maintain outward control. Sadness, despair, crying, and feeling forlorn are not always experienced all at once. They seem to come in bits and pieces. People around the bereaved may be unaware that they are not doing well. Long afterward, most people say they were not really in charge at this point.

After the initial period, mourners find themselves asking the same questions about the continuation of life as they knew it. As they become aware that nothing is the same, they express their stress as tension and anxiety. These feelings may be accompanied by a sense of being afloat and losing direction, in part because the typical ways of coping are no longer effective. Bereaved persons realize that their sense of order in the world is challenged. Even if their faith provides an understanding of the place of death in life, and they see the deceased as having gone to a better place, this may not suffice to comfort them at this time. Faith may help in the long run, but bereaved persons must also continue to live their lives on a day-to-day basis. This requires new skills and new ways of organizing their lives.

For older adults, how they proceed may depend in part on their own physical health and ability to move about in their communities. In addition, many of the current generation of older adults may not have been socialized to deal with their feelings in a direct manner. They may be unaware of how contemporary bereavement theory suggests they mourn. It becomes critical to ask how they understand the experience and what they expect from themselves and others.

Facing the New Reality

The period sometimes called *recoil* refers to a time when the numbing lifts, sometimes in a dramatic way, as if a spring snaps. It now seems possible for the new reality to come into the full consciousness of the bereaved. These feelings may have emerged from time to time earlier but were pushed aside. Each person finds his or her own way of visiting the fullness of the loss. For some, there is a dramatic confrontation. They may forget and set an extra place at the table or come home to an empty house after having kept themselves occupied in other settings. This could be the period when people feel most depressed, as if they have hit bottom.

It becomes clear during this period that life is going to be very different. The profound changes are rarely talked about as part of the bereavement process, so mourners may not be prepared to deal with the new reality. They may feel inadequate because, six months to a year later, people ask why they are not over their grief. Most of their friends and relatives have returned to their lives, and the bereaved can feel very alone. Adult children who may themselves be mourning may not know how to help. They may become overprotective. Neither those offering support nor the mourners themselves are aware that the process has only just begun.

One of the most difficult things that all mourners need to do is to bear the pain—the strong, upsetting, and strange feelings that they are experiencing. They may look for ways of avoiding the feelings to give themselves respite. Learning to cope with these feelings will take time, education, and an ability to acknowledge the changed context of their lives.

Accommodation

Over time, people make an accommodation to the death. This is not an end to grieving. It is a time when people have a sense of their own ability to prevail, to deal with the pain, and to find new ways of living in the world. It is a continuing process. Most people seem to reach a point where grief no longer runs them; rather, they run it. They still feel pain associated with the loss, but it is no longer the driving force in their lives. There is still a place in their hearts and minds that feels the pain of the loss and is connected to the deceased. This is not an atrophied spot, but a place where a changing relationship with the deceased is constructed, nourished, and sustained. Faith and religion often provide meaning and comfort that earlier may have eluded mourners (Cook & Wimberly, 1983; Kushner, 1989). McCrae and Costa (1993, p. 205) found the older widowed men and women they studied quite resilient, stating "this was remarkable only in comparison with our expectations." Gallagher-Thompson and colleagues (1993) found that bereavement lasts longer than might be expected. This can be better understood by looking at the way the bereaved think about themselves, how they remain attached to the deceased, and what sort of support they may have from family, friends, and the community. These factors may be an essential part of the bereaved person's ability to make a meaningful accommodation.

A Shifting Sense of Self

What is involved in finding a new way of living in the world? In part, it involves not only reorganizing the details of daily life but also finding a new sense of self. The self is the ability to process and connect experiences, to direct behavior, and to know who we are and what we are doing. Our sense of self changes as a result of how we differentiate ourselves from others and how we include others in our lives. As stated by Clinchy (1996), the self is not something finished that one carts about from one relationship to the next. Selves are always being reconstructed in the context of relationships. Social context and significant others affect the direction and nature of this movement. Age does not limit older people from developing a new sense of self and a new place in their world (Doress-Worters & Siegel, 1994; Jacobs, 1991). One goal in helping older bereaved people is to find ways to facilitate their learning. There is nothing inherent in being old that prevents learning.

According to Piaget (1954), there is an ongoing conversation between an individual and his or her world. This back-and-forth leads to a process of adaptation that can go several ways. When death occurs, the self that is formed *by* and *in* the relationship to the deceased is lost, at least in the context of what was possible before. What is mourned when someone dies is both the lost relationship and the self as reflected in that relationship. In their roles as husbands and wives, men and women find ways of framing and focusing their daily lives and of supporting each other. Exactly what is lost depends not only on how these individuals constructed their marriage. For example, a year after her husband died one widow said,

> I know I am still my children's mother. I am still a grandmother. But I feel like I don't know who I am any more, now that Jim is dead. If I am not his wife, then who am I?

Her sense of self was embedded in this relationship. She lost the self she knew in her relationship with her husband. She needs to learn to acknowledge this dilemma and consider what she can do about it.

It is impossible to understand how people cope with death without examining some aspects of how they define themselves in relationship to others. We typically associate growth and change with children, in whom it is easy to chart emotional and cognitive movement that coincides with physical development. But human development is a process that extends from birth to death, and it is important to look at the direction and movement in adults' lives (Kegan, 1982). Bereaved adults report a changing ability to reflect on their own behavior and the role of others in their lives (Silverman, 2000). As the bereaved begin to recognize the need to change, they find new ways of organizing and making sense of their experiences. This results in a new sense of self and a new place in the world. A 70-year-old widower described his own evolving sense of self:

> I worry more about others. I am not so concerned with me. I'm different, I can't always explain it. If I want a social life now, it is up to me, and I'm reaching out.

Like this man, many bereaved persons talk about feeling a new voice, a new ability to act on their own behalf—a new sense of empowerment. While stress can cause an emotional downturn, it can also lead to just such a positive outcome. If stress is viewed not so much as what happens to people, but as what they do about it, then this period can be an opportunity for growth, regardless of where they are in their life cycle. In the words of one 79-year-old widow,

> I never thought I would find myself speaking up this way. I always deferred to my husband. Now I find that if I don't speak up, no one will do it for me. I have a new voice and I am getting used to people reacting differently to me. I was even able to explain to my children what I need, and how I have changed so they can understand and be supportive. I began to see their point of view and could explain that I didn't need that much protection, even at my age.

Continuing Bonds

New research reflecting the experience of the bereaved highlights the ways in which they maintain an ongoing connection to the deceased (Silverman & Klass, 1996). Silverman and Nickman (1996) observed that bereaved families were not letting go of their attachment to the deceased as bereavement theories had previously encouraged. The surviving family did not withdraw their energy from the deceased. Instead, they constructed a new relationship. This was a different relationship, but an ongoing relationship nonetheless. The continuing bond with the deceased is dynamic and changing, typically providing the bereaved with solace (Nickman, Silverman, & Normand, 1998; Silverman, 2000; Silverman & Klass, 1996).

Most mourners struggle with the need to find a place for the deceased in their lives and are often embarrassed to talk about it for fear of others thinking there is something wrong with them (Klass, 1984; Silverman, 2000). But, as Robert Anderson (1974) wrote of his deceased wife more than 10 years after her death, "I have a new life...Death ends a life but it does not end a relationship, which struggles on in the survivor's mind toward some resolution which it never finds." With this statement he legitimated his own experience and that of other mourners as well. Without a sense of the past and an understanding of its place in people's lives, it is difficult to move ahead.

Walters (1999) observed that it was not only important for the bereaved to find a way to relate to the deceased, but for the community to do so as well. Just as an individual's personal life is profoundly disrupted by a death, so is the social world of which the deceased was a part. Walters noted the importance of ritual in helping to find a place for the dead in the life of the bereaved and the community. Ritual helps those who participate to reconstitute their world. In Catholicism, for example, mourners are expected to have a memorial mass on the anniversary of the death. In Judaism, the mourners remember deceased family members by participating in a synagogue ritual on five occasions during the year, including the anniversary of the death. These traditions and rituals help mourners keep the memory of the deceased alive.

The changing nature of this relationship is not related to age. Adult children have similar needs to connect to their now dead parent, just as their surviving parent may need to do. Mourners talk about feeling the presence of the deceased in many ways and report ongoing conversations with the deceased. When people are widowed in later life, they likely had a long life together with the deceased and their sense of self is more clearly defined by this relationship. They will find their own way to keep the presence of the deceased alive in their lives. This might include talking about the deceased, memorializing them, participating in activities that honor their memories, or following in their footsteps in work (Campbell & Silverman, 1996). Moss and Moss (1996) studied widowed persons who had remarried. In the successful marriages, there was a place for the deceased spouse in the new relationship. In another example of maintaining a relationship with the deceased, a widow I met told how she remembered her husband and created opportunities to talk about him. He had collected neckties to remind him of places he had been and things he had done. She cut up the ties and from them she made small quilted pillows for each of her grandchildren. Each piece in the pillow represented an aspect of their grandfather's life, and they came to know him in ways they could not have during his lifetime. In this way he became a vital part of their lives. His widow drew comfort from telling his story over and over again to her eager young audience.

There is paradox in this view of grief that needs to be recognized (Silverman & Nickman, 1996). People cannot live in the past. There has to be some giving up of the deceased, since the very nature of their daily lives is changed by the death. The deceased are both present and very absent, and this creates tension in the bereavement process. Nonetheless, the concept of continuing bonds changes the way we approach grief. It becomes clear that grief is not something from which people recover. They do not get over it. There is no closure. They do not live life as they once lived it. It is a disservice to tell older people to put the past behind them and to stop talking about the deceased. Remembering and honoring the dead provides comfort and solace to them and others who are mourning with them, as they go on living.

Support Networks

Considering how communities respond to a death raises the question of how to help the bereaved live through this difficult period in their lives. Humans live in a web of relationships that provide support and care during difficult periods in our lives. Family members help out of a sense of obligation. There is often a mutuality and exchange involved and, typically, they offer very concrete kinds of help. Neighbors and friends are also part of this network based on mutuality and exchange of goods and services. Beyond family and friends, helpers can be more specialized, and may include clergy, health professionals, and the like. Each member of a network offers different types of care. In considering what kind of help might be needed after a death, it is important to try to match the help available with the needs of the bereaved.

The first place the bereaved turn to for assistance is family members, friends, and neighbors. They help plan the funeral, bring food, and take care of some of the physical and emotional needs of the bereaved. The bereaved need each other and their families to share their feelings about the deceased, to remember together, and to support each other as they acknowledge their pain and loss. They need friends to help with the concrete tasks of living and managing their family from the time before the funeral until afterward. They need the funeral director and the clergy to help with burial and mourning rituals. Younger family members may try to protect older family members by taking care of things for them, but older family members need to be involved. A better way to protect them is to consult with them and respect their wishes.

With time, as the bereaved person's needs change, this network is not always able to respond. Often the mourner is referred to professionals for assistance (Osterweis, Solomon, & Green, 1984). These professionals may be clergy, physicians, or mental health therapists. Clergy offer prayer and address the spiritual issues related to the death. Physicians usually prescribe medication to relieve some of the physical symptoms, like insomnia. Mental health professionals generally focus on the psychological aspects of the process (Jacobs, 1991). Some professionals may convey the notion that something is wrong with the mourner who consults with them and may suggest that with the right professional help, the bereaved will get over his or her grief. This is not helpful and may reflect generational differences in response to psychological counseling. If the bereaved feel that something is wrong with them because their grief lasts beyond a month or two, this can make them feel worse. When such a profound and complex disruption has occurred, however, no single type of assistance is usually sufficient.

There is still another dimension of support, which may not be available from anyone who has not had a personal experience with bereavement. Meeting others who have had a similar experience can help the bereaved understand that theirs is not a unique experience.

A helper who has lost a loved one can be a role model by demonstrating that people do survive. We talk often about peer influence on adolescents, but we need to consider that this may be a need throughout the life cycle. At every phase of life, people seek others who have gone before to learn from them what Goffman (1963) has called "the tricks of the trade," or what they need to know to cope with the loss and the changes in their lives.

If the widowed do not have people in their network who have been widowed, then they may seek others outside this network. Often, these people can be found in self-help or mutual help organizations. The growth of these organizations has made increasingly clear the bereaved person's need for others who have had a similar experience. Hamburg and Adams (1967) point out that learning is made easier when the helper is one step ahead of the person in need and has personal experience with the problem to use as a guide. Mutual help organizations are based on the premise that in times of stress, people need others who have had a similar experience as role models and teachers (Silverman, 1978, 1980; Gartner & Riesman, 1977; Lieberman & Borman, 1979; Powell, 1987).

Caserta, Lund, and Rice (1999) found that many older widowed persons, often living alone, did not have sufficient information to maintain a healthy lifestyle. To remedy this, they set up an educational health program designed specifically for older persons. They met on a regular basis, using classroom techniques to provide their constituents with appropriate information. These sessions encouraged the participants to take charge of their own health and their own lives. The program became an invitation for people to set up a mutual help network. They made new friends and felt empowered to deal with their bereavement and themselves in new ways, achieving a new sense of well-being. This is a good example of how professionally led programs can help the bereaved take over for themselves.

Historically, bereaved people have been helping each other for as long as people have been living in communities and mourners have needed solace. Habits of the past often fall into disuse, however, and as society has become more specialized, services that people once performed for each other have been taken over by professionals. People became self-conscious about their lack of credentials to help in times of stress and no longer recognized as legitimate the experience they may have amassed from living. Informally, however, people have continued to help each other. We see communities of the widowed in programs for older people and in various settings where older people live. They vacation together, go to lunch together, do quilting together, and find various other ways to share their lives. They exchange skills. They often set up programs to help each other in churches and community centers.

The Widow to Widow Program (Silverman, 1966, 1986; Vachon, 1979) demonstrated the effectiveness of the widowed helping the widowed. Widowed helpers in this program used the knowledge they gained from personal experience to help newly widowed women. They built on a sense of mutuality and that they were peers of the women they helped. The model was adopted by the AARP.

In recent years, there has been a proliferation of mutual help programs for the bereaved organized primarily by and for each other (White & Madera, 1995). Whether they join together in a small local group or as part of a national organization, they often develop some organizational structure that gives their efforts continuity. Rather than clients of an agency, people become members of an organization with a structure resembling a club or other type of voluntary association. As members, they control the resources and determine what help the organization will provide and who will provide that help.

In mutual help organizations, members are peers who make their own decisions about what happens and who can move from the role of recipient of help to that of helper. Help is offered in many ways: through one-to-one outreach, telephone hotlines, social activities, newsletters, educational meetings, group discussions, legislation and advocacy activities, and through becoming leaders and helpers in turn. Lieberman (1993) observed that there may be a difference in the help parents who lose a child get as members of Compassionate Friends. He suggests that this may be due to the fact that when a child dies, his parents, in today's world, confront such issues as the ultimate meaning of their lives.

Mutual help is different from the help available through professional agencies. In a professionally led support group, members are screened by the agency and are in the subordinate role of client. They have no ongoing relationship to the agency and are not responsible for the continuing life of this helping experience. Help is primarily through psychological or educational counseling, either in group or in individual sessions (Lieberman & Borman, 1979; Silverman, 1978, 1980).

By contrast, a mutual help setting has its own dynamic. Members themselves are responsible for the continuing life of the group and the program with which it is associated. Help is effective because people (1) find others so that they feel less alone and less unique, (2) have their feelings legitimized, (3) get specific information about their problems and a sense that there is something they can do about them, (4) have role models who can provide alternative ways of solving problems and with whom they can identify, (5) can and do assume responsibility for the ongoing life of the organization, and (6) find the ability to help others. As they move away from the death event, meaningful help also involves extended social activity. Their affiliations provide the opportunity to "repeople their lives" (Silverman, 1970). Help in this context becomes a part of community life that focuses on people caring for each other and being present in each other's lives as they live through a difficult life cycle event.

Conclusion

In developing resources that facilitate and legitimate this change and growth, there is sufficient evidence to recognize the unique value of bereaved persons using their own experience to help each other. In so doing, they normalize the grieving process and provide support, resources, and learning opportunities that help people develop realistic goals for themselves consistent with their experience. They learn that they do not recover or get over their grief but are changed by it. ■

Phyllis R. Silverman, PhD, LCSW, is Professor Emerita at the MGH Institute of Health Professions, and has spent the better part of her professional life pioneering the study of how people deal with death over the life cycle. She developed the concept of the widow-to-widow program, and from 1964 through 1972 she directed the research project that demonstrated its effectiveness. This research was the model for the Widowed Person's Service, a national program sponsored by the American Association of Retired Persons (AARP), which honored her for this work on AARP's 25th anniversary. She was one of the first to look at gender differences in the bereaved. Her work has led her to focus on the meaning of relationships in the lives of both men and women. Dr. Silverman has a PhD from Brandeis University, a public health degree from Harvard School of Public Health, and a social work degree from Smith College School for Social Work. Her work has been recognized both nationally and internationally. She has published extensively in professional journals and written several books on her work, among them Widower: When Men are Left Alone. *She co-edited* Continuing Bonds: A New Understanding of Grief.

References

Anderson, R. (1974). Notes of a survivor. In S.B. Troop & W.A. Green (Eds.), *The patient, death and the family.* New York: Scribner.

Belenky, M., Clinchy, B., Goldberger, N., Tarule, J. (1996). *Women's ways of knowing.* New York: Basic Books.

Bowlby, J. (1961). Process of mourning. *International Journal of Psychoanalysis, 42,* 317-340.

Campbell, S., & Silverman, P.R. (1996). *Widower: When men are left alone.* Amityville, New York: Baywood.

Caserta, M.S., Lund, D.L., & Rice, S.J. (1999). Pathfinders: A self-care and health education program for older widows and widowers. *The Gerontologist, 39,* 615-620.

Clinchy, B. (1996). Connected and separate knowing: Towards a marriage of two minds. In N. Goldberger, J.M. Tarule, B. Clinchy, and M. Belenky (Eds.), *Knowledge, difference and power* (pp. 205-247). New York: Basic Books.

Cook, J.A., & Wimberly, D.W. (1983). If I should die before I wake: Religious commitment and adjustment to the death of a child. *Journal for the Scientific Study of Religion, 22*, 222-238.

Doress-Worters, P., & Siegel, D.L. (1994). *The new ourselves, growing older.* New York: Simon and Schuster.

Gallagher-Thompson, D., Futterman, A., Farberow, N., Thompson, L.W., & Peterson, J. (1993). The impact of spousal bereavement on older widows and widowers. In M.S. Stroebe, W. Stroebe, & R.O. Hansson (Eds.), *Handbook of bereavement: Theory, research and intervention* (pp. 227-239). New York: Cambridge University Press.

Gartner, A., & Riesman, F. (1977). *Self-help in the human services.* San Francisco: Jossey-Bass.

Goffman, E. (1963). *Stigma: Notes on the management of spoiled identities.* Upper Saddle River, NJ: Prentice Hall.

Hamburg, D.A., & Adams, J.E. (1967). A perspective on coping: Seeking and utilizing information in major transition. *Archives of General Psychiatry, 17*, 277-284.

Jacobs, R.H. (1991). *Be an outrageous older woman.* Manchester, CT: Knowledge, Ideas and Trends.

Kegan, R. (1982). *The evolving self.* Cambridge, MA: Harvard University Press.

Klass, D. (1984). Bereaved parents and The Compassionate Friends: Affiliation and healing. *Omega, 15* (4), 353-373.

Kushner, H.S. (1989). *When bad things happen to good people* (2nd ed.). New York: Schocken Books.

Lieberman, M. (1993). Bereavement self-help groups: A review of conceptual and methodological issues. In M.S. Stroebe, W. Stroebe, & R.O. Hansson (Eds.), *Handbook of bereavement: Theory, research and intervention* (pp. 411-426). New York: Cambridge University Press.

Lieberman, M., & Borman, L. (1979). *Self-help groups for coping with crisis.* San Francisco: Jossey-Bass.

Lund, D.A. (1989). *Older bereaved spouses: Research with practical applications.* New York: Taylor & Francis.

McCrae, R.R., & Costa, P.T. (1993). Psychological resilience among widowed men and women: A 10 year follow-up of a national sample. In M.S. Stroebe, W. Stroebe, & Hansson, R.O. (Eds.), *Handbook of Bereavement: Theory, research and intervention* (pp. 196-207). New York: Cambridge University Press.

Moss, M.S., & Moss, S.Z. (1996). In D. Klass, P.R. Silverman, & S.L. Nickman (Eds.), *Continuing bonds: New understandings of grief.* Washington, DC: Taylor & Francis.

Moss, M.S., Moss, S.Z., and Hansson, R.O. (2001). Bereavement and old age. In, M.S. Stroebe, R.O. Hansson, W. Stroebe, H. Schut (Eds.), *Handbook of bereavement research: Consequence, coping and care* (pp. 241-260). Washington, DC: American Psychological Association.

Neimeyer, R.A. (1998). *Lessons of loss: A guide to coping.* New York: McGraw Hill.

Nickman, S.L., Silverman, P.R., & Normand, C. (1998). Children's construction of their deceased parent: The surviving parent's contribution. *American Journal of Orthopsychiatry, 68* (1) 126-141.

Osterweis, M., Solomon, F., & Green, M. (1984). *Bereavement reactions: Consequences and care.* Washington, DC: National Academy Press.

Parkes, C.M. (1996). *Bereavement studies in adult life* (3rd ed.). London: Routledge.

Piaget, J. (1954). *The construction of reality in the child.* New York: Basic Books.

Powell, T. (1987). *Self-help organizations and professional practice.* Washington, DC: National Association of Social Workers.

Silverman, P.R. (2001). It makes a difference. Invited paper for special issue on Women in Thanatology. *Illness, Crisis and Loss, 9* (1), 11-128.

Silverman, P.R. (1978). *Mutual help groups and the role of the mental health professional.* Washington, DC: U.S. Government Printing Office, NIMH, DHEW Publication No. (ADM) 78-646, Reprinted 1980.

Silverman, P.R. (1980). *Mutual help: Organization and development.* Beverly Hills: Sage Publishing Co.

Silverman, P.R. (2000). *Never too young to know: Death in children's lives.* New York: Oxford University Press.

Silverman, P. R. (1966). Services for the widowed during the period of bereavement. *Social Work Practice.* New York: Columbia University Press.

Silverman, P.R. (1970). The widow as caregiver in a program of preventive intervention with other widows. *Mental Hygiene, 54* (4), 540-547.

Silverman, P.R. (1986). *Widow to widow.* New York: Springer Press.

Silverman P.R., & Klass, D. (1996). Introduction: What's the problem? In D. Klass, P.R. Silverman, & S.L. Nickman (Eds.), *Continuing bonds: New understandings of grief.* Washington DC: Taylor & Francis.

Silverman P.R., & Nickman, S.L. (1996). Concluding thoughts. In D. Klass, P.R. Silverman, & S.L. Nickman (Eds.), *Continuing bonds: New understandings of grief* (pp. 349-355). Washington DC: Taylor & Francis.

Vachon, M.L.S. (1979). *Identity change over the first two years of bereavement: Social relationships and social support in bereavement.* Unpublished doctoral dissertation,York University, Toronto.

Walters, T. (1999). *On bereavement: The culture of grief.* Philadelphia: Open University Press.

White, B.J., & Madera, E. (1995). *The self-help sourcebook* (5th ed.). Denville, NJ: Northwest Covenant Medical Center.

CHAPTER 18

Effects of Grief on a Survivor's Health

J. Richard Williams

INTRODUCTION

Last year I helped take care of a friend, a thoracic surgeon, who was terminally ill but who expressed the desire to live until his granddaughters were baptized. He was being cared for in his home. One morning, a priest who was a close friend and who was staying in the home baptized the granddaughters. My friend went into a coma shortly afterward and died that night. In hospice we have seen events like this time after time—someone who is terminally ill lives until an important event takes place, a major life event that they anticipate with pleasure, such as a wedding or a birth, and then they die.

In early 2000, national attention was drawn to this phenomenon when Charles Schulz, creator of the comic strip *Peanuts*, died of colon cancer the day before his final strip was to appear. Multiple studies document altered death rates around major life events. Sociologist David Phillips of the University of California, San Diego, found that women are less likely to die the week before their birthday than in any other week of the year. Conversely, male mortality peaks shortly before the birthday (Phillips, Van Voorhees, & Ruth, 1992). Based on this and other studies, Phillips suggests that "Death can be briefly postponed until after the occurrence of a significant occasion." (Phillips & Smith, 1990)

These observations and studies suggest that, even in a person with terminal illness, the length of survival may be flexible, depending on both physiological and psychological variables that affect the will to live. If we can understand what influences the will to live, both generally and following the loss of a spouse, we will be in a better position to support bereaved spouses effectively. If, in fact, social and psychological factors influence survival, this may explain the ways in which bereavement affects health, suggesting intervention strategies to assist the bereaved.

Three questions then guide this chapter: How does bereavement affect health? What factors seem to mitigate the effect of a significant loss (such as the loss of a spouse) or the health of survivors? Finally, are there intervention strategies that can protect the health of survivors?

How Does Bereavement Affect Health?

By age 65, about 10% of all men have been widowed at least once. Because men die at a younger age than women, more than half of all 65-year-old women have lost at least one husband (Anonymous, 2000).

A review of the literature clearly supports the fact that a relationship exists between bereavement and mortality and morbidity. This relationship, in a few studies, seemed especially pronounced for men. For example, in a major survey, researchers measured the mortality of the surviving spouse among more than 12,000 couples (Schaefer, Quesenberry, & Wi, 1995). From 1964 to 1987, 1,453 men and 3,294 women lost their spouses. During this period, bereaved men died twice as often as bereaved women: 30% of men versus 15% of women. Mortality increased the most from 7 months to 12 months after the loss, but it remained elevated for more than two years. Healthy men who lost a wife were twice as likely to die as healthy men who were not bereaved, even after other predictors of mortality were taken into account.

Similar results were observed in the Caregiver Health Effects Study (Schulz & Beach, 1999). Here the mortality rate for men increased twofold.

Mitigating Factors

Clearly, bereavement does have an effect on health. Less obvious are factors that exacerbate or lessen the intensity of these effects. A number of factors may account for the rise in mortality, among them are the levels of depression and stress felt by the survivor. Conversely, maintaining an active social life and seeking spiritual solace through religious observance seem to have a salutary effect on the health of the bereaved. A discussion of these various factors and how they affect survival follows.

Psychological and Physical Mortality

In addition to increasing mortality, the loss of a spouse also increases psychological morbidity. The relationship between psychological morbidity and physical health is evidenced in several studies. One study found a high rate of depression at 6 months and 12 months after the loss of a spouse: 32% and 27%, respectively (Jacobs, Hansen, Berkman, Kasl, & Ostfeld, 1989). In most instances, depression lasted considerably longer than one month, and the depression was often associated with anxiety, restlessness, psychomotor retardation, and intense grief. Post-loss depression was more common in widows than in widowers and was unrelated to a personal history or family history of depression. In a follow-up to the initial report (Jacobs et al., 1990), the investigators found that during the first year of bereavement, 44% of surviving spouses reported at least one type of anxiety disorder, such as panic disorder and generalized anxiety, associated with depression and severe grief.

A more recent study compared rates of depression in married or recently bereaved persons over age 70 (Turvey, Carney, Arndt, Wallace, & Herzog, 1999). Individuals who had recently lost a spouse had a ninefold higher risk for syndromal depression and a fourfold increased incidence of depressive symptoms. Depressive symptoms could last for as long as two years after spousal loss. An observation pertinent to the hospice situation is that the incidence of depressive symptoms was not mitigated by the expectation of death. The authors concluded that "recent bereavement is a significant risk factor for syndromal depression in the elderly."

In a survey among older people who were recently widowed or recently married, or widowed or married for several years, Lawton and colleagues (Winter, Lawton, Casten, & Sando, 2000) found that depressive affect was greatest among recently bereaved persons, while positive affect was greatest among recently married individuals.

This propensity to depression or other mental illness certainly seems to influence physical health. Older persons who lose a spouse are at risk for both mortality and depression. Several questions arise from these observations: When a survivor dies in a short time after the death of a spouse, does the survivor die as a result of a pre-existing illness, or some new cause? Are these deaths associated with any particular cause, such as cardiovascular disease (CVD)? Is the higher mortality risk independent of the increased rate of depression, or could depression be acting as an intermediating variable, making the survivor more vulnerable to organic disease? At least partial answers to these questions can be derived from published data showing the following:

- Many excess deaths soon after losing a spouse are due to CVD.
- Depression increases mortality generally.
- Depression is associated specifically with increased CVD mortality.
- Social isolation increases mortality specifically from CVD, although it is proving difficult to determine how.

Bereavement-associated mortality has been shown to result in part from CVD. In their 1988 editorial, "On the Health Consequences of Bereavement," Rogers and Reich (1988) wrote: "In their so-called broken-heart study in 1969, Parkes et al. described an increase in deaths among widowers within the first six months after bereavement—nearly half of them the result of coronary heart disease." They also cited a Finnish study in which post-bereavement mortality was twice the expected rate, "primarily from ischemic heart disease." Not all studies have found this association, but it does seem to have validity.

In a study conducted in The Netherlands, depression was found to be associated with excess mortality generally in older persons (Schoevers et al., 2000). These investigators calculated the adjusted six-year mortality risk accompanying neurotic and psychotic depression among 4,051 community-living older men and women. They reported that "psychiatric depression was associated with significant excess mortality in both men and women." Neurotic depression was associated with a 1.67-fold higher mortality risk in men only.

Excess mortality following depression has also been documented in an extensive meta-analysis conducted by Wulsin, Vaillant, and Wells (1999). These authors reviewed 57 studies of depression and mortality, focusing on 21 that were most rigorous. Combined data suggested that "depression substantially increases the risk of death," but the researchers judged that there were not enough data to derive a sound estimate of the mortality risk associated with depression.

These investigators also reported that depression increased CVD mortality. They noted that suicide, which might be expected to predominate as the cause of death in depressive populations, accounted for <20% of deaths even in psychiatric samples and <1% in medical and community samples. However, depression did appear to increase the risk of CVD death, especially for men.

A high level of depressive symptoms has been so well established as a risk factor for death in persons with coronary artery disease (CAD) that one group of researchers attempted to determine which symptom groups on depression rating scales were most strongly associated with survival (Barefoot, Brummett, Helms, Mark, Siegler, & Williams, 2000). Five factors were evaluated: well-being, negative affect, somatic symptoms, appetite, and hopelessness. Among patients who had been in the hospital for coronary angiography, over a 19.4-year follow-up, only hopelessness and negative (depressive) affects remained as independent predictors of mortality due to CAD after adjusting for disease severity.

A recent article in the *Harvard Heart Letter* (Anonymous, 2001) described two new studies extending the associating between depression and CVD to heart failure. In the first, investigators showed that depressed persons with isolated systolic hypertension were significantly more likely to progress to heart failure over 4.5 years of observation. In the second study, conducted among patients hospitalized for severe heart failure, the likelihood of dying or deteriorating in function was positively correlated with the severity of depressive symptoms.

Based on these data, we can safely say that the development of depression following the loss of a spouse has serious health implications. In addition to not being willing or able to diagnose depression generally, most physicians do not know to look for depression in this population. Moreover, most physicians may not know how to advise someone who has lost a spouse and are not aware of the severity of this complication. We in hospice need to think about how to address these problems.

Stress and Grief

Bereavement can influence survival in other ways. One is stress. A major loss and its accompanying life changes create stress, and heightened stress does seem to be associated with higher morbidity and mortality.

Even before bereavement, being the caregiver of a disabled spouse can be a risk factor for mortality (Schulz and Beach, 1999) among older persons. In the *Caregiver Health Effects Study* (CHES), which included more than 800 couples, one partner was disabled in about half of the couples. Spouses of disabled persons ranged from 66 to 96 years and were either not helping to care for the disabled partner, helping with no reported strain, or helping but experiencing physical or emotional strain. Over four years, about one in eight participants died. Partners who were providing care and experiencing caregiver strain had a significantly increased risk of mortality, 1.6 times higher relative to non-caregiving controls. On the other hand, participants who were giving care but not experiencing strain or who had a disabled spouse but were not providing care did not experience increased mortality. "Being a caregiver who is experiencing mental or emotional strain is an independent risk factor for mortality among older spousal caregivers," the authors concluded.

A previous report from CHES had documented that strained caregivers had significantly higher levels of depressive symptoms and lower levels of perceived heath, in addition to getting less rest and less exercise. All of these factors could increase vulnerability and mediate the observed association between strained care giving and mortality.

Stress is only one factor from the experience prior to death that should be examined. The second factor that should be considered is the general lifestyle prior to the onset of illness. Many contemporary diseases have lifestyle components: diet, exercise, tobacco use, or substance abuse. Thus whatever affected one spouse's health may have a direct or indirect role on the other spouse's health. Spouses could benefit by examining and, sometimes, modifying pre-morbid lifestyles.

Positive Effect of Social Networks

Research has clearly demonstrated that one of the most critical factors affecting health is social networks. In many prospective studies, a higher level of social interrelationship and social activity is associated with a higher rate of survival and vice versa. It is not unreasonable to suppose that we can favorably influence our clients' will to live by providing appropriate social support.

A pioneering report in this field was the 1979 publication by Berkman and Syme from the Alameda County (California) study (1979). These authors reported that "People who lacked social and community ties were more likely to die in the [nine-year] follow-up period than those with more extensive contacts." For men, the risk of death was increased 2.3 times; for women, 2.8 times. For both sexes the risk of death was independent of health status, socioeconomic status, smoking, alcohol, and other known risk factors.

Data from the 17-year follow-up of the Alameda County study (Seeman, Kaplan, Knudsen, Cohen, & Guralnik, 1987) verified the initial finding and showed that the form of social tie was most important and differed relative to age at baseline. For those under 60 years at the start of the study, marital status was critical, for those over 60, ties with close friends and/or relatives were paramount.

Confirmatory data on the value of social networks for men came from the Tecumseh (Michigan) Community Health Study (House, Robbins, & Metzner, 1982). Over 9 to12 years, "Men reporting higher levels of social relationships and activities [at baseline] were significantly less likely to die during follow-up," the researchers reported. Among women, there was a nonsignificant trend in the same direction. Again the health benefit of social relationships was independent of age and health status.

Other research also has supported the positive role played by social networks (Cerhan & Wallace, 1997; Zuckerman, Kasl, & Ostfeld, 1984). The importance of social networks also correlates with another component of enhanced survival: social activity. For example, in one study subjects were asked about their participation in both social activities, such as church attendance, concerts, card games, and fitness activities. When subsequent mortality was related to the levels of these two types of activities, what emerged was that purely social and productive activities lowered the risk of all cause mortality to the same degree as fitness activities. To the authors, this suggested that "activity may confer survival benefits through psychosocial pathways." While this was not an intervention study, it does suggest that low-stress interventions for frail surviving spouses may provide them with survival benefit.

A series of studies from Umea, Sweden, (Bygrn, Konlaan, & Johansson, 1996; Johansson, Konlaan, & Bygren, 2001; Konlaan et al., 2000; Konlaan, Bygren, & Johansson, 2000) make this same point; engaging frequently in such activities as reading books or periodicals, attending cultural events, making music, and singing in a choir were associated with a lower nine-year mortality risk. In a second, 14-year follow-up, survival was favorably influenced by cultural events—attending the cinema, concerts, museums, or art exhibits—even after controlling for age, level of exercise, income, and education.

Significant associations between social activity and survival also were found in many other studies conducted among a range of populations in several countries (Ceria, Masaki, Rodriguez, Chen, Yano, & Curb, 2001; Jylha & Aro, 1989; Avlund, Damsgaard, & Holstein, 1998; Grand, Grosclaude, Bocquet, Pous, & Albarede, 1990; Maier & Smith, 1999; Gognalons-Nicolet, Derriennic, Monfort, & Cassou, 1999; Armenian, Saadeh, & Armenian, 1987).

From all these reinforcing studies, it seems clear that spending enjoyable time with other people is a hallmark of a longer life. Little evidence exists to explain this consistent finding, although considerable research links psychological stress with adverse health effects, and it seems plausible that spending pleasant time with other humans can provide substantial survival benefits. However social relationships exert their salutary impact, providing opportunities for social interaction for recently bereaved persons and encouraging them to take part in these activities or in others of their own devising seem appropriate.

A significant loss, then, especially one associated with depression, can disrupt activities and networks, adversely influencing survival. Men may be at particular risk because their wives may have had the dominant role in sustaining networks and planning and maintaining levels of social activity.

Spirituality, Survival, and the Will to Live

Spirituality and meaning, as well as activity, also seem to influence survival. We are postulating that the timing of a person's death is sometimes influenced by that person's will to live. In this formulation, wanting to experience a pleasurable major life event can allow an ill person to extend life, while the loss of a spouse can reduce the will to live and shorten life. Some research on the will to live was been done by the late M. Powell Lawton and his colleagues under the rubric "valuation of life." Lawton and colleagues characterized valuation of life as a "cognitive-affective schema" that is a "mediator and moderator between health and end-of-life decisions" (Lawton et al., 2001).

In one study (Lawton et al.,1999), Lawton's group posed health utility questions about years of desired life to 600 healthy or chronically ill persons who were 70 years or older. In 8 out of 10 health conditions, longer years of desired life was significantly correlated with valuation of life, after adjusting for background, health, quality of life, and mental health status. The researchers concluded that "valuation of life is an internal representation of the many positive and negative features of the person and her everyday life that is necessary to comprehend how people may cling to life or welcome its end." Considering valuation of life may provide predictive information regarding years of desired life beyond that which can be predicted by considering physical or mental status alone. It also may help explain the relationship between spirituality and survival. Spirituality is a broad concept, referring to the ways that an individual imparts meaning to life. While spirituality is different and broader than religion, most of the present studies have focused on the role of religiosity on survival.

Two recent publications showing the health benefits of religiosity have come from Koenig and colleagues. In the first, it was shown that weekly attendance at religious services significantly prolonged survival in older persons (>64 years) over a period of 6 years. Regular attendance at religious services reduced the relative hazard of mortality by about 50% for women and almost 40% for men. When adjusted for health, social connections, and other pertinent variables, the benefit was attenuated somewhat, to a 35% mortality reduction for women and 17% for men (Koenig et al., 1999).

In a second investigation (Helm, Hays, Flint, Koenig, & Blazer, 2000), these investigators found that private religious activity—prayer, meditation, bible, study—also prolonged survival in unimpaired older persons over a six-year period, but not among those impaired in activities of daily living (ADL). Among ADL-unimpaired persons, mortality adjusted for demographic and health variables was significantly increased, 1.63-fold, for subjects "rarely or never participating in private religious activities." After adjusting for health practices, social support, and other known factors, relative risk was reduced to 1.47, or just significant (Cl 1.07–2.03). Religious activity in ADL-unimpaired individuals "may reflect habit and not simply prayer under duress," the authors suggested. A secondary finding was that "males were nearly three times more likely than females to be low private religious participants." This is interesting in light of the observations that males are twice as likely as females to die soon after loss of a spouse.

While many studies have been done linking religious observance to improved health or survival, much of this research has been criticized for poor design. However, Helm and colleagues (Helm, Hays, Fling, Koenig, & Blazer, 2000) cite six well-done studies showing a reduction in mortality for frequent church attendees "even after controlling for....factors known to impact mortality." In an interview, Dr. Koenig suggested that perhaps religious practice extends survival because a religious worldview is "a positive belief system" and that it "gives people hope and encourages support." Whether this is substantially different from the mechanism by which social networks exert their beneficial effect is difficult to determine without a deeper understanding of how each behavior or attitude operates. Again, a similar risk remains for bereavement; it may challenge beliefs, negatively influence a will to survive, and disrupt relationships with faith communities.

Intervention Strategies for Professionals

The research clearly shows the increased risk to health of bereavement and suggests reasons that health may be at risk. These risk factors include the fact that bereavement affects mental health, disrupts lifestyle, including social networks and activities, challenges meaning, perhaps even causing spiritual alienation, and increases stress. All of these factors may well interrelate with one another in complex ways.

Naturally, careful assessment of bereaved individuals is needed. While it is beyond the scope of this chapter to indicate the full protocol of a bereavement assessment, it should include an assessment of physical, psychological, and social reactions as well as current physical and mental health, including signs of depression and any risk for suicidal behavior. Certainly the effects of the death on the lifestyle of the surviving spouse need to be examined. This includes not only changes in diet, exercise, sleep, and adherence to medical regimens but more broadly changes in social activities, interactions with others, and church attendance. Physicians and others should listen carefully for comments that suggest that life satisfaction, subjective well-being, and a sense of personal meaning may be impaired. Persistent interrupted sleep and persistent inability to concentrate lasting more than three months after the death of a spouse should be considered warning signs and trigger referral to a physician for screening for depression.

Following an assessment, we can begin to develop a broad range of interventions that may not only enhance adaptation to bereavement but to survival as well. These interventions may include multiple strategies, for example, medication has a place in managing some patients' grief. In a personal communication, Keith Meador, Director of the Duke Institute on Care at the End of Life, wrote, "The increased risk of mortality during bereavement is compelling, with substantial evidence that the risk is mediated through a stress reaction that is frequently manifested through symptoms commonly interpreted as depression and anxiety." The relationship of these symptoms to increased mortality in cardiac patients and the potential to reduce this risk with antidepressant therapy is a point of active investigation. Meador pointed out that "Symptom relief is a legitimate goal in the care of grieving persons, as long as we are not implying an unwillingness to share in the necessary and inevitable expressions of grief common to loss."

While bereavement groups also may be an effective strategy, we need to keep examining the complexity hidden behind the phrase "social support." It is important to recognize the wide range of activities that constitute effective social support—churchgoing, singing, playing cards, attending concerts. Some of the persons who most need social support may be the hardest to reach, because they do not recognize that they need help (Brummett et al., 2001). Further research is needed to identify the impact of health effects in grieving spouses who refuse bereavement services.

In short, we need to have an eclectic mix of strategies tailored to the needs of bereaved individuals. But in this mix, it is not enough to emphasize the disruptive nature of loss and stress. Rather, it is critical to assist individuals in acknowledging their own resistance and reaffirming the power of life (Rogers & Reich, 1988). ■

J. Richard Williams, MD, is Chairman and President of the Foundation for End of Life Care and a founding benefactor of Duke University's Institute on Care at the End of Life. Dr. Williams serves as Executive Vice President and Chief Patient Care Officer of VITAS Healthcare Corporation and is a recognized authority on noninvasive symptom management of the terminally ill. He is board certified in oncology, internal medicine, and hospice and palliative medicine. Dr. Williams has concentrated his medical career on caring for terminally ill patients in both institutional and home settings.

References

Anonymous. (2000). Coping with Loss. *Harvard Men's Health Watch, 5*, 1-3.

Anonymous. (2001). Depression and heart failure. *Harvard Heart Letter, 26*, 3-4.

Armenian, H.K., Saadeh, F.M., & Armenian, S.L. (1987). Widowhood and mortality in an Armenian church parish in Lebanon. *American Journal of Epidemiology, 125*, 127-132.

Avlund, K., Damsgaard, M.T., & Holstein, B.E. (1998). Social relations and mortality. An eleven-year follow-up study of 70-year-old men and women in Denmark. *Social Science and Medicine, 47*, 635-643.

Barefoot, J.C., Brummett, B.H., Helms, M.J., Mark, D.B., Siegler, I.C., & Williams, R.B. (2000). Depressive symptoms and survival of patients with coronary artery disease. *Psychosomatic Medicine, 62*, 790-795.

Berkman, L.F., & Syme, S.L. (1979). Social networks, host resistance, and mortality: a nine-year follow-up study of Alameda County residents. *American Journal of Epidemiology, 109*, 186-204.

Brummett, B.H., Barefoot, J.C., Siegler, I.C., Clapp-Channing, N. E., Lytle, B.L., Bosworth, H.B., Williams, R.B., Jr., & Mark, D.B. (2001). Characteristics of socially isolated patients with coronary artery disease who are at elevated risk for mortality. *Psychosomatic Medicine, 63*, 267-272.

Bygren, L.O., Konlaan, B.B., & Johansson, S.E. (1996). Attendance at cultural events, reading books or periodicals, and making music or singing in a choir as determinants for survival: Swedish interview survey of living conditions. *British Medical Journal, 313*, 1577-1580.

Cerhan, J.R., & Wallace, R.B. (1997). Change in social ties and subsequent mortality in rural elders. *Epidemiology, 8*, 475-481.

Ceria, C.D., Masaki, K.H., Rodriguez, B.L., Chen, R., Yano, K., & Curb, J.D. (2001). The relationship of psychosocial factors to total mortality among older Japanese-American men: The Honolulu Heart Program. *Journal of the American Geriatric Society, 49*, 725-731.

Gognalons-Nicolet, M., Derriennic, F., Monfort, C., & Cassou, B. (1999), Social prognostic factors of mortality in a random cohort of Geneva subjects followed up for a period of 12 years. Journal of *Epidemiology and Community Health, 53*, 138-143.

Grand, A., Grosclaude, P., Bocquet, H., Pous, J., & Albarede, J.L. (1990). Disability, psychosocial factors and mortality among the elderly in a rural French population. *Journal of Clinical Epidemiology, 43*, 773-782.

Helm, H.M., Hays, J.C., Flint, E.P., Koenig, H.G., & Blazer, D.G. (2000). Does private religious activity prolong survival? A six-year follow-up study of 3,851 older adults. *Journals of Gerontology, Biological Sciences and Medical Sciences, 55A*, M400-405.

House, J.S., Robbins, C., & Metzner, H.L. (1982). The association of social relationships and activities with mortality: prospective evidence from the Tecumseh Community Health Study. *American Journal of Epidemiology, 116*, 123-140.

Jacobs, S., Hansen, F., Berkman, L., Kasl, S., & Ostfeld, A. (1989). Depressions of bereavement. *Comprehensive Psychiatry, 30*, 218-224.

Jacobs, S., Hansen, F., Kasl, S., Ostfeld, A., Berkman, L., & Kim, K. (1990). Anxiety disorders during acute bereavement: risk and risk factors. *Journal of Clinical Psychiatry, 51*, 269-274.

Johansson, S.E., Konlaan, B.B., & Bygren, L.O. (2001). Sustaining habits of attending cultural events and maintenance of health: a longitudinal study. *Health Promotion International, 16*, 229-234.

Jylha, M., & Aro, S. (1989). Social ties and survival among the elderly in Tampere, Finland. *International Journal of Epidemiology, 18*, 158-164.

Koenig, H.G., Hays, J. C., Larson, D. B., George, L. K., Cohen, H. J., McCullough, M. E., Meador, K. G., & Blazer, D. G. (1999). Does religious attendance prolong survival? A six-year follow-up study of 3,968 older adults. *Journals of Gerontology, Biological Sciences and Medical Sciences, 54A*, M370-376.

Konlaan, B.B., Bjorby, N., Bygren, L.O., Weissglas, G., Karlsson, L.G., & Widmark, M. (2000). Attendance at cultural events and physical exercise and health: a randomized controlled study. *Public Health, 114*, 316-319.

Konlaan, B.B., Bygren, L.O., & Johansson, S.E. (2000). Visiting the cinema, concerts, museums or art exhibitions as determinant of survival: A Swedish fourteen-year cohort follow-up. *Scandinavian Journal of Public Health, 28*, 174-178.

Lawton, M.P., Moss, M., Hoffman, C., Grant, R., Ten Have, T., & Kleban, M.H. (1999). Health, valuation of life, and the wish to live. *Gerontologist, 39*, 406-416.

Lawton, M.P., Moss, M., Hoffman, C., Kleban, M.H., Ruckdeschel, K., & Winter, L. (2001). Valuation of life: A concept and a scale. *Journal of Aging and Health, 13*, 3-31.

Maier, H., & Smith, J. (1999). Psychological predictors of mortality in old age. *Journals of Gerontology, Psychological Sciences and Social Sciences 54B*, 44-54.

Meador, K. (2001 October 28). Personal communication via e-mail.

Phillips, D.P., & Smith, D.G. (1990). Postponement of death until symbolically meaningful occasions. *Journal of the American Medical Association, 263*, 1947-1951.

Phillips, D.P., Van Voorhees, C.A., & Ruth, T.E. (1992). The birthday: Lifeline or deadline? *Psychosomatic Medicine, 54*, 532-542.

Rogers, M.P., & Reich, P. (1988). On the health consequences of bereavement. *New England Journal of Medicine, 319*, 510-512.

Schaefer, C., Quesenberry, C.P., Jr., & Wi, S. (1995). Mortality following conjugal bereavement and the effects of a shared environment. *American Journal of Epidemiology, 141*, 1142-1152.

Schoevers, R.A., Geerlings, M.I., Beekman, A.T., Penninx, B.W., Deeg, D.J., Jonker, C., & Van Tilburg, W. (2000). Association of depression and gender with mortality in old age. Results from the Amsterdam Study of the Elderly (AMSTEL). *British Journal of Psychiatry, 177*, 336-342.

Schulz, R., & Beach, S.R. (1999). Caregiving as a risk factor for mortality: The Caregiver Health Effects Study. *Journal of the American Medical Association, 282*, 2215-2219.

Seeman, T.E., Kaplan, G.A., Knudsen, L., Cohen, R., & Guralnik, J. (1987). Social network ties and mortality among the elderly in the Alameda County Study. *American Journal of Epidemiology, 126*, 714-723.

Turvey, C.L., Carney, C., Arndt, S., Wallace, R.B., & Herzog, R. (1999), Conjugal loss and syndromal depression in a sample of elders aged 70 years or older. *American Journal of Psychiatry, 156*, 1596-1601.

Winter, L., Lawton, M.P., Casten, R. J., & Sando, R.L. (2000). The relationship between external events and affect states in older people. *International Journal of Aging and Human Development, 50*, 85-96.

Wulsin, L.R., Vaillant, G.E., & Wells, V.E. (1999). A systematic review of the mortality of depression. *Psychosomatic Medicine, 61*, 6-17.

Zuckerman, D.M., Kasl, S.V., & Ostfeld, A.M. (1984). Psychosocial predictors of mortality among the elderly poor. The role of religion, well-being, and social contacts. *American Journal of Epidemiology, 119*, 410-23.

CHAPTER 19

Facing Life Alone: Loss of a Significant Other in Later Life

Dale A. Lund and Michael S. Caserta

INTRODUCTION

How older adults face life alone after the loss of a spouse is likely to be influenced by how they managed to adjust to life losses and transitions throughout the course of their life. Nearly everyone who lives a long life will experience many situations that help to develop or challenge their coping skills. Infants become temporarily separated from parents and siblings when they leave the familiar surroundings of the home to attend day care and school. Children also lose toys, clothes, pets, and valued belongings. With increased geographic mobility, it is common for children to move several times from one neighborhood to another, changing friends and familiar surroundings with each move. Young adults have lost relationships with teachers, clubs, organizations, and peers, as they advance from elementary grades, through high school and college. In later life adults continue to lose more friendships and relationships because of relocations, deaths, and retirement. With divorce rates of about 40% in the United States (Macionis, 2001), millions are experiencing the loss of marital relationships, parents, and family life. Due to physiological changes associated with aging, people often lose hair, hearing, sight, muscle tone, independence, and mobility. Each loss has the potential of disrupting patterns of behavior, initiating grief-related feelings, and requiring adjustments, but such losses also add to the course of human development.

Older adults have many opportunities to develop their coping skills or become overwhelmed by life's cumulative losses. It is much easier to understand how people cope with their current bereavement situations if we recognize how they have managed their previous losses. In the case of older bereaved spouses, effective interventions need to take into account how they experienced relocation, physical, and relationship losses earlier in their life (Lund, 1989). If they relied on task-oriented strategies in handling these previous situations, then a similar approach might be effective again. For example, the young boy who is told to be strong and not to cry after his father's death might easily grow up to be the unexpressive and isolated widower in later life. At the same time we need to appreciate the uniqueness of each loss or bereavement experience and not assume that the loss of personal belongings is the same as a divorce or death of a parent.

Research on spousal bereavement, widowhood, and other forms of partner loss over the past 20 years has greatly expanded our understanding of the short- and long-term grief process. It has also helped identify factors that have led to more effective ways to adjust to a new and very different life. This growing knowledge base can be very helpful to the bereaved and to a variety of professionals who help guide them through the adjustment process. This chapter highlights the results and implications of some recent research and offers several suggestions for helping those who are facing life alone.

Spousal Bereavement

The death of a spouse is an increasingly common experience among older adults, particularly women. Only 2% of the men in the United States between the ages of 18 and 64 were widowed in 1998 compared with 7% of similar aged women. These percentages increase dramatically with advancing age so that 9% of the men were widowed between the ages of 65 and 74, 20% at ages 75 to 84, and 42% at age 85 and over. For women, the percentages are much higher at every age. Between the ages of 65 and 74, 32% of the women were widowed, at ages 75 to 84, 56% were widowed, and by age 85 and older, 77% were widowed (U.S. Bureau of the Census, 1998). These high percentages actually underestimate the number of persons who experience the death of a spouse because they do not include those who remarried. In short, death-related bereavement is a common and expected experience for older adults.

Although the death of a spouse might be the most stressful event that a person will experience, many bereaved spouses, including those who are older, do find ways to manage and rebuild their lives. The course of spousal bereavement is often characterized by resiliency, which allows depression, loneliness, and sadness to be followed by feelings of pride, confidence, and personal growth. Although it has been estimated that between 15 and 25 percent of bereaved spouses have long-term difficulty in coping, many more gradually discover effective ways of dealing with their loss (Lund, 1989).

Resiliency following the death of a spouse might best be explained by a life course or developmental perspective that emphasizes the importance of growth, maturation, adaptability, and previous life experiences in coping with stressful events. When people experience bereavement at earlier times in the life course, it comes at an unexpected time and they are likely to be less prepared to make the needed adjustments. By contrast, spousal bereavement in later life is considered to be more timely because death occurs more frequently in older adults and is more expected. Older adults also have had more opportunities than younger adults to successfully manage a variety of losses and thereby develop effective strategies and interpersonal skills.

This advantage, however, does not mean that older adults automatically cope better than others. Unsuccessful coping with earlier losses can lead to poor coping skills later. Another problem is bereavement overload, in which coping becomes exceedingly difficult because several losses or deaths occur in a very short time. The key to resiliency during bereavement is developing successful interpersonal coping strategies to deal with each new loss.

Recent studies have revealed that the bereavement process is more like a roller coaster ride than an orderly progression of stages with clear time frames associated with each stage. The bereavement roller coaster is characterized by the rapidly changing emotions of grief; meeting the challenges of learning new skills; recognizing personal weaknesses and limitations; developing new patterns of behavior; experiencing fatigue, loneliness, and helplessness; and forming new friendships and relationships.

Research has been unable to identify clear time markers associated with these many ups and downs. In fact, the highs and lows can occur within minutes, days, months, or years. Fortunately, for most bereaved spouses the roller coaster ride becomes more manageable over time, with fewer abrupt highs and lows. This gradual improvement may never lead to an end or resolution, however, because as many bereaved spouses report: "You never get over it—you learn to live with it."

Our own research has also documented that there is considerable diversity among and within bereaved persons. Not all people experience the same feelings, thoughts, and actions as they move through the process. For example, a 65-year-old widow described herself in the following way 4 weeks after her husband's death: "I am a very lonely person. Lousy, all washed out, despondent, feel deserted, angry, hurt, hopeless, alone, mixed-up, cannot concentrate, very emotional, very tired, cry a lot, hateful, very bitter, misfit, nobody, very miserable, very much of a loner." This same woman described herself in much the same troubled way two years into the bereavement process. She added that she was concerned about herself and really hurt inside. She noted that she was sick of living alone and didn't care about life. In contrast, another 69-year-old widow described herself at 6 months after her husband's death as being "independent, excited about keeping busy, enjoying the company of others, and working in my yard and doing handiwork." This diversity in bereavement reactions also is found within each individual. It is not unusual to find a person simultaneously experiencing a full range of feelings and behaviors. For example, a bereaved person can feel angry, guilty, and lonely, yet at the same time feel personal strength and pride in how he or she is coping. A 70-year-old woman described herself at length as being busy, enjoying many different activities, and doing things with other people, but her final self-descriptive comment was that she still feels lonely. It is common for bereaved persons to experience simultaneously both positive and negative feelings.

Loneliness and problems associated with managing the tasks of daily living are two of the most common and difficult adjustments for older adults. These problems are even more difficult for the spousally bereaved because the daily lives of spouses are so closely connected. In later life, especially, spouses frequently become dependent on each other for conversation, love, and sharing of tasks. Loneliness is problematic because it involves missing, sadness, and a void that does not go away simply by being with or among other people. Many bereaved persons report feeling lonely but not being alone. In the case of experiencing the death of a parent, child, or sibling who may live many miles away, the bereaved often describe how lonely they feel when they realize they can no longer call their loved one on the phone or hear his or her voice again. In a study by the authors, 70% of the bereaved spouses reported that loneliness was their single greatest difficulty during the two years following their partners' deaths (Lund, 1989).

Unfortunately, most older adults have not learned to do many of the tasks of daily life that are important to maintaining their health, well-being, and happiness. Many older men have not learned how to prepare meals, wash clothes, and clean house because they left these tasks to their wives. Similarly, many older women have not learned how to do home repairs, maintain or sometimes even drive an automobile, and manage finances. Research has shown that these deficiencies further complicate the bereavement process because grief requires physical and mental energy, which can be additionally depleted by worrying about how these tasks will be done (Lund, Caserta, Dimond, & Shaffer, 1989). The lack of skills in daily living lends itself to a promising focus for future interventions because these skills can be easily taught. In future, perhaps, as the current generation of middle-aged adults begins to age and lose spouses, they will be better equipped to deal with a much broader range of tasks of daily living, having lived in a time when roles and tasks have been less gender-bound.

Other Forms Of Partner Loss

Most of the literature on partner loss in later life has focused on spousal bereavement and widowhood. Losses associated with other forms of partnered relationships, however, do occur and need to be mentioned here. Some of the most common instances are within same-sex relationships and those engaged in unmarried cohabiting heterosexual relationships. There has been little if any focus on these types of losses exclusively in later life, but it is likely that much of what has been observed transcends age.

Although not as much is known about this form of bereavement, many aspects of the loss of a gay or lesbian partner are comparable to what has been reported for the loss of a spouse. Similar to bereaved widows and widowers, the more commonly mentioned negative consequences associated with same-sex partner bereavement include loss of companionship, loneliness, depressed mood, and the distress associated with taking on new daily tasks and challenges in which the surviving partner may not be adequately skilled (de Vries, 2001; Shernoff, 1997). Like those who have lost a husband or wife (Lund et al., 1989), the bereaved partner may have difficulty managing many of those tasks of daily living that were the primary responsibility of the person who has died, whether it is managing finances or other aspects of the household. It is very likely that these challenges can add to the emotional stressors mentioned above, making coping with the loss even more difficult.

Particular attention has been focused on partner loss due to AIDS. Again, there are some parallels between AIDS-related bereavement and other forms of partner loss, particularly reports of increased incidence of depressive symptoms, more physical health complaints, and more frequent visits to health care providers (Martin & Dean, 1993). What makes AIDS-related bereavement particularly unique, however, is that these bereaved partners are more susceptible to bereavement overload due to multiple losses of friends, former partners, and others with whom they had emotional attachments within a relatively short period of time (Martin & Dean, 1993). Older adults are especially susceptible to bereavement overload because the likelihood of multiple losses is greater in later life (Moss, Moss, & Hansson, 2001).

Although same-sex relationships and those of cohabiting heterosexual partners have many similarities to traditional marriages, when a loss occurs in such a relationship, the survivor can experience what Doka (1989) has termed *disenfranchised grief*. "A person experiences a sense of loss but does not have the socially recognized right, role, or capacity to grieve…The person suffers a loss but has little or no opportunity to mourn publicly" (Doka, 1989, p.3). In addition to the grief over the loss of a gay or lesbian or cohabiting life partner, the grief of losing a partner in an extramarital affair, as well as an ex-spouse, can be potentially disenfranchised.

Typically, the intensity of the grief reactions is greater when the partners are more invested—both emotionally and in terms of commitment—in the relationship. While not a marital relationship in the traditional or legal sense, those who behave as if it were a marriage tend to experience a stronger grief response to the loss than those who are not as committed at the time of the death. Oftentimes, particularly in the case of extramarital affairs, ex-spouses, and in some cohabiting relationships, the bereaved may be excluded from many of the rituals, opportunities for support, and legal benefits of survivorship. This could complicate the grief further because these additional stressors may exacerbate an already distressing situation (Doka, 1989).

Bereavement As Process

It is generally accepted that bereavement is an ongoing, long-term process with no clear stages or endpoints. Although the most difficult period typically is soon after the death of a spouse or partner—and that varies among individuals—instances of distress and painful memories can occur for many years after the loss (Barrett & Schneweis, 1980; Wortman & Silver, 2001). One study, for instance, reported that it took anywhere from 10 to 20 years for some aspects of widows' sense of well-being to approach the levels of those who were not bereaved (Wortman, Silver, & Kessler, 1993).

Even among those who have been widowed for a long time and feel that they have adapted to life without their partner, certain events or occasions can precipitate distress associated with the past loss. These can be anniversaries or other special occasions when the deceased partner's presence is missed, as well as encountering certain photographs, letters, and other memorabilia (Weiss, 2001). The bond the survivor has with the one who has died can continue for years, well after the initial grief experience wanes, and may even continue for the survivor's lifetime (Horacek, 1995; Weiss, 2001).

Most empirical evidence suggests that it is not necessary to dissolve former bonds or attachments to the deceased. Certain memories can trigger a renewed sadness, but at the same time they can provide a sense of connection to the deceased that may be a source of comfort and reassurance suggesting an ongoing but transformed relationship with them (Horacek, 1995; Weiss, 2001; Worden, 1991). Consequently, this continuing attachment often is associated with positive adaptation rather than a pathological failure to achieve resolution (Klass, Silverman, & Nickman, 1996; Wortman & Silver, 2001).

Essentially, the long-term outcomes of partner loss depend upon an evolving process of adaptation, often completely transforming the life of the bereaved person. Widowhood frequently marks the beginning of a new phase of life that could last several years, especially for women, given increasing life expectancies and fewer opportunities for remarriage. As with any life transition, a widowhood career, that is, learning new life skills, presents both challenges and opportunities for personal growth (Hansson, Remondet, & Galusha, 1993). Other features of the aging process, however, can affect how well a person functions as a widow or widower, particularly in later life. For example, chronic health problems and potential social isolation could adversely influence the person's sense of personal control. Those who lack the personal, social, and environmental resources to meet the daily demands of widowed life can experience greater difficulty managing their widowhood career than they would if those resources were available to them (Hansson et al., 1993).

As discussed earlier, those who adapted effectively to prior losses are more likely to have the personal resources and resilience to successfully meet the demands and challenges of widowhood well into the life course (Hansson et al., 1993; Moss et al., 2001). Older widows and widowers who have successfully lived independently for years after becoming widowed often report enhanced feelings of self-efficacy or the confidence to meet future challenges that might confront them (Arbuckle & de Vries, 1995). Some, but not all, eventually grow beyond merely adapting and positive functioning; they try new things and explore new interests (hobbies, classes, or career or volunteer opportunities) that they otherwise may not have tried had they not been widowed. These instances of personal growth can result in a more meaningful and balanced life for many who have lost a partner (Lieberman, 1996; Schaefer & Moos, 2001).

How To Help

People often say that the passage of time heals a wound. This statement is problematic in that it implies that little or no effort is required to cope with the situation—that simply allowing time to pass will bring about successful adjustment. Although it is a fact that most bereaved persons have less difficulty and more positive adjustments over time, it is important to recognize that it is what people do with their time that determines the outcome. Successful adjustments require active rather than passive coping strategies.

Many bereaved persons have said that it is most helpful to take one day at a time and to remain active, busy, and socially connected with other people. Being physically and socially active can help to reduce the feelings of despair, helplessness, loneliness, and being overwhelmed that often contribute to a long-term strategy of waiting—often in vain—for time to bring about healing. In addition to these active coping strategies, it is important to have social support from others and opportunities for self-expression, especially in the early months of bereavement. Some of the most difficult and stressful bereavement experiences occur in the first few months when grief issues are especially intense.

Researchers have also learned that how a person copes with loss early in the process is one of the best predictors of long-term coping. Those who report effective coping in the first couple of months usually cope better than others a few years later. Bereaved persons therefore are likely to benefit most from social support that they receive early in the process and from opportunities to express how they feel at this time. Some of the most appreciated support comes from those who allow the bereaved to openly express anger, sadness, and other emotions without passing along advice and counsel. It is important for bereaved persons to know that their reactions are common and that others respect their feelings and care about their well-being. Self-help groups for bereaved persons provide good opportunities for self-expression, particularly for those who do not have someone in whom they can confide.

The importance of internal coping resources is supported by research that has focused on the role of self-esteem and self-efficacy. Both concepts represent personal coping resources that individuals develop throughout their lives. Self-esteem refers to the positive or negative judgments or evaluations that one makes about self-worth. Self-efficacy refers to a person's ability to meet the changing demands of everyday life and feeling confident in doing so.

The way people feel about themselves and how skilled they are in managing the many tasks of daily living—maintaining a household, paying bills, driving a car, knowing how to access resources, and so on—will influence how effectively they adjust to the loss of a loved one. People who develop positive self-esteem and competencies such as social, interpersonal, and instrumental skills are likely to have more favorable bereavement outcomes that those who develop negative self-images and lack self-efficacy.

Self-esteem and self-efficacy are highly interrelated; people who are confident and have pride in themselves are usually more motivated to learn new skills, and the process of becoming more competent in daily life itself creates more positive self-esteem. Bereaved persons with these positive characteristics are likely to cope quite well because they will not be content using a passive approach to coping. Conversely, bereaved people who never developed these personal coping resources are likely to experience long-term difficulties because they are more inclined to believe that they deserve to remain depressed, lonely, and incapacitated. These people tend to feel overwhelmed and take few constructive actions on their own behalf.

The predictors of adjustment to bereavement are similar for both men and women and for young and older adults. Age and gender are not the most influential factors in the course of bereavement. Of greater importance is developing self-esteem early in life, continuing to enhance these views over the life course, and developing skills that help in meeting the changing circumstances and demands of daily living. People with these traits are more likely than others to adjust well to nearly any major life stress or transition. Human development is a life-long process. In the case of late-life bereavement, the developmental process is challenged. During this transition period, the bereaved person can remain physically, psychologically, and socially disrupted or he or she can emerge with a sense of growth from learning new skills, becoming more independent, and developing a clearer self-identity.

Although it is tempting to conclude that most bereaved persons will need help with their adjustment process, this is not the case. Research has shown that many bereaved persons do not want or need intervention services (Lund, 1993). This point is important to recognize, because it is frequently assumed by clinicians and service providers that older bereaved persons are depressed, socially isolated, and incapacitated by their loss. The research evidence (Wortman & Silver, 2001) does not support this assumption, although certainly some bereaved persons are depressed, isolated, and incapacitated. The tasks for those developing intervention services are many; among their first should be to focus on those who are at greater risk—to seek them out rather than simply announcing the existence of the service—and encourage their participation by explaining how and why the service will be helpful. It is critical to recognize that many, perhaps most, of the potential population of bereaved persons will not want to participate. This can be discouraging to those who are committed to the value of their services, but their motivation to continue their efforts will probably be less adversely affected if they anticipate the lack of enthusiasm among many potential clients. For example, only 44% of the bereaved spouses who completed a study by the authors said that they would have liked the opportunity to attend self-help groups (Lund, Dimond, & Juretich, 1985). In a later study (Lund, Redburn, Juretich, & Caserta, 1989), only 27% of those assigned to self-help groups actually agreed to participate.

Interventions need to be available early in the bereavement process and continue over relatively long periods of time. There is a good deal of research evidence that the first several months (usually 1 to 4 months) are the most difficult and that early adjustments will influence outcomes much later. Also, because bereavement may last for many years and some people may not be ready for early interventions, it would be most helpful to have services available over long periods of time. This does not mean that the same people need to continue receiving services for many years, although some will have this need: rather, bereaved persons need to have an opportunity to participate when they are ready.

Because the impact of bereavement is multidimensional, it is imperative that interventions offer comprehensive and diverse services. No one intervention can provide all that is needed, and each intervention should clearly identify which needs are being targeted so that the grieving person is aware of what help is not being provided. For example, the death of a spouse or a partner in later life can impact emotions, psychosocial functioning, health, family life, interpersonal relationships, work, recreation, and financial situations. Those who design interventions that provide primarily an opportunity for self-expression (such as self-help groups) should recognize that some dimensions are not likely to be addressed. Ideally, all communities would have available a variety of interventions or services so that each person's unique skills, resources, and circumstances could be matched to the most appropriate set of services. Unlikely as this possibility is, communities can at least strive to offer interventions with the broadest scope of impact. With this in mind it would be worthwhile, whenever possible, to address several dimensions simultaneously by providing opportunities for self-expression and the enhancement of self-esteem; teaching new skills to complete the tasks of daily living; enhancing and mobilizing already existing social support networks; providing education and assistance regarding health, nutrition, and exercise; and encouraging social participation.

Various intervention formats and professionals are needed to ensure that appropriate services are available. Not all people experience bereavement in the same way; similarly, not all people will use or benefit from the same interventions. In terms of format, some people will want only a one-on-one type of intervention. They may feel the uniqueness of their situation can be dealt with more effectively one-to-one because they are reluctant to express personal and sensitive feelings in group situations. Others have reported that they particularly enjoyed being in a self-help group because they learned from others, recognized some commonalities in their situations, and enjoyed the socializing and friendships that developed.

Many people have skills and expertise that are well suited for helping the bereaved. Phyllis Silverman (1986), who developed the widow-to-widow program, has shown that widows are quite capable of assisting each other. An experienced widow can reveal to a new widow that she knows how it feels to grieve. Also, there are important contributions that can be made by researchers, gerontologists, psychologists, psychiatrists, physicians, social workers, nurses, occupational therapists, art therapists, hospice workers, counselors, clergy, and many other professionals such as social scientists, lawyers, accountants, educators, and direct service providers. Again, because bereavement has a multidimensional impact, interventions can be developed by many different professional and trained team members. Other bereaved persons can provide a sharing of experiences while trained persons assist with legal, financial, health, spiritual, and educational issues. A multidimensional team approach increases the likelihood of developing interventions that address a diversity of needs and lead to greater success.

It should be understood that bereavement is a common and natural experience that we all share. Unfortunately, many people are not well prepared for the pain, threats, and challenges that it presents. Because bereavement occurs in broader contexts, we do not all have the same experiences and needs. What appears to help one person may have an entirely different impact on someone else. The best way to help bereaved persons is to be educated about the process; assess the context in which it occurs; become familiar with a wide range of resources; and be patient, nonjudgmental, and a good listener. ■

Dale A. Lund, PhD, is a Professor of Gerontology and Sociology and Director of the University of Utah Gerontology Center. Dr. Lund is internationally known for his research, publications, and presentations on coping with difficult transitions in later life, particularly family caregiving and spousal bereavement. He edited and authored Older Bereaved Spouses and Men Coping with Grief. *Dr. Lund is the founder of Bereavement Interest Group within the Gerontological Society of America and is a member of the International Work Group on Death, Dying and Bereavement. He has received numerous awards including the Utah Hospice Person of the Year, Charles Redd Prize from the Utah Academy of Sciences, Arts and Letters, and the 1996 Outstanding Researcher Award from the Association for Death Education and Counseling.*

Michael S. Caserta, PhD, is an Associate Professor at the University of Utah Gerontology Center in Salt Lake City. He has co-authored numerous journal articles and book chapters in the areas of spousal bereavement, family caregiving, and health promotion and self-care. His most recent work is the development of Pathfinders, *a program designed to improve the self-care practices of older widows and widowers. He is an active member of the Association for Death Education and Counseling, the American Society on Aging, the American Association for Health Education, and the Gerontological Society of America where he has co-convened an interest group on death, dying, bereavement, and widowhood.*

References

Arbuckle, N.W., & de Vries, B. (1995). The long-term effects of later life spousal and parental bereavement on personal functioning. *The Gerontologist, 35*, 637-647.

Barrett, C.J., & Schneweis, K.M. (1980). An empirical search for stages of widowhood. *Omega, 11*, 97-104.

de Vries, B. (2001). Grief: Intimacy's reflection. *Generations, 25*, 2, 75-80.

Doka, K.J. (1989). *Disenfranchised grief: Recognizing hidden sorrow.* Lexington, MA: Lexington Books.

Hansson, R.O., Remondet, J.H., & Galusha, M. (1993). Old age and widowhood: Issues of personal control and independence. In M.S. Stroebe, W. Stroebe, & R.O. Hansson (Eds.), *Handbook of bereavement: Theory, research, and intervention.* New York: Cambridge University Press.

Horacek, B.J. (1995). A heuristic model of grieving after high-grief deaths. *Death Studies, 19*, 21-31.

Klass, D., Silverman, P.R., & Nickman, S. L. (1996). *Continuing bonds: New understandings of grief.* Washington, DC: Taylor & Francis.

Lieberman, M. (1996). *Doors closed, doors open: Widows grieving and growing.* New York: G.P. Putnam's Sons.

Lund, D.A. (1989). *Older bereaved spouses.* Washington, DC: Taylor & Francis.

Lund, D.A. (1993). Widowhood: The coping response. In R. Kastenbaum (Ed.), *The encyclopedia of adult development.* Phoenix, AZ: Oryx.

Lund, D.A., Caserta, M. S., Dimond, M.F., & Shaffer, S.K. (1989). Competencies, tasks of daily living, and adjustments to spousal bereavement in later life. In D.A. Lund (Ed.), *Older bereaved spouses: Research with practical applications.* New York: Taylor & Francis/ Hemisphere.

Lund, D.A., Dimond, M.F., & Juretich, M. (1985). Bereavement support groups for the elderly: Characteristics of potential participants. *Death Studies, 9,* 309-321.

Lund, D.A., Redburn, D.E., Juretich, M., & Caserta, M.S. (1989). Resolving problems implementing bereavement self-help groups. In D.A. Lund (Ed.), *Older bereaved spouses.* Washington, DC: Taylor & Francis.

Macionis, J. (2001). *Sociology* (8th ed.). Upper Saddle River, NJ: Prentice-Hall.

Martin, J.L., & Dean, L. (1993). Bereavement following death from AIDS: Unique problems, reactions, and special needs. In M. S. Stroebe, W. Stroebe, & R. O. Hansson (Eds.), *Handbook of bereavement: Theory, research, and intervention.* New York: Cambridge University Press.

Moss, M.S., Moss, S.Z., & Hansson, R.O. (2001). Bereavement and old age. In M.S. Stroebe, R.O. Hansson, W. Stroebe, & H. Schut (Eds.), *Handbook of bereavement research: Consequences, coping, and care.* Washington, DC: American Psychological Association.

Schaefer, J.A., & Moos, R.H. (2001). Bereavement experiences and personal growth. In M.S. Stroebe, R.O. Hansson, W. Stroebe, & H. Schut (Eds.). *Handbook of bereavement research: Consequences, coping, and care.* Washington, DC: American Psychological Association.

Shernoff, M. (1997). *Gay widowers: Life after the death of a partner.* New York: Harrington Press.

Silverman, P. (1986). *Widow to widow.* New York: Springer.

U.S. Bureau of the Census. (1998). Marital status and living arrangements of adults: March 1998. Washington, DC: Government Printing Office.

Weiss, R.S. (2001). Grief, bonds, and relationships. In M.S. Stroebe, R.O. Hansson, W. Stroebe, & H. Schut (Eds.), *Handbook of bereavement research: Consequences, coping, and care.* Washington, DC: American Psychological Association.

Worden, J.W. (1991). *Grief counseling and grief therapy: A handbook for the mental health practitioner* (2nd ed.). New York: Springer.

Wortman, C.B., & Silver, R.C. (2001). The myths of coping with loss revisited. In M.S. Stroebe, R.O. Hansson, W. Stroebe, & H. Schut (Eds.), *Handbook of bereavement research: Consequences, coping, and care.* Washington, DC: American Psychological Association.

Wortman, C.B., Silver, R.C., & Kessler, R.C. (1993). The meaning of loss and adjustment to bereavement. In M.S. Stroebe, W. Stroebe, & R.O. Hansson (Eds.), *Handbook of bereavement: Theory, research, and intervention.* New York: Cambridge University Press.

Additional Reading

Books

Campbell, S., & Silverman, P.R. (1996). *Widower: When men are left alone.* Amityville, NY: Baywood.

Davidson, J.D., & Doka, K.J. (1999). *Living with grief: At work, at school, at worship.* Levittown, PA: Brunner/Mazel.

Glick, I.O., Weiss, R.S., & Parkes, C.M. (1974). *The first year of bereavement.* New York: John Wiley & Sons.

Kushner, H.S. (1981). *When bad things happen to good people.* New York: Avon Books.

Lopata, H.Z. (1996). *Current widowhood: Myths and realities.* Thousand Oaks, CA: Sage.

Lund, D.A. (2001). *Men coping with grief.* Amityville, NY: Baywood.

Martin, T.L., & Doka, K.J. (2000). *Men don't cry…women do.* Philadelphia: Brunner/Mazel.

CHAPTER 20

Faces of Grief and Intimacy in Later Life

Brian de Vries, Rosemary Blieszner, and John A. Blando

INTRODUCTION

Imagine a multisided prism, suspended on a cord in sunlight and shadow. The facets give off rainbow glints of colors, suggesting the multiple forms of intimate relationships, each distinct, yet sharing common features. The relationship prism twists and turns throughout the span of life and the light to which it is exposed is stronger and weaker at varying times owing to changes in relationships, including death. The prism takes on special features in the later years. This image of a prism, of flashing colors that come and go, symbolizes the many forms of intimacy and the many faces of grief in later life.

As Brehm (1985) commented, multiple kinds of intimate relationships exist. "There are many, many different individuals who join together, who influence each other's lives, who fulfill each other's needs, who love each other...for a day, for a year, or for a lifetime" (p. 6). These influences and connections are seen in the commitment individuals share, the deep sense of caring and compassion, the sharing of values, the desire to be near each other, and the experience of interdependence (Moss & Schwebel, 1993). Relationships are, in turn, shaped by the individual's characteristics and the contexts in which interaction takes place. In the later years of life, changes in either partner's roles, health status, living arrangements, finances, or other aging-related aspects of life can affect intimate relationships. Certainly, the chances of losing loved ones to debilitating illness and death increase with advanced aging.

Study of intimate relationships in old age has flourished in recent years; at the same time, significant research interest has arisen in the experience of those bereft of loved ones. Research on grief has focused on intrapersonal issues, such as the stages and phases of grief and recovery, on the search for biological processes underlying the manifestations of grief, and on interpersonal issues, such as social risk factors and possible interventions in the course of grief (Stroebe, Hansson, Stroebe, & Schut, 2001).

These parallel literatures have mostly developed and proliferated independently, obscuring the perspective that grief is a reflection of intimacy (de Vries, 2001). That is, the simultaneous consideration of grief and intimacy is rarely undertaken, rendering incomplete our understanding of both. As Deck and Folta (1989) observed, grief "is the study of people and their most intimate relationships" (p. 80). To this we would add that grief is the study of intimacy in people's relationships (de Vries, 2001).

Embedded in the following brief and selective review of issues of intimacy in later-life relationships are some of the intimate experiences of grief. This simultaneous consideration of intimacy and grief is intended to serve as a reminder that death marks the end of a life, not the end of a relationship. It is intended to enrich our understanding of intimate relationships and loss in later life. The five facets of the relationship prism included in this analysis are romantic, parent-child, grandparent-grandchild, sibling, and friend relationships. In each case, we present some special features of the relationships in old age and attendant consequences of their loss when at least one of the partners is old.

Romantic Relationships

The first facet of the prism, romantic relationships, represents the quintessential form of intimacy (Huyck, 2001). Even romantic relationships assume many forms, including heterosexual marriages and remarriages, same-sex partnerships, cohabiting relationships, living apart together relationships (i.e., partners who do not maintain a common household), romantic and sexual affairs, and abandoned and unrequited relationships. The form these relationships take may influence the expression and experience of intimacy therein.

Traditionally, romantic relationships also are ones in which couples search for and achieve physical arousal and sexual satisfaction, the extent and nature of which varies over time and by age and circumstance. Intimately interconnected lives, however, are not restricted to physical acts. Typically, it is in romantic relationships that couples develop a sense of cohesion and compassion. In such relationships, personal confidences are exchanged, although (in heterosexual relationships) the flow tends to be from husbands to their wives rather than from wives to their husbands (Strain & Chappell, 1982). Companionship and feeling needed, secure, and respected are frequently mentioned as important aspects of intimacy, particularly in later life. The loss of one's partner means missing the shared activities and comfortable feelings of belonging and being cared about. It also means confronting myriad daily tasks alone and facing the world alone.

Lehman and associates (1999) found that, in contrast with other bereaved individuals, bereaved spouses reported that concomitant stressors, including home care, household duties and maintenance, financial management, and decision making on one's own, had caused them the most trouble in dealing with the partner's death. Loneliness was also mentioned frequently. The small, daily acts of intimacy that characterize couples across the life course become the source and substance of grief reactions following the death. One bereaved spouse reported, "He is not here to do things with me, [such as] eating together, working together. Now I'm alone. I've lost my husband. I'm lonely, I'm lost, and I'm miserable" (Lehman et al., 1999, p. 126). The many kinds of intimate couples, across the life course and in later life, and the many forms of intimacy expressed by these couples, are mirrored in the many faces of grief.

Parent-Adult Child Relationships

The intimate relationship between aged parents and their adult children, the second facet of the relationships prism, is similarly fluid, cultivated, and complex. The sharing of a deep and genuine concern for another person is typical of the intimacy experienced between older parents and their adult children, balanced by an awareness of the other person as an individual with unique strengths and weaknesses. These two features are said to be key to understanding the intimacy of the parent-child relationship in later life (Fingerman, 2001), characterized in a variety of reports as satisfying (Bengtson & Harootyan, 1994) and consistent over the course of adulthood (Leigh, 1982).

Fingerman (2001) described the intimacy between parents and their children in later life as the paradox of distant closeness. For example, parents no longer attempt to direct the affairs of their children, and children seek to protect their parents from worry. These guarded efforts entail recognition of what has changed in the relationship and how best to proceed. Both parents and children learn of topics to avoid in conversation based on the knowledge that such topics may introduce disharmony or disagreement. In both these examples, a certain degree of distance serves to enhance the intimacy of the relationship.

Intimacy also may be enhanced, however, by expressions in safe topics. For example, parents may enjoy hearing about their offspring's daily affairs and feel included in their lives through stories of work and family. In fact, parents may bask in the reflected glories of the accomplishments of their children and relish the children's fulfillment of the parents' developmental stake (Bengtson & Kuypers, 1971). Parents are the reporters of family history and the footprints for children's futures; children often enjoy hearing about the formative years of their parents and learning about and experiencing their own histories through these stories (Fingerman, 2001). Such temporal, narrative inclusions help form the bridge over the distances mandated in other areas of interaction and communication. "Intimacy between parents and offspring in late life includes a sense of self-validation, steeped in a sense of identity over time" (Fingerman, 2001, p. 28).

This sense of self and time is paramount to understanding both the intimacy between parents and children and their grief experiences. When a child dies, parents feel as though their foundations have been rocked. The natural order of the universe is violated; after all, the old are supposed to die before the young (Perkins & Harris, 1990). Parents ask, "How is it my child could be taken when I am old and still here?" (de Vries, Dalla Lana, & Falck, 1994). Children are the extensions of parents, with potential for fulfilling parents' unattained hopes and dreams; Yalom (1989) described children as the immortality projects of parents. Parents of deceased offspring frequently report an amputation-like experience assuming the form "of an empty historical track" (Klass & Marwitt, 1989, p. 41). They spend time keeping track of what the child would have accomplished or where the child would be in life had he or she lived. In such ways, the child continues to occupy a symbolic presence in the parent's inner world. A parent reported, "I don't think you can lose a child and ever get over the loss. You learn to live with it, but you never get over it" (Lehman et al., 1999, p. 127).

Similarly, adult children grieve in ways that reflect the meaning, nature, and timing of the parental death. Moss and Moss (1989) reported that the parent is a composite of a child's perceptions across the life course: the protector of the child in early life, the competent adult of midlife, and the model for living the advanced years. The death of a parent is the loss of that protected past and of the model for living out old age. It is a concrete reminder of the passage of time and of one's own mortality. According to a bereaved son, aged 62:

> There is less family now, less connections with the past. We [siblings] cling to each other more. There's loss of a real link with the past...we grew up in a small town. When I left the funeral we passed the house where I grew up, and I recalled early days of childhood. It was a happy childhood. There is a remote past for which [mother] was the link. (Moss & Moss, 1989, pp. 107–108)

Marshall (1980) described a parent's death as a life-span marker that structures expectations of the timing of one's own life events and personal death. Moss and Moss (1989) reported that "a 57-year-old woman whose parents both died at age 55, has said that she now celebrates two occasions on her birthday: her chronological age and the number of years she has lived beyond the age when her parents died" (p. 107).

The themes of response to parental death may seem contradictory in that they depict profound loss yet gains in personal development, deep caring and desire for intimacy with strong negative feelings, and wishes for independence and distance (Moss & Moss, 1989). This observation elaborates on the paradox of distant closeness described by Fingerman (2001) and attests to the complex and fluid nature of intimacy and grief in parent-adult child relationships.

Grandparent-Grandchild Relationships

An intimately distant form of closeness is replicated, in many similar ways, in the third facet on the relationship prism, interactions of grandparents and grandchildren. Troll (1983) referred to grandparents as the "family watchdogs" and Hagestad (1985) likened them to the "national guard." In both of these similes, the implication is that although grandparents may not be integrally involved in the daily lives of their grandchildren, they are available and on call when the need arises; their interactions with the family range from noninterference to mobilization (White, 1999).

Grandparent-grandchild interactions are governed by how grandparents interpret the meaning of their family roles. Neugarten and Weinstein (1964) observed that grandparents derived meaning from their roles through emotional self-fulfillment, a sense of biological renewal, being a resource person to their grandchildren, and enjoying vicarious achievement through the activities of their grandchildren. In addition, Kivnick (1983) believed that grandparents experienced feelings of personal immortality through the continuity of their families over the generations. Bengtson (1985) asserted that grandparents assisted in the social construction of the family biography: the building of connections among the past, present, and future, in part as represented by the generations of the grandparents, the parents, and the grandchildren, respectively.

The key to understanding the grandparent-grandchild relationship is recognizing its skip-generational nature, crossing generational divides. Grandparents achieve their role through the activities of others. The path to "grandma's house" is developed and maintained by the parents, illustrating the contingent nature of the grandparent role. Parents create the contexts within which grandparents and grandchildren interact, and parents mediate access between the elder and younger generations, at least when grandchildren are young. This multilevel influence affects the nature of grandparent-grandchild ties and the grief trajectories of grandparents and grandchildren.

When this multilevel influence is interrupted by untimely death, the effect is wide ranging. Fry (1997) studied the personal accounts of grandparents who had lost a grandchild within the previous six months. Like widowed persons, bereaved grandparents spoke of their feelings of disbelief and shock, and they expressed a need to restructure relationships with other family members and with living grandchildren. Like parents, they spoke of shattered belief systems, the unfairness of life, and the guilt of surviving. A grandmother said:

> Your grandchild dying is worse than any death I've experienced before… You look at a healthy young person, and you say 'that's not fair.' Fair would be if I could have died, 'cause I am old. I've had my life, but he was so young, you know, wasn't supposed to go before his grandparents and parents. (Fry, 1997, p. 129)

The complexity of the grief response is exacerbated by the dimension of generations. That is, bereaved grandparents report a sense of helplessness and pain arising out of their concern for their adult child and their inability to shield their offspring from the pain of losing a child. Fry (1997) offered the following quote reflecting the double grief of a grandmother: "The pain of missing my grandchild, Sarah, and the pain of not being able to comfort Martha, my daughter, just eats away at me" (p. 129). This is an example of how the family watchdog is unable to fulfill his or her role and the consequence of such inability.

Intimacy and grief are experienced by grandparents in ways that reflect the reactions of both bereaved spouses and parents and in ways that are unique to their multigenerational ties. These ties both direct and exacerbate the experiences of grandparents and add another dimension to our understanding of intergenerational lives and loss.

Sibling Relationships

There is little research on the fourth prism facet, sibling relations in later life. This is surprising given the length and prevalence of this relationship among older adults. Siblings experience a unique bond based on a shared generation, near equal status, and reciprocal interactions (Bedford & Avioli, 2001). Nevertheless, a certain ambivalence can be found in sibling relationships. Competition, rivalry, and sometimes envy characterize them, as well as the strengths and benefits of shared history, legacy, and identity.

These latter characteristics are particularly evident in later life (Johnson & Barer, 1997). Gold, Woodbury, and George (1990) found, in their study of older sibling dyads, that approximately 80% revealed positive attachment that was stronger in intensity than in the middle years and about as intense as in childhood. Several authors have drawn attention to this hourglass pattern of sibling ties.

Older siblings represent a safety net for each other (Bedford, 1995), coming to each other's aid in times of crisis. Siblings are most frequently called upon for emotional support. They may also be each other's social companions and co-biographers, having been a part of each other's life story and life time (Connidis, 1989). Few others have had the history of siblings that enables communication about parents, other relatives, family pets, childhood events and issues, and family holidays. Siblings can share insights into the past and may offer perspectives on events that can serve to clarify meaning; they can retell old family jokes and family folklore.

These same features, of course, are evident in the nature of grief experienced by siblings. With the death of a sibling in later life, an individual may feel that his or her own mortality is threatened (Hays, Gold, & Pieper, 1997), based on their shared generation, history, and genetic legacy. Hays and colleagues (1997) suggested that "elders weigh the death of kin very highly when calculating their overall health status" (p. 37). Moss and Moss (1989) reported on this theme of the impact of a sibling's death on the survivor's sense of self with the following quote from one of their respondents:

> My first memory of childhood was when I was 3 with my brother...When he left me [died], there was part of my childhood that went. There were things I couldn't verify... Suddenly I was alone with my memories. (p. 104)

As Bedford and Avioli (2001) noted, the death of a sibling may simultaneously serve to increase and decrease the sense of vulnerability in the surviving sibling through the loss of personal validation and self-evaluation functions the sibling provided, in the former case, and the resultant increase in family contact and concomitant relations in the latter. As Moss and Moss (1989) indicated, however, not all siblings realign; if the sibling who died performed the kin-keeping functions of the family, connections may dissipate. Most connections persist, however, as evidenced in the following quotes: "[His] last wish was that his wife be closer with the family, so I call her every day," and "There are so few of us left, we like each other more" (Moss & Moss, 1989, p. 105).

Later-life siblings share a long and sometimes ambivalent history, but they frequently see each other as "there for the long haul" and as co-biographers of family life. These important later-life resources form the substance of grief following the death of a sibling and illustrate the importance of sibling ties in later life.

Friend Relationships

In many ways, the significance of friends, at least from society's point of view, lies in what they are not. That is, those on the fifth facet of the relationship prism are not relatives and as such are free of some the more formal role prescriptions that govern family interaction (de Vries, 1996). Friends assume their position in each other's lives by choice; friendships arise out of shared values, interests, activities, and experiences (Adams, Blieszner, & de Vries, 2000). Friendship interactions promote self-esteem, self-awareness, a sense of belonging, life satisfaction, and even empowerment. Friends serve as a sort of yardstick against which individuals can map their progress, gauge their goals, and check their assumptions. With friends, individuals may freely offer and receive affection, companionship, and empathy (de Vries, 1996). For older gay men and lesbians, the role of friendship may be even more pronounced. Being a friend is a life-long role, persisting even as other roles cease or change; in fact, changes in family and work roles may heighten the importance of friendship (Blieszner, 2001).

Even though friends play very significant roles in the lives of older adults, the grief experienced by individuals following the death of a friend has received only scarce research attention. Friends of all ages may be described as the neglected or abandoned grievers (de Vries & Johnson, in press), as evidenced by the absence of a term by which this loss might be characterized, notwithstanding the high frequency of experiencing such a loss in later life (Johnson & Barer, 1997).

Deck and Folta (1989) suggested that the death of a friend may evoke complex emotions, including a combination of the fear that "it could have been me" with the relief that "it wasn't" (Deck and Folta, 1989). The death of a friend is not only the loss of the relationship, one's role in it, and mattering to someone chosen as an intimate, it is the loss of an important self-referent.

Our research (de Vries & Johnson, in press) has explored the experiences of the death of a friend among the oldest-old and showed that they do display many of the reactions just described. Moreover, bereaved very old persons placed the loss of friends in the context of their history of loss and in the context of their life course; they reported a profound sense of survivorship, having outlived all that was important to them. One woman commented that she missed "not being necessary to anyone." One man, describing the circumstances following the death of his friend, said:

> His family didn't seem to care much about him in his life. After his accident, they all came out to the coast, formed a sort of human shield around him denying us access to him or even knowledge about his condition. They swept through the house taking his belongings and left us with nothing—not even a chance to speak at the funeral.

Pogrebin (1987) also quoted an individual's experience of the death of his friend:

> When Josh was dying, his wife and children monopolized every last minute for themselves; they couldn't share him. Someone from the family was always around the hospital bed. I wanted to ask them to leave us alone for a minute, but they seemed to resent that I was there at all. I wasn't able to tie up the loose ends before he died. People should realize that friends too need to say good-bye. (p. 107)

These older adults experience a loss that takes place in a society in which grief "is an emotional role whose rights, privileges, restrictions, obligations, and entry requirements tend to be confined to family members" (Sklar, 1991, p. 110). Friends are largely unsupported in a world of grief; health care facilities, employers, and other social institutions often exclude friends during the dying process and grieving rituals (de Vries, 2001). We heard from one older woman that "One friend that I didn't hear from for quite a while...when I called I found out that she passed away during the holidays. Her husband didn't call to tell me." Such losses leave open the possibility for unfinished interpersonal business. Additionally, respondents in our research commented on how the death severed their connections to other places and other times—to their other selves. Understanding the ways in which individuals respond to the death of a friend offers a vehicle for understanding friendships in general, an individual's role in this relational context, and the intimacy that is a part of this experience.

Summary and Conclusion

A complete depiction of the relationship prism of later-life relationships requires focusing on the many facets and forms of intimate interaction, while recognizing the associated multiple faces of intimate grief. This simultaneous focus on both intimacy and grief is considered infrequently in the gerontology research literature, yet attending to both the rainbows and the shadows increases our understanding of intimate relationships and their loss and in later life. It reveals that grief is more than sadness, that faded rainbows can still carry meaning and bring consolation.

For example, grief among spouses represents lost companionship, no longer mattering in the life of another, diminished security, and reduced respect. It also means confronting myriad daily tasks alone and facing the world alone. For parents and children, grief reflects a rocking of fundamental assumptions about self and time as well as about giving and receiving care. Grandparents experience such loss both directly and vicariously, complicated by a sense of guilt for surviving. Siblings grieve the demise of their co-biographers of family life. Friends experience grief as the absence of an important self-referent, a chosen other, and they do so in the absence of social support and recognition of the meaning of their bereavement.

Grief and intimacy assume additional faces and forms not described here. Parts of who we are, parts of our relationships, and parts of our worlds change daily and we may grieve these changes. Further, intimacy may be experienced with objects, places, and other living creatures. Companion animals are a relevant and poignant example. Animals may provide security and help in adapting to changing environments; they engender nurturing experiences, and they offer companionship without the fear of rejection (Suthers-McCabe, 2001). In many ways, companion animals become family members and friends; yet similar to the death of a friend, pet-loss goes unrecognized by the larger society.

Another facet of grief and intimacy, as suggested by Troll (2001) is that intimacy may continue to characterize relationships between those still living and those who have predeceased them. In her research with women and men aged 70 and older, she demonstrated that strong, enduring attachments were expressed by participants with their mothers, now long dead, as well as with their deceased spouses. The data suggested that deceased individuals, along with living intimates, are included when people describe their networks of social support. "Individuals who appear alone need not have an empty set characterizing their network of support" (Troll, 2001, p. 57).

When examining the intimate experiences of the later years, much can be gained from studying the relationship prism and all its twists and turns through sunlight and shadow. Integrating accounts of close relationships and their loss enables a fuller understanding of both intimacy and grief and a deeper understanding of individuals and their intimate relationships at the end of life. ■

Brian de Vries, PhD, is Professor and Director of Gerontology at San Francisco State University. He received his doctorate in life-span developmental psychology from the University of British Columbia. He is Associate Editor of The International Journal of Aging and Human Development, *and has guest-edited a special issue of* Omega: Journal of Death and Dying *and* Generations. *Additionally, he is the Editor of* End of Life Issues: Interdisciplinary and Multidimensional Perspectives *and of* Narrative Gerontology: Theory, Research, and Practice. *He has authored or co-authored more than 50 journal articles and book chapters on topics including grief and bereavement, life review, and social relationships in later life.*

Rosemary Blieszner, PhD, is a Professor of Gerontology and Family Studies in the Department of Human Development, and Associate Director of the Center for Gerontology, at Virginia Polytechnic Institute and State University. She received her PhD in human development—family studies from Pennsylvania State University and her research focuses on family and friend relationships, life events, and psychological well-being in adulthood and old age. She is co-editor of Older Adult Friendship: Structure and Process *and* Handbook of Aging and the Family, *co-author of* Adult Friendship *and* Spiritual Resiliency in Older Women: Models of Strength for Challenges through the Life Span, *and author of numerous journal articles and book chapters.*

John A. Blando, PhD, is Assistant Professor of Counseling at San Francisco State University. He received his PhD in educational psychology from Stanford University and has additional training in clinical psychology. Professor Blando is the winner of a National Institute of Mental Health-San Francisco State University Faculty Development Award. He writes in the areas of disenfranchised grief, the Internet, and gay and lesbian aging. Recent publications include "Twice hidden: Older gay and lesbian couples, friends, and intimacy," "The times of our lives," in Narrative gerontology: Theory, research and practice, *and "Disenfranchised grief on the World Wide Web" in* Family Focus.

References

Adams, R.G., Blieszner, R., & de Vries, B. (2000). Definition of friendship in the third age: Age, gender, and study location effects. *Journal of Aging Studies, 14,* 117-133.

Bedford, V.H. (1995). Sibling relationships in middle adulthood and old age. In R. Blieszner & V.H. Bedford (Eds.), *Handbook on aging and the family* (pp. 201-222). Westport, CT: Greenwood.

Bedford, V.H., & Avioli, P.S. (2001). Grief: Intimacy's reflection. *Generations, 25,* 34-40.

Bengtson, V.L. (1985). Diversity and symbolism in grandparental roles. In V.L. Bengtson, & J.F. Robertson (Eds.), *Grandparenting* (pp. 11-29). Beverly Hills, CA: Sage.

Bengtson, V.L., & Kuypers, J.A. (1971). Generational difference and the developmental stake. *Aging and Human Development, 2,* 249-259.

Bengtson, V.L., & Harootyan, R.A. (Eds.) (1994). *Intergenerational linkages: Hidden connections in American society.* New York: Springer.

Blieszner, R. (2001). She'll be on my heart: Intimacy among friends. *Generations, 25,* 48-54.

Brehm, S.S. (1985). *Intimate relationships.* New York: Random House.

Connidis, I.A. (1989). *Family ties and aging.* Toronto: Butterworths.

de Vries, B. (2001). Grief: Intimacy's reflection. *Generations, 25,* 75-80.

de Vries, B. (1996). The understanding of friendship: An adult life course perspective. In C. Magai and S. McFadden (Eds.), *Handbook of emotion, adult development, and aging* (pp. 249-268). New York: Academic Press.

de Vries, B., & Johnson, C.L. (in press). The death of friends in later life. In R. Settersten & T. Owens (Eds.), *Advances in life-course research: New frontiers in socialization.*

de Vries, B., Dalla Lana, R., & Falck, V.T. (1994). Parental bereavement over the life course: A theoretical intersection and empirical review. *Omega: Journal of Death and Dying, 29,* 47-68.

Deck, E.S., & Folta, J.R. (1989). The friend-griever. In J.K. Doka (Ed.), *Disenfranchised grief: Recognizing hidden sorrow* (pp. 77-89). Lexington, MA: Lexington Books.

Fingerman, K.L. (2001). A distant closeness: Intimacy between parents and their children in later life. *Generations, 25,* 26-33.

Fry, P.S. (1997). Grandparents' reactions to the death of a grandchild: An exploratory factor analytic study. *Omega: Journal of Death and Dying, 35,* 119-140.

Gold, D.T., Woodbury, M.A., & George, L.K. (1990). Relationship classification using grade of membership (GOM) analysis: A typology of sibling relationships in later life. *Journal of Gerontology, 45*, S43-S51.

Hagestad, G.O. (1985). Continuity and connectedness. In V.L. Bengtson, & J.F. Robertson (Eds.), *Grandparenting* (pp. 31-48). Beverly Hills, CA: Sage.

Hays, J.C., Gold, D.T., & Pieper, C.F. (1997). Sibling bereavement in late life. *Omega: Journal of Death and Dying, 35*, 25-42.

Huyck, M.H. (2001). Romantic relationships in later life. *Generations, 25*, 9-17.

Johnson, C.L. & Barer, B.M. (1997). *Life beyond 85 years: The aura of survivorship*. New York: Springer.

Kivnick, H.Q. (1983). Dimensions of grandparenthood meaning: Deductive conceptualization and empirical derivation. *Journal of Personality and Social Psychology, 44*, 1056-1068.

Klass, D., & Marwitt, S. (1989). Toward a model of parental grief. *Omega: Journal of Death and Dying, 19*, 31-50.

Lehman, D.R., Wortman, C.B., Haring, M., Tweed, R.G., de Vries, B., DeLongis, A., Hemphill, K.J., & Ellard, J.H. (1999). Recovery from the perspective of the bereaved: Personal assessments and sources of distress and support. In B. de Vries (Ed.), *End of life issues: Interdisciplinary and multidimensional perspectives* (pp. 119-144). New York: Springer.

Leigh, G.K. (1982). Kinship interaction over the family life span. *Journal of Marriage and the family, 44*, 197-208.

Marshall, V. (1980). *Last chapters: A sociology of aging and dying.* Monterey, CA: Brooks/Cole.

Moss, B.F., & Schwebel, A.I. (1993). Defining intimacy in romantic relationships. *Family Relations, 42*, 31-37.

Moss, M.S., & Moss, S.Z. (1989). The death of a parent. In R. Kalish (Ed.), *Midlife loss: Coping strategies* (pp. 89-114). Beverly Hills, CA: Sage.

Moss, S.Z., & Moss, M.S. (1989). The impact of the death of an elderly sibling: Some considerations of a normative loss. *American Behavioral Scientist, 33*, 94-106.

Neugarten, B.L., & Weinstein, K.K. (1964). The changing American grandparent. *Journal of Marriage and the Family, 26*, 199-204.

Perkins, H. & Harris, L. (1990). Familial bereavement and health in adult life course perspective. *Journal of Marriage and the Family, 52*, 233-241.

Pogrebin, L.C. (1987). *Among friends.* New York: McGraw Hill.

Sklar, F. (1991). Grief as a family affair: Property rights, grief rights, and the exclusion of close friends as survivors. *Omega: Journal of Death and Dying, 24*, 109-121.

Strain, L.A., & Chappell, N.L. (1982). Confidants: Do they make a difference in quality of life? *Research on Aging, 4*, 479-502.

Stroebe, M.S., Hansson, R.O., Stroebe, W., & Schut, H. (2001). Introduction: Concepts and issues in contemporary research on bereavement. In M.S. Stroebe, R.O. Hansson, W. Stroebe, & H. Schut (Eds.), *Handbook of bereavement research: Consequences, coping, and care* (pp. 3-22). Washington, DC: American Psychological Association.

Suthers-McCabe, H.M. (2001). Take on pet and call me in the morning. *Generations, 25*, 93-95.

Troll, L.E. (1983). Grandparents: The family watchdogs. In T. Brubaker (Ed.), *Family relationships in later life* (pp. 63-74). Beverly Hills, CA: Sage.

Troll, L.E. (2001) When the world narrows: Intimacy with the dead. *Generations, 25*, 55-58.

White, D. (1999). Grandparent participation in times of family bereavement. In B. de Vries (Ed.), *End of life issues: Interdisciplinary and multidimensional perspectives* (pp. 145-166). New York: Springer.

Yalom, I. (1989). *Love's executioner and other tales of psychotherapy.* New York: Basic Books.

CHAPTER 21

Voices

Adult Orphans

Jack D. Gordon

When we see the word *orphan* it conjures a mental picture of Oliver Twist holding out his bowl for more food. Many other books, photo essays, and movies have made the word synonymous with children and poverty. Yet there are more orphans than just poor children, a fact brought home to me by a friend who told me after the death of his remaining parent, "Here I am at age 65, an orphan." That brought home to me the vast numbers of adult orphans who are themselves Medicare eligible. As a matter of fact, I am one of that group. I am 79 years old.

My father died when I was 15. My mother died 19 years later. I still mourn for my parents every so often when an event in my life or that of my family reminds me of one or both of them or what they would have said. The death of a close family member, certainly of a parent, leaves a very big hole in your life. Over time you learn to walk around the hole, it tends to get smaller, but it is always there.

Now, with the cohort from age 80 to 90 a rapidly growing age group, there are going to be more and more people in their 60s who will have the same realization as my friend. They will have to deal with that empty hole. There are complications with being an older orphan. Given the advanced age of the parents' generation, many of them die of lingering degenerative diseases, including Alzheimer's Disease. The child's last memories of the parent may be troubling, a picture of decrepitude and decline that crowds out earlier images. Elie Wiesel once described the course of dying for an Alzheimer's patient who was a friend that it is like taking a favorite book and tearing out a page every day until you are left with just the cover.

Others remain in full control of their faculties, even though terminally ill, and can provide much help to their children's way of dealing with their death. For very often the older person is much more realistic about impending death, while children are beset with myriad emotions, often including both denial and guilt. The denial comes naturally because the initial reaction is to cling to hope that some medical miracle will take place, regardless of how unlikely that is. The children's guilt comes from remembering the missed opportunities to spend time with the parent, an often unavoidable situation given the demands of their own family and work responsibilities.

Denial and guilt may combine, it should be noted, to make referral to a hospice program as late as possible, thus depriving the dying and their caregivers the opportunity to come to understand at a deeper level the events taking place. A last month, or six months, in hospice care instead of a last few days gives the hospice staff a chance to know the patient and family well enough to be much more helpful. In addition, because continuing bereavement counseling is part of the hospice obligation for a year after death, knowing the family better makes the counselor that much more effective. Even more important for the survivors is the fact that bereavement starts with the diagnosis and the concomitant realization, denied and understood at the same time, that the end is near.

One of the things of lasting benefit that children can do in the last month or two of their parents' life, if it hasn't been done already, is help them compile their life story. This is most important for the parents to bring some closure to their lives and affirm the value of the life they have led. Dr. Robert Butler describes the importance of life review in greater detail and with great understanding in his chapter in this book.

At the Hospice Foundation of America, we were so taken with his concept seven years ago that we funded the Center on Aging at Florida International University in Miami to create a self-help book titled *A Guide for Recalling and Telling Your Life Story.* Using this book or your own tape recorder or camcorder to help your parent create a life story will give you and your family a priceless remembrance for many generations to come.

I particularly mention this activity because it gives everyone something to do that's enjoyable and useful. It is a way of being positive in the face of a negative situation. It is better, however, not to wait to compile a personal or a family history until the central character is on his or her deathbed. Do it now. It will provide a lasting legacy, a continuing bond that can make your life as an orphan easier and provide a great experience for grandchildren and generations to follow. ■

Senator Jack D. Gordon was the President of the Hospice Foundation of America from 1990 until 2000, and since has served as its Chairman and CEO. He was elected to the Florida State Senate in 1972 and served until his retirement in 1992. While in the Senate, he was involved in health and education issues, including sponsoring the first hospice licensure-law in the nation. In 1997, Senator Gordon was invited to join the International Work Group on Death, Dying and Bereavement. He serves on the Financing Task Force and the Provider Education Task Force of the Last Acts Campaign. Senator Gordon is on the Board of the Center for Policy Alternatives and is a Member of the Carter Center Mental Health Task Force.

■ CHAPTER 22 ■

Voices

A Grandmother's Grief

Judy Mann

The phone call came about 12:30 p.m. on September 8, 2000, a lovely late summer day in the Shenandoah Valley, where my husband and I live on a farm. My husband picked up the call in the main house at the same time I picked up the phone in my office in the guesthouse.

"Mom!" The voice was so strangled I could not tell which one of my two sons was calling. Then he broke down and started to cry so hard that I found myself saying, "Who is this? What's wrong?"

"It's me, mom, Devin." And the tears overwhelmed him again as he choked out the most awful news. "Charlie's dead."

■

Charles Edward Mann had been born 21 months earlier, 10 weeks prematurely. He was an identical twin, and within three weeks of his birth, he was diagnosed with a condition known as periventricular leukomalasia. Devin got the diagnosis from a radiologist, and he had called me in my office in the newsroom of *The Washington Post* to see if I could go on the Internet to find out what this was. With the help of one of our researchers, I found out. As I sat next to her, reading the information on the screen, tears just poured out of my eyes. It is brain damage— damage to the neurons, a kind of damage that so far has not been repairable in humans. It is one of the causes of cerebral palsy. I faxed the devastating information to my son. That evening, my daughter-in-law Sophie called. She asked me to come out to Los Angeles, where they live. "I think your son could use his mother right now," she said in an unsteady voice. Sophie is British and her family lives in England. I was the closest mum. That was Wednesday. My husband drove me to the airport Friday morning. "You have to be strong for them," he warned me. "You cannot break down or fall apart. You are all they have right now. You can break down when you get back here, but not while you are with them. You've got to help them understand what this is and what they can do. They aren't going to be thinking clearly. You have to do that." I clung to his words during the five-hour flight. Yet, when I saw Devin and Sophie I wept with them. None of us could help it.

I went with them that afternoon to see a pediatrician who was also an expert on twins. Devin had talked to him earlier on the phone and I watched him weep as he listened to the news. PVL, as this condition is known, can cause minor, medium, or major disability. It affects each child differently. Even experts hesitate to predict the degree of impairment from brain scans. Their pediatrician was frank about this, and he was frank about everything else as well. He told them that the scan showed massive bilateral involvement. He had never seen a scan that showed as much damage. I saw my son and daughter-in-law's hopes for healthy children vanish in the breath of a single phrase.

So began our family's journey into a loss no one could have prepared us for. All the dreams Charlie's parents had for him had to be put away and they had to grieve for the life that poor little boy would likely have. Oliver, who survives, and Charlie would spend the first three months of their lives in the Neonatal Intensive Care Unit at Cedars Sinai, overcoming one medical crisis after another, struggling to live. Sophie and Devin went through months of worry and agony before they were finally able to bring the babies home, Charlie first and a couple of weeks later, Oliver, who had weighed a mere 2 pounds,

3 ounces, at birth and had to have a hernia repaired before he could go home.

The days after we got the news about Charlie were simply terrible. We were overwhelmed by sadness. One thing that helped me understand what Devin and Sophie were going through was that I'd had breast cancer two years before this happened. I, too, had had to face a grave loss: not just my breast, but my sense of immortality, of invulnerability. Loss and uncertainty about the future had become part of my emotional fabric. I could listen to them and help them realize that their feelings were normal. I think that helped all of us.

We had to find out about the different kinds of care available to families with disabled children. Sophie, riddled with guilt and anxiety, had to schedule meetings with social workers and therapists. She learned quickly to write everything down because in grief, you forget things. Twenty-one months later, when Charlie died, a wise woman would tell me that for a grandmother these losses are very hard: "You grieve for your grandchild," she said, "just like your children. But you also grieve for the terrible loss your children have taken."

After I returned home, my assignment was to find out everything I could about PVL and whether anyone in the world was making any progress in treating it. I found that there was promising research being done in Mexico in reversing neuron damage. There was some hope on the horizon. We clung to that. And as the months progressed, Charlie entered into more intensive therapies. His eyesight was very poor. Devin and Sophie were told at one point he would probably be blind, another of many devastating blows.

With the hope of each new therapy and the crush of every setback, I listened and grieved. Mourn for the baby. Mourn for his parents. Keep yourself together, listen well, try to offer encouragement when it can be honest. Helping your children cope in whatever way you can lets you feel a little less powerless. Stay as informed as you can about the problems your grandchild is having. Don't butt in or second-guess. Charlie was in some form of therapy nearly every day. Sophie became an expert on different forms of therapy and she continued doing them at home.

Oliver, who has mild cerebral palsy, was also in therapy, but on a much less intensive level. The babies were surrounded by caring adults and by parents who were utterly devoted to them and to making sure they were getting the best medical care possible.

Charlie threw up a lot, as did Oliver. Charlie's swallowing mechanism was affected by the PVL. Both babies had immature digestive systems, and both had trouble gaining weight. On the morning of September 8, Sophie had crept into the babies' room and gathered Oliver from his crib to take him to an early morning feeding clinic. She tried to keep Oliver quiet so he would not wake Charlie. She took him into the master bedroom to dress him and then she left. About 8:30 that morning, Los Angeles time, my son went in to wake up Charlie, and he found him in his crib, not breathing. He called 911 for an ambulance and immediately started to do cardiopulmonary resuscitation. It was too late. The strangled call came less than an hour later, from the hospital.

I broke down completely. Charlie was so special, so sweet, so brave—he had captured all of our hearts. For Devin and Sophie to be delivered another such shattering loss was beyond anything life should deal such sweet people. At some point, perhaps in that conversation, I said it outright: "You don't deserve this." Devin told me as best he could what had happened. Then I said the stupidest thing I've said in my life: "Do you want me to come out?"

"I don't know, Mom," he said. "I've got a dead child on my hands and I don't know what to do." I told him I would call him back.

I sat there on the floor of the guesthouse crying my heart out. I was in shock. I wasn't thinking clearly. I could not absorb what had happened, much less accept it. My husband came into the guesthouse almost immediately after he hung up the phone in the main house. I stood up and clung to him, sobbing, simply sobbing. This was too terrible for words. When I finally stopped, he said to me: "You've got to go out there right away. I want you to give me the phone number for your travel agent, I'll make the arrangements, and you start packing, but you must get out there as soon as we can get you on a plane." He said he would come out as soon as we needed him. We made the two-hour drive from the farm to National Airport and I got on a 6:00 p.m. plane to Los Angeles. At one point the flight attendant, serving beverages, asked politely how I was. "Fine, thank you," I said, automatically. Then, I said, "Actually I'm not fine."

"What's wrong," she asked kindly.

Then I choked it out: "I lost a grandchild today, a baby boy."

I got to Devin and Sophie's home around midnight their time. Devin was, mercifully, sleeping. Two friends had stayed with Sophie until I arrived. We held onto each other, joined by tears of unspeakable grief. "You came," Sophie whispered. "You came." And we went into the garden to talk, to weep together, and finally to bed.

The days ahead were very difficult: We did not know when the coroner would release Charlie's body, Devin and Sophie had trouble deciding between burial and cremation, a decision that would force them to fully confront the horror that had happened. Sophie's mother, Sally, and her sister Anna arrived from England and they were a huge help. But none of us had ever dealt with the death of a child. A woman named Barbara in the coroner's office put me in touch with Heather Aitken, who had lost a baby, and went on to found Little Heroes, a project that helps Los Angeles families both financially and emotionally with final arrangements when they have lost a child. Heather was the lifeline who helped us with the difficult decisions. She was the wise woman who told me how hard it was on grandparents.

I am not a religious person, but I am a spiritual person. Reverend Charles, who had been a neighbor of Devin and Sophie's, came by their home to comfort them and he agreed to officiate at the memorial service. He talked about Charlie's purpose in life, why he had come to our family. He said he was an angel, he had finished his work, and God had moved him on to another purpose. For once, the questioning journalist shut down. The grieving grandmother took enormous comfort in this appreciation of Charlie. I took comfort in the nearly full church, the amazing floral arrangements, the fact that my nephew, David, who lives in Santa Cruz came down to be with us, along with his young daughter.

My younger son, Jeff, who also lives in Santa Cruz came down. Devin's step-brother, Don, came down from Washington State. At a time of great sadness and loss, the next generation was there for the family, there for two of their own.

How do you mourn such a tragedy? Very slowly, I discovered. I returned to the farm to grieve not only for Charlie but for Devin and Sophie's unimaginable loss. There is no hurt like what a parent feels for a lost child or what a grandparent feels for one's own hurt child. It's a hurt that needs soothing, or else you go mad. The one consolation we can give ourselves is that Charlie never suffered the cruelties that life would likely have had for him.

It has been more than a year now, since Charlie died, and I still find myself thinking about him and sometimes weeping at unexpected times. Writing this piece brought its share of tears. We spent time with Devin and Sophie and Oliver at the end of August and Sophie and I spent private time talking, weeping, listening to each other, and I think that helped both of us. I think Charlie made us better people. I have the deepest admiration for my son and daughter-in-law and how they have coped with such courage and so much love for those babies. I take comfort in that, too. Charlie taught us about patience and about bravery. My son gave the eulogy for Charlie at his memorial service, and he said it best: He told of how a small, severely disabled child had taught an entire family about unconditional love. ■

Judy Mann, a columnist for The Washington Post *for 23 years, is the author of two books,* The Difference: Growing Up Female in America, *and* Mann for All Seasons, *a collection of essays and columns. She has three grown children and is married to Richard T. Starnes, a retired newspaper executive and columnist.*

CHAPTER 23

Suicide in Older People

Patrick Arbore

INTRODUCTION

Suicide in older people is a tragic public health problem in the United States. Of the 30,575 suicide deaths of people of all ages in 1998, 19.0% of these, or 5,809 people, were 65 years of age or older (Murphy, 2000). Caregivers and community members often assume, incorrectly, that younger people have the highest suicide rates. This simply is not true. In an examination of suicide rates for 1997, White adolescent males age 15 through 19 had a rate of 16 per 100,000. Older White adult males age 85 and older had a rate of 65 per 100,000 during that same year (Pearson, 2000). White males age 85 and older have the highest rate of suicide of any age population, an astonishing figure that is six times the nation's age-adjusted rate. In The *Surgeon General's Call to Action to Prevent Suicide* (Satcher, 1999), five population groups were targeted as being at high risk for suicide, including older persons.

While men in general have suicide rates that surpass the rates among women, older adults demonstrate the greatest gender differences. The male-female suicide ratio is approximately 5:1 for the 65 through 74 year age group, 8:1 for the 75 through 84 year age group, and 10:1 for those aged 85 and older (Brogden, 2001). Suicide is the 13th leading cause of death for people 65 years of age and older. Brogden (2001) estimates that one older person dies by suicide every 80 minutes. The ratio of attempts to completed acts of suicide among older persons is about 4:1 as compared to 8:1 for the general population or 200:1 among younger people.

The implication of these ratios is that older adults are less likely to engage in nonfatal suicidal behaviors, have greater intentionality, and less desire for attention. Furthermore, older adults are less likely to express their suicidal ideation directly and exhibit more complex motives than younger individuals. Because older adults make fewer suicide attempts, express their suicide intention less frequently, and appear to be more determined to die, there is an urgent need to respond aggressively and efficiently to an at-risk older adult (Conwell, 2001).

Prevention: Recognizing Who Is At Risk

Although older people do not readily avail themselves of mental health services, they do regularly see their primary care providers (PCPs). Conwell (2001) and Pearson (2000) both acknowledge studies wherein older adults who completed suicide had seen a primary care physician within a month of their death (Carney et al., 1994; Clark, 1991; Conwell, 1994; and Frierson, 1991). Many of these older adults saw their PCPs a week prior to their deaths. While they may not talk about their subjective states, older adults do at least have contact with individuals who may be in a position to help them.

Clark (1991) discovered that 48% of the older suicide victims in his study had spoken to someone directly about their suicidal thoughts in the last six months of their lives, while another 26% had stated explicit thoughts of death. Despite these warning signs, 89% of the "knowledgeable informants" stated that they were surprised by the suicidal act.

In a controlled study by Conwell et al. (2000), 42 individuals 60 years of age and older who died by suicide and had seen a PCP within 30 days of their deaths were compared with 196 patients age 60 years and older from a group practice of general internal medicine or family medicine. The two groups were compared to determine whether physical and psychiatric illness, functional status, and treatment history distinguished older primary care patients who committed suicide from those who did not.

Results of the study indicated that measures of psychiatric illness and symptom severity strongly distinguished the two groups. Major depression was the most frequent psychiatric diagnosis in both groups, although it was significantly more prevalent in the suicide completer group. Although alcohol and drug use disorders were infrequent, they were significantly more prevalent in the suicide completer group. Older people who died by suicide had significantly greater physical health burdens and disability. Regarding mental health care, 92.9% of those older adults who died by suicide had been in either inpatient or outpatient psychiatric care at some time in their lives, in significant contrast to the 26.5% of the older adults who did not die by suicide. Despite the prevalence and severity of mental illness in the suicide completer group, only six (14.6%) were currently seeing a psychiatrist or other mental health professional at the time of their death.

Conwell and his colleagues (2000) defined some important implications based upon the results of their study. First, the depressed older adults who died by suicide escaped adequate diagnosis and treatment of their affective disorder. Second, suicide risk in older ambulatory individuals is associated with the burden of their physical illness and functional limitations. Third, a reduction in suicides among older adults hinges on the development of more sensitive and specific methods to assess suicide risk through research on the interplay of depression, physical illness, and functional impairment.

■

Uncapher and Arean (2000) investigated whether PCPs recognize suicide potential in their patients and their degree of willingness to treat older and younger suicidal patients. Results of the study suggested that while the PCPs recognized the presence of depression and suicidal ideation in both older and younger patients, they were less willing to conclude that the suicidal ideation of the older patient was as serious a problem as the suicidal ideation of the younger patient. The PCPs in this study perceived depression in older patients as being less responsive to treatment. This lack of faith about the efficacy of depression treatment for older adults may be a serious obstacle in the prevention of late-life suicides (Uncapher & Arean, 2000).

One contributing factor to the inability of professional caregivers to recognize and respond to suicidal older adults is *ageism*. Ageism, a process of systematic stereotyping and discrimination against people because they are old, makes it easier for people in society to ignore older adults. Ageism blinds us to the many problems experienced by older adults (Osgood, 1992). Professional caregivers may share the same negative stereotypes about older adults as that of nonprofessionals. If professional caregivers do not explore their own ageism, they may fail to respond effectively to the suicidal thoughts of the older adult in their care, and a tragedy may result. Older adults themselves may have ageist views and struggle to manage their own internalized ageism. According to Palmore (1999), they may commit suicide, which might be the ultimate escape from ageism.

What would motivate an older person to commit suicide? Edwin Shneidman (1998), Professor Emeritus at the University of California, Los Angeles, and the author of numerous books and articles on suicide, states that the suicidal individual is in pain. This pain, according to Shneidman, can be called despair, loneliness, fear, anxiety, guilt, shame, depression, angst, fear of growing old, or fear of dying badly. The pain may also be described in more technical terms as depression, alcoholism, mental illness, or bereavement. Despite the label, the suicidal person is experiencing a level of pain that is defined as intolerable. The suicidal person's unfulfilled psychological needs must be addressed and mitigated if the person is going to choose to live.

The following suicide note, written by a 75 year-old man (whom I will refer to as J.K.), illustrates the type of pain referred to by Shneidman.

> No one knew that I was going to do this. No one helped me in any way.
>
> This is solely and completely my doing, and has nothing to do with anyone else.
>
> No one is at fault for this happening, except me.
>
> I apologize to the people who loved me.
>
> I am an old man, my life is lived. I am in pain with my knee, shoulder, and neck.
>
> My hearing is shot, and my eyesight is poor, and will not be getting any better.
>
> My physical health and mental health all together will not improve, but rather I face a long slow decline into chronic illness and death anyway, and I would rather save my self, and my family, that wrenching, expensive, inevitable path to my demise. I would like to be cremated, and I don't care what is done with my ashes. I believe that I will see all of you in heaven, I surely hope so.

One of the ways J.K. defined pain was through fear of dying badly when he wrote, "but rather I face a long slow decline into chronic illness and death anyway." J.K. had a history of depression that was not being treated aggressively. Unfortunately, J.K. did die, leaving his wife and family to cope with the devastating aftermath of suicide.

While I agree with Conwell (2001) that there is no single cause for suicide and, therefore, no single intervention that can be universally applied, I strongly agree with his research that unipolar major depression is the most common psychiatric syndrome of older suicide victims, including J.K. Depression can be treated; however, there is an urgent need to respond quickly before a suicidal crisis erupts.

What is depression? Styron (1990) may have best described this emotional state when he wrote of his own depression "the pain of severe depression is quite unimaginable to those who have not suffered it, and it kills in many instances because its anguish can no longer be borne. The prevention of many suicides will continue to be hindered until there is a general awareness of the nature of this pain. Through the healing process of time—and through medical intervention or hospitalization in many cases—most people survive depression, which may be its only blessing; but to the tragic legion who are compelled to destroy themselves there should be no more reproof attached than to the victims of terminal cancer."

In addition to depression, substance abuse disorders can place older adults at greater risk of suicide (Conwell, 2001). Osgood (1992) has referred to the relationship among alcoholism, depression, and suicide as the deadly triangle. Alcohol problems in older people, similar to depression, are often unrecognized by professional caregivers and family members. Older adults may be overlooked for alcohol problems because they may do their drinking at home. Caregivers might mistake symptoms of substance abuse for those of diabetes, dementia, depression, or other issues that face the older adult population (Levin & Kruger, 2000). Other barriers to identifying substance abuse problems among older people include ageism, lack of awareness, clinician behavior, and comorbidity (Blow, 1998).

Community prevalence rates for heavy alcohol use among older people range from 3 to 25% and for alcohol abuse from 2.2 to 9.6% depending on the older population being sampled (Liberto et al., 1992). Blow (1998) asserts that alcohol and prescription drug abuse is one of the fastest growing health problems facing older adults today. Liberto et al. (1992) predict that alcohol problems among older people will continue to increase.

Additional factors that may place older adults at risk for suicide include hopelessness, some personality traits, social circumstances, physical illness, and functional impairment (Conwell, 2001). It is important to note, however, that certain risk factors that may be associated with a unique individual may have no significance whatsoever (Motto, 1999). Loss of a loved one in the life of an older person may be an important and difficult transition, but it may not predispose this person to contemplate suicide. The person may have successfully integrated other losses, demonstrating his or her ability to cope with loss in healthy ways. On the other hand, ungrieved losses could trigger suicidal ideation. Motto (1999) asserts that there is no one assessment tool for suicide risk that has been widely accepted by the professional community. Instead of adding up risk factors, Motto suggests that it may be better to make a personal connection with the individual. Through a more intimate connection, the caregiver will develop a better understanding of the older person's suicidality.

Intervention: Treating Those At Risk

Once an older adult has been identified as being at risk for suicide, there is an opportunity for intervention. In addition to improving the recognition of depression, alcohol problems, and suicidal ideation in the primary care setting, a growing body of research demonstrates that psychotherapy, pharmacotherapy, and electroconvulsive therapy techniques can be effective (Fiske & Arbore, 2000).

When thoughts of suicide turn deadly, crisis intervention is initiated. Crisis intervention is associated most frequently with suicide prevention centers. While suicide prevention centers do attract high-risk clients, they do not show a measurable effect on the suicide rates in their communities (Dew, Bromet, & Brent, 1997). Older adults, however, are underrepresented among those individuals who call traditional suicide prevention centers (Mercer, 1989). Volunteers who staff suicide prevention centers also do not have as much knowledge about older at-risk callers. Only a third of the counselors studied by Adamek and Kaplan (1996) were aware that older adults had the highest suicide rates of any age population.

One community outreach agency, the Center for Elderly Suicide Prevention & Grief Related Services (CESP), now a program of the Goldman Institute on Aging in San Francisco, California, was created specifically to prevent suicide among older at-risk adults and provide grief and traumatic loss services for the bereaved. The 24-hour telephone outreach and visiting program, known as the Friendship Line, was begun in 1973 to serve depressed, lonely, isolated, abused, bereaved, and/or suicidal older adults and their advocates in San Francisco. Suicide bereavement support groups were added in 1986; a toll-free number was added in 2000; and traumatic loss groups were implemented in 2000. Each month CESP logs approximately 1,300 incoming calls, 1,800 outgoing calls, and 150 face-to-face visits. Services are provided by professionally supervised volunteers, many of whom are psychology, counseling, and clinical social work practicum students. In addition to training in suicide intervention skills, volunteers learn to recognize depression, bereavement, alcohol or medication abuse, personality disorder, psychosis, and dementia. Volunteers also receive training in the developmental changes associated with late life.

Results of a program evaluation that compared clients and a control group on depressive symptoms, hopelessness, and life satisfaction before and after clients received one year of services from CESP revealed a significant reduction in hopelessness among the clients (Fiske & Arbore, 2000). For the clients, there were no significant changes in life satisfaction or symptoms of depression, suggesting, perhaps, that maintaining a consistent level of depressive symptoms in the face of great difficulty represents success.

One important finding was the association between changes in health and changes in depressive symptoms among the clients. Clients with changes in vision, hearing, and mobility showed changes in depressive symptoms and hopelessness in the expected directions (Fiske & Arbore, 2000).

Researchers have also identified the Gatekeepers program of the Spokane Community Mental Health Center's Elderly Services unit in Washington State as an example of a comprehensive model of community outreach (Conwell, 2001; Fiske & Arbore, 2000). The Gatekeepers model includes a comprehensive clinical case management system, which is equipped to respond with clinical referrals; in-home medical, psychiatric, family, and nutritional assessments; medication management and respite services; and crisis intervention.

Intervention efforts need to include collaboration among medical, mental health, and social services if suicides among older people are going to be prevented. Osgood (1992) advocates for the implementation of pain clinics for older adults who suffer from painful conditions. There is a great need for geriatric mental health services of all kinds, including geriatric alcoholism and addiction services, bereavement counseling, retirement and life review groups, peer self-help groups, and suicide survivor groups (Osgood, 1992).

Caregivers need to be aware of the programs in their communities that provide needed social support for older adults, including adult day health programs, senior centers, creative arts programs, and other programs that reduce the loneliness that many older adults experience.

Because older adults both male and female die by suicide most frequently through the use of firearms, caregivers must be able to discuss a suicidal older adult's access to a gun (Kaplan et al., 1994). With 200 million guns in homes across the nation, identifying those older individuals who are depressed and suicidal is an urgent need. The following vignette is from a case in which an older patient with suicide ideation had access to a gun.

> J.C. is an 82-year-old widower living alone in a modest home where he has lived for the last 44 years. J.C. had been the primary caregiver for his wife who died recently after a 10-year struggle with dementia. J.C. and his wife had no children. After his wife had been diagnosed with dementia, J.C.'s world narrowed significantly. Trips to the doctors were his only outings as the years passed. Now that his wife has died, J.C. is devastatingly lonely and bereaved. He talks often of joining his wife and wonders why he has not yet died. I ask him directly about suicide. "Have you had thoughts of suicide since your wife died?"

"Yes," J.C. responds quietly, "I think of suicide all the time."

"How would you kill yourself," I inquire.

J.C. looks away from me as he says "I don't know…maybe I'd…I don't know."

I can see that J.C. is uncomfortable. He doesn't know how far he can go in this conversation. I am aware of his ambivalence and explore further. "I can sense that there is a part of you that wants to die and a part of you that wants to live."

"Maybe" J.C. responds.

"Sometimes," I continue, "the pain feels so bad that a person just might want to shoot himself, overdose on pills, hang himself or attempt suicide by some other method. Have you had thoughts like these?"

J.C. looks relieved as he says, "I think about shooting myself. I have a gun right here." J.C. opens a drawer in the coffee table that we are seated near and pulls out a handgun. J.C. places the gun on the coffee table and says, "I have had this gun for about 20 years. I bought it for protection. Now I want to kill myself with it. I don't know what I'm doing anymore (cries and holds his head). I just can't stand any more sorrow. I have had all the sorrow I can take."

J.C. permits me to call the nearby police station and two police officers arrived shortly. Because J.C. owns the gun, the officers remove the bullets (the gun was loaded) and discuss safety issues. After they leave, J.C. and I agree that the gun might better be held in a safety deposit box at his bank, at least until this crisis is resolved. J.C. agrees to call his doctor in my presence to set up an appointment for a medical examination. We discuss symptoms of depression as well as symptoms of grief. I give J.C. the Friendship Line number,

> promising him that a volunteer would call him each day and that I would return tomorrow for another visit. J.C. thanks me for caring as he says, "I don't know why anyone would be interested in an old man like me, but I am glad you're here."

J.C. did not commit suicide that day, and maybe he would never use the gun. Yet, as Osgood (1992) writes, "Handguns are the firearm most frequently used to commit suicide. They are easier to use for suicide than rifles or shotguns...are more often kept loaded and close at hand, and are viewed in our culture as a personal weapon."

Survivor Intervention: Dealing With The Aftermath

The suicide of an individual does not end with that person's death. Suicide affects the family members or friends of the individual who dies by suicide. These people are referred to as suicide survivors and represent the largest group of mental health casualties related to suicide (Shneidman, 1972). The American Association of Suicidology reports that for every suicide death, there are at least six survivors. Based on this estimate, there are now approximately 4.7 million survivors of suicide in the United States. Each year more than 186,000 new individuals are added to the roster of survivors.

While it is often suggested that suicide bereavement is a more difficult experience than the grief that accompanies other forms of death, there are few studies that compare suicide survivors with survivors of natural or accidental deaths (Farberow, 1991). What we do know about suicide death is that suicide is voluntary, while other forms of death are involuntary, for the most part. The person who dies by suicide severs all ties with family or friends, leaving the survivors without any opportunity to intervene. The following case demonstrates that unanswered questions plague the survivors, triggering enormous feelings of guilt, anger, disbelief, denial, shock, self-criticism, shame, anxiety, abandonment, anguish, horror, and deep sorrow.

M.C., a 75 year-old woman, wanted to join CESP's Suicide Bereavement Support group after the death of her husband. M.C. stated that her husband had slashed himself to death in the bathroom of their home while she frantically tried to stop him from the other side of the locked door. M.C.'s husband was 15 years her senior. They had been married for 42 years. They had two sons who lived in other parts of the state. M.C.'s husband had been ill for some time. Because M.C. herself had to have hip surgery, she would not be able to care for her husband for several months while she recovered. M.C. spent a great deal of time locating a facility that would be suitable for her husband during her recovery period. Although M.C.'s husband was not happy about the temporary need for him to be placed in a nursing home, his distress appeared to be relieved when it was agreed that he could come home on the weekends after M.C.'s surgery. If M.C.'s convalescence went well, her husband could return full time to their home within six months. The weekends would be viewed as a trial period, testing M.C.'s strength. Two months after M.C.'s hip replacement, her husband returned to their home for the first trial weekend. On Saturday M.C.'s husband locked himself inside their bathroom and slashed himself. By the time the police, paramedics and coroner arrived, M.C.'s husband was dead. The way he died horrified and shocked M.C. She refused to tell anyone, other than her two sons and the group members, how her husband died. M.C. told neighbors, friends, and relatives that her husband died suddenly of a heart attack. There was no funeral. M.C. stated that she felt her entire marriage had been called into question since her husband killed himself. She said, "How can I trust that he didn't make other decisions during our marriage without telling me? If he could kill himself, lock himself in the bathroom, without telling me what he was planning, our whole marriage is in question. What will happen to our sons? Didn't he love them? Why did he do this?"

M.C.'s anguished questioning demonstrates the fact that suicide is very hard for survivors to reconcile. In six categories—searching, guilt, stigma, identification with suicide, loss of trust, and anger—Farberow (1991) addresses the concerns of M.C. and others that are found among survivors of all ages and all kinds of relationships with the person who died by suicide.

Searching

M.C. constantly asked the question "Why?" This questioning drove her to seek constantly for any clue that would make this horrible experience disappear. M.C. probed into their marriage, searching for reasons for her husband's deadly decision in a desperate attempt to understand the rejection and to find some logic behind her husband's death. Caregivers need to evaluate whether the ruminating is a helpful exercise for the survivor or a way to avoid closure.

Guilt

In suicide death, these feelings tend to be more intense than in other types of death. "If only I had known," or "What if I could have..." are familiar laments of survivors. Caregivers are advised not to attempt to take the guilt away from the survivors. Reassurance is needed rather than absolution from blame. Guilt needs to be worked through, not taken away.

Stigma

No other type of death carries as much of a burden than suicide death. Like M.C., many survivors cannot disclose to others how the loved one died. The shame, whether fueled by cultural, religious, tradition, or societal beliefs, causes the survivor to hide behind half truths or total silence. The survivor may believe that others will judge them as a psychologically damaged person, a bad spouse, an uncaring adult child, an unloving grandchild. Caregivers must be aware of their own feelings and guard against displaying a judgmental attitude about suicide death so that they do not unconsciously discourage the survivor from revealing their feelings.

Identification with the Suicide

Some survivors, unable to cope with feelings of loss or abandonment, identify strongly with the person who died by suicide and threaten to join the person. Underlying mental health problems that were present prior to the suicide death may predispose the survivor to thoughts of their own suicide. The caregiver needs to carefully assess the survivor's coping ability and emotional health prior to and since the death. Assessing for suicide ideation in the survivor may need to be an ongoing part of the grief work.

Loss of Trust

The sudden, often violent suicide death affects the survivor's capacity to trust. Survivors often feel betrayed; they felt they knew their loved one's thoughts and motives and may now find it difficult to trust again. In CESP's Suicide Bereavement Support Groups, participants are encouraged to make a commitment to attend all eight sessions. The commitment is stated in front of the other participants at the end of the first session to support the group's ability to trust that each of them will be present during the next seven sessions.

Anger

Feelings of anger may be much too intense and experienced much too frequently by the survivor. The survivor may feel angry feelings towards the deceased and, at the same time, judge these feelings to be unacceptable. The survivor may also experience murderous feelings towards anyone whom they believe was in some way responsible for the death. Caregivers must help the survivors learn to accept their feelings of anger. Exploring how survivors feel about anger is a good first step. At CESP, participants are invited to reflect on their earliest memories about anger. How did the participant learn about anger? How does the participant currently manage his or her anger? Does the participant believe that anger must be directed at the deceased? Perhaps the anger is related more to the deceased's absence. Learning to deal effectively with his or her own anger may be an important step for the survivor in order to accept and to understand the suffering that must have contributed to the loved one's death.

CONCLUSION

At CESP, our Suicide Bereavement Support Groups are seen as prevention for the generations. On many occasions, grandchildren will be participants in the group. One such grandchild remarked, "My grandfather killed himself when he was 75; my father killed himself at the age of 72; I guess I have to do the same thing when I am their age." Working through grief will teach participants how to cope with tragic losses, particularly in families where more than one suicide death has occurred. Because a loved one died by suicide does not mean that other members of the family or friends will inevitably follow. Suicide does not have to happen.

What issues does a caregiver need to know about suicide prevention among older persons and suicide bereavement?

1. Caregivers need to be aware of their attitudes about aging, death, and suicide. They must be aware of their limitations around these issues.

2. Caregivers must notice whether they are in any way blaming the survivor. Does the caregiver think that the survivor was responsible for the death of the loved one? Holding onto this type of belief will interfere with the survivor's ability to grieve in a safe way with you.

3. If the deceased was depressed at the time of the suicide, caregivers need to be alert to any stigmatizing attitudes they experience in relationship to mental health issues.

4. Caregivers must be able to encourage repetitive accounts of the death. If the caregiver is uncomfortable with descriptions of traumatic, violent, and sudden death, the survivor will shut down and not discuss how the loved one died.

5. Caregivers need to be knowledgeable about what symptoms characterize both normal and difficult bereavement. Caregivers need to know when it is appropriate to refer a survivor to a professional for a depression assessment.
6. Caregivers need to know how to assess for suicide risk and for misuse of alcohol or other drugs. The survivor may become dependent on substances in order to avoid the pain associated with the loved one's death.

When caregivers work with older adults who are depressed and possibly suicidal or with those individuals who are experiencing the loss of a loved one to suicide, they must be able to accompany hurting people into some painful places. By being present with the individual, the caregiver is saying "I am with you. We are alike. We are human. We will get through this hurt together." If we can reduce the pain of a suicidal older adult just a little bit, the vital balance can change sufficiently to save a life (Shneidman, 1996). ■

Patrick Arbore is the Director and Co-founder of the Center for Elderly Suicide Prevention and Grief Related Services at the Goldman Institute on Aging in San Francisco. He began his career in crisis intervention, bereavement, and aging in 1973. Mr. Arbore is a lecturer in the Human Services Division at the College of Notre Dame in Belmont, California, and the 1998 recipient of the American Society on Aging's Award for outstanding contributions in the field of aging. Mr. Arbore conducts local and national workshops and lectures on elderly suicide prevention, alcohol and aging, bereavement, difficult clients, shame and guilt, crisis intervention; depression, change and transition, and forgiveness. He is the author of numerous articles and book chapters on these topics, including a recent article, "Future Directions in Late Life Suicide Prevention," co-authored with Amy Fiske, in Omega: The Journal of Death and Dying.

REFERENCES

Adamek, M.E., & Kaplan, M.S. (1996). Managing elder suicide: A profile of American and Canadian crisis prevention centers. *Suicide and Life-Threatening Behavior, 26* (2), 122-131.

Blow, F.C. (1998). *Substance abuse among older adults: Treatment improvement protocol (TIP) Series #26.* Rockville, MD: U.S. Dept. of Health and Human Services.

Brogden, M. (2001). *Geronticide.* London & Philadelphia: Jessica Kingsley Publishers.

Carney, S.S., Rich, C.L., Burke, P.A., & Fowler, R.C. (1994). *Journal of the American Geriatrics Society. 42,* 174-180.

Clark, D.C. (1991). *Suicide among the Elderly.* Final report to the AARP Andrus Foundation, Washington, DC.

Conwell, Y. (1994). Suicide in elderly patients. In L.S. Schneider, C.F. Reynolds, III, B. Lebowitz, and A.J. Friedhoff (Eds.). *Diagnosis and treatment of depression in late life,* pp. 397-418. Washington, DC: American Psychiatric Press.

Conwell, Y., Lyness, J., Duberstein, P., Cox, C., Seidlitz, L., DiGiorgio, A., & Caine, E. (2000). Completed suicide among older patients in primary care practices: A controlled study. *Journal of the Americam Geriatrics Society 48,* 23-29.

Conwell, Y. (2001). Suicide in later life: A review and recommendations for prevention. *Suicide and Life-Threatening Behavior, 31,* 32-46.

Dew, M.A., Bromet, E.J., & Brent, D. (1997). A quantitative literature review of the effectiveness of suicide prevention centers. *Journal of Consulting and Clinical Psychology, 2,* 239-244.

Farberow, N.L. (1991). Adult survivors after suicide: Research problems and needs. In A. Leenaars (Ed.) *Life span perspectives of suicide: Time-lines in the suicide process,* pp. 259-279. New York: Plenum.

Fiske, A., & Arbore, P. (2000). Future directions in late life suicide prevention. *Omega, 42* (1), 37-53.

Frierson, R.L. (1991). Suicide attempts by the old and very old. *Archives of Internal Medicine, 151*, 141-144.

Kaplan, M.S., Adamek, M.E., & Johnson, S. (1994). Trends in firearm suicide among older American males: 1979-1988. *The Gerontologist, 34* (1), 59-65.

Liberto, J.G., Oslin, D.W., & Ruskin, P.E. (1992). Alcoholism in older persons: A review of the literature. *Hospital and Community Psychiatry, 43* (10), 975-984.

Mercer, S. (1989). *Elder suicide: A national survey of prevention and intervention programs.* Washington, DC: American Association of Retired Persons.

Motto, J. (1999). Critical points in the assessment and management of suicide risk. In D.G. Jacobs (Ed.), T*he Harvard Medical School guide to suicide assessment and intervention*, (pp. 224-238). San Francisco: Jossey-Bass.

Murphy, S.L. (2000). *Deaths: Final data for 1998, National Vital Statistics Report, 48* (11), Hyattsville, MD: National Center for Health Statistics: DHHS Publication No. (PHS) 2000-1120.

Osgood, N. (1992). *Suicide in later life.* New York: Lexington Books.

Palmore, E. (1999). *Ageism: Negative and positive.* New York: Springer Publishing Co. Inc.

Pearson, J. (2000). Suicidal behavior in later life. In R. Maris, S. Canetto, J. McIntosh, and M. Silverman (Eds.) *Review of Suicidology 2000*, (pp. 202-225). New York: The Guilford Press.

Satcher, D. (1999). *The Surgeon General's call to action to prevent suicide 1999.* Washington, DC: U.S. Public Health Service.

Shneidman, E.S. (1972). Foreword. In A.C. Cain (Ed.) *Survivor of suicide*, (pp. ix-xi). Springfield, IL: Charles C. Thomas.

Shneidman, E.S. (1996). Psychotherapy with suicide patients. In J.T. Maltsberger and M.J. Goldblatt (Eds.), *Essential papers on suicide*, (pp. 417-426). New York: NY University Press.

Shneidman, E.S. (1998). Suicide on my mind, Britannica on my table. *The American scholar, 67*, 93-104.

Styron, W. (1990). *Darkness visible: A memoir of madness.* New York: Random House.

Uncapher, H., & Arean, P.A. (2000). Physicians are less willing to treat suicidal ideation in older patients. *Journal of the American Geriatrics Society, 48*, 188-192.

CHAPTER 24

Voices

Reflections on Post-Traumatic Stress

Myra MacPherson

The Vietnam War has been called the first "living room war" because the evening news brought dispatches from its front lines into our living rooms every night. And yet, despite such nightly news realism, most Americans, and even those in the medical field, could not comprehend the living nightmares of returning combat soldiers who were scarred with a legacy of shock and grief. Veterans Administration hospitals treated these soldiers as hallucinating schizophrenics, not as normal men who had experienced abnormal trauma and were reliving horrific real events as flashbacks. We owe a debt of gratitude to a handful of pioneering veterans who forced the medical profession to understand and treat their condition—post-traumatic stress disorder (PTSD), now accepted worldwide as a syndrome caused by traumatic experiences. Today experts counsel the victims of floods and earthquakes, refugees from wars in Bosnia and Baghdad, rape victims, and survivors from Oklahoma City and Columbine High School on coping with their PTSD symptoms. These include unresolved grief, pain, anger, withdrawal, and depression, which may not surface until months or years later.

The grim legacy of Vietnam veterans and other PTSD victims found resonance on September 11, 2001—but with a difference. This time, nonstop television coverage, endless commentaries by talk show pundits, and repeated viewings of the crashing planes and collapsing World Trade Center (WTC) towers branded those images on our national consciousness. The enormity of the events, the emotional fallout, the false alarms of further attacks, and the threat of anthrax challenge mental health professionals to help traumatized survivors live with their emotions of fear, anxiety, and grief. One psychiatrist counseled his devastated patients to stop watching television and reading newspapers.

One group that has been ignored in the 24-hour coverage of the terrorist crisis needs special consideration. The traumatic grief experienced by the older parents of the adults who perished in the World Trade Center—whether stockbrokers or kitchen helpers at Windows on the World—claims a special poignancy. These are parents who lived through the bruised knees, high fevers, and broken bones of childhood, as well as the sleepless nights worrying about car accidents, juvenile depression, and rebellion of the teenage years. For their adult children to vanish in an instant left a traumatic ending that superseded any good memories.

To know only that the ashes of their children could be mingled with those of the demolished buildings, to have no body for a healing funeral service, is a heavy burden for these parents. They don't need to see the videos of the towers collapsing, surrounded by smoke and fire, to feel traumatic stress. The terrible memories play over and over again in their consciousness.

Those directly affected by the loss of a child or other loved one are not the only elders experiencing traumatic stress in the wake of September 11. My 92-year-old father and his companion, who is 84, are a case in point. "This is all so hard on the elderly," she says. They have lived a long life, but now they feel anxious, depressed, and helpless as they face their final years. They are terrified at the thought of leaving their children and grandchildren to face the new uncertainties of a shattered world.

For older Americans, who are already threatened with the illnesses of old age and the constancy of loss as their friends and relatives die, the terrorist attacks can trigger memories of the traumas accumulated during a lifetime. Such traumas can be difficult to treat, because the memories are so layered and because the ability to bounce back diminishes with the passing years. Moreover, our elders come from an era when people seldom sought psychological help. And even if they were willing to do so, many are too housebound to make the effort. Therapists across the country should conduct outreach programs targeting elders who have been affected by the recent events.

■

Although I always empathized with Vietnam veterans as I researched their experiences of PTSD for a book on the Vietnam generation (*Long Time Passing: Vietnam and the Haunted Generation*, 1980), I never really understood what they were going through. Then my husband Jack Gordon, President of the Hospice Foundation of America, had triple bypass surgery one Monday morning at Washington Hospital Center in Washington, DC. I was standing beside him when he awoke the next morning in the intensive care unit just as the planes hit the WTC towers.

In hospitals, the television is always on. In the waiting room, crowds watched in disbelief. Then there were moans and cries of "Oh my God!" as the first tower collapsed. When the plane hit the nearby Pentagon, it felt like an earthquake's strongest aftershock. At that moment, "What next?" was the question in the minds of many Washingtonians.

The hospital immediately went on Code Orange, which meant that all personnel were called in for around-the-clock duty and all elective services were suspended. As Jack was moved to the cardiac recovery unit, I felt as if I were in Saigon. From his room I could see a billowing dark mass of smoke above the Pentagon, an ominous cloud on a mockingly beautiful morning of blue skies. His room looked down on the hospital's helicopter landing pad. Throughout the day, helicopters left and returned with stretchers filled with white-shrouded burn victims.

But there were all too few casualties as the Pentagon dead far exceeded the injured.

No phone lines were open, so my cell phone didn't work when I tried to reach my son Mike, who works as spokesman for the U.S. Senate Finance Committee. The evacuation of the Capitol was announced. I didn't know what was happening next. Later we heard that the downed plane in Pennsylvania probably had been headed for the Capitol, but at that early point, no doubt, many were afraid that would be the next target.

Later, I helped answer phones at the blood bank as people swarmed in to donate blood. I did such a miserable job of dealing with the blinking buttons that I suspect they were eager to take my contribution next. I gave my one measly pint, wishing I could do more, as I talked to my daughter Leah on a cell phone that finally worked. She had covered the Monday night football game in Denver as a producer for ESPN. On Tuesday morning at 7 a.m. Denver time, just before the planes hit New York, she boarded a plane. As the flight headed toward Dallas, the pilot announced that the plane might need to make an emergency landing because all planes were being ordered to the ground. Leah heard about the Pentagon and imagined all of Washington under siege. She finally got to Dallas only to witness attacks on Muslims and anyone who looked Arabic.

Three weeks after his operation, my husband was recuperating beautifully and we went out to dinner. As the meal progressed, Jack said he felt warm and uncomfortable. As we stood up to go, he fell forward, crashing into a plate glass window, which fortunately did not shatter, and then to the floor. As I cradled him in my arms, I felt in my bones that he was dead. But by the time the ambulance had arrived, he was beginning to wake up. After a frantic ride to the hospital and two days of tests, we were given the good news that nothing was wrong with his heart. He had been so overmedicated that his blood pressure dropped, triggering the dizziness and fainting.

I had just gotten over that shock when another struck. My son Mike was at his desk in the office of Senator Max Baucus in the Capitol when

Senator Tom Daschle received an anthrax-contaminated letter. As fate would have it, Mike was in the only Capitol area that was seriously endangered: the three offices and corridors that the Centers for Disease Control and Prevention (CDC) dubbed the "hot zone," where anthrax spores were found. For me, a nerve-wracking experience came from watching a film clip of my son played over and over in a CNN montage of those being evacuated. That vision just flattened me, making it seem even more real. I stared at the screen and cried, unable to turn it off.

CDC immediately put Mike on a 60-day prescription of CIPRO at a dosage highly toxic to the liver and kidneys. Although other doctors suggest less invasive antibiotic treatments, CDC said that those in the hot zone were at too great a risk for anything less. His first test finally came back negative, but even so they kept him on the antibiotic treatment because there are often false negatives as well as false positives. Now he awaits follow-up tests.

My new slogan is, "A hawk is a pacifist whose child has just been terrorized." Some of my reactions have been embarrassing. Even as I write these words, six weeks after September 11, my heart is beating fast. I remember every detail. I can hear my husband hitting the glass. My mind races through the night with relived fears. My children chide me for being overly anxious about them.

I felt guilty at not being able to put the fears aside, knowing that they were small compared to the devastation experienced by survivors closer to Ground Zero in Manhattan. Yet I was an elderly mother, concerned for her adult children. I went to a psychiatrist, and he assured me that many people were anxious and I had more reason than most to feel that way after the combined traumas I had experienced. Reliving the scenes was normal, he pointed out. Then he told me that I ought to try EMDR.

■

EMDR is an acronym for Eye Movement Desensitization and Reprocessing, a controversial psychological treatment promulgated 14 years ago by Francine Shapiro, a licensed psychologist who was then a senior research fellow at the Mental Research Institute in Palo Alto, California, and is now the executive director of the EMDR Institute, which trains clinicians in the method. EMDR is driven by alternating bilateral brain stimulation of the eyes, or by other pulsing stimuli, as the therapist asks the patient to think about the distressing memories. During therapy, many patients vividly relive and then move through a traumatic experience as they process dark memories.

It helps to understand EMDR by remembering that desensitization is the opposite of sensitization. Vietnam combat soldiers needed to be sensitized to the threats of jungle warfare, otherwise they would be killed. They had to be very focused at every moment. Sensitizing is a coping mechanism of the moment. When the wholly unexpected terror of September 11 happened, some survivors coped well in the initial stages; their brains either denying the horror or becoming sensitized to the enormity of destruction. Only later did some survivors experience nightmares, severe headaches, and flashbacks; fearful about driving into New York City, they quit their jobs.

Why EMDR works is a mystery, which explains, in part, why this new technique is still controversial. On the other hand, enthusiastic practitioners claim it can work successfully for problems ranging from devastating PTSD experiences to performance anxiety in athletes and actors. The method is used at many distinguished institutions and has been praised by UNICEF, the Red Cross, international refugee organizations, and the Domestic Violence Institute.

■

One of the platitudes repeated often during this uncertain period is that we should "get back to normal." But what was "normal" has been shattered. Traumatic reactions have spread across this land as Americans try to grasp a hard truth: Our lives have been changed forever by this horrific attack on our soil by an enemy. We know we will have to live closer to the edge; we will have to become less trusting, more vigilant, more sensitized in many ways. There is a sense of anxiety, of helplessness, of danger; we are waiting for the other shoe to drop as we are warned of the possibility of other terrorist acts, such as a smallpox attack.

EMDR is an individually oriented therapy that complements family and grief therapy in assisting survivors of trauma. Other examples include Thought Field Therapy, Visual/Kinesthetic Disassociation, and Trauma Incident Reduction. These and a variety of other approaches are being used in concert with group, individual, and cognitive techniques to help traumatized people process and desensitize their terrible memories. In these troubled times, let's give thanks to those who can help diminish the worst traumatic memories, leaving room for calmer, happier remembrances to soar. ■

Myra MacPherson is the author of two books pertaining to trauma, grief, and death. Her award-winning Long Time Passing: Vietnam and the Haunted Generation *was among the first trade books to examine post-traumatic stress disorder in Vietnam veterans. An updated version was published by Indiana University Press this year. Her latest book,* She Came to Live Out Loud: An Inspiring Family Journey Through Illness, Loss and Grief, *traces the personal and instructive aspects of grief and dying, including the hospice movement.*

CHAPTER 25

Culture and Loss

Hosam K. Kamel, Charles P. Mouton, and Deborah R. McKee

INTRODUCTION

Culture is the constellation of values, norms, and behavior guidelines that are shared by a group of individuals (Brislin, 1993). The word *culture* is most often used in reference to specific ethnic or religious groups. End-of-life views and practices are greatly influenced by individuals' cultural beliefs. When faced by death, individuals often look to their culture to help them find a meaning for death and to guide them on how to act and how to express grief. They often find comfort in the rituals that the culture prescribes when a death occurs (Johnson & McGee, 1991; Smith, 1991).

Recent medical advances, although making it possible to prolong human life by artificial means, greatly complicate the medical, legal, and ethical issues at the end of life. In addition, the U.S. population, especially its older segment, is becoming more culturally diverse. Health care providers are more likely than ever before to interact with patients and families whose cultural beliefs are different from their own. Ignorance or insensitivity to patients' cultural beliefs may lead to cross-cultural clashes that can greatly impair the patient-doctor relationship. This is particularly true for dying patients and their families, as cultural patterns have great influence in the period surrounding death. This chapter reviews the beliefs and practices surrounding the time of death from the perspective of major religious and ethnic cultural groups in the United States.

Death and Grief among Major Religious Beliefs

Religious beliefs in relation to suffering, death, and the afterlife can greatly influence the grieving process. Health care providers should educate themselves in the basic beliefs of the different religions and on how they may affect their patients' medical care. This is particularly important when providing care for a dying patient, as individuals often revert to their religious roots when faced with death. It is important to recognize that religious beliefs evolve continuously to meet changing cultural conditions and that wide variations in beliefs and practices exist even within specific religious subgroups. The best way to assess the likely impact of religious beliefs on the grieving process is to directly ask the patient and/or family.

Christianity is the most common religious belief around the world, followed by approximately 28% of the world's population (Markham, 1996; Brail & Mori, 1990). Most Christians believe that suffering may be a punishment for committing sins and that it can be relieved through God's grace and by believing in God's love for humankind and the promise of eternal life. Death is viewed by many Christians as a temporary separation of the body and the soul. Christians believe that the bodies of the dead will rise up after Christ's second coming and rejoin their souls for final judgment that will determine if an individual will be sent to heaven, where he or she will enjoy eternal bliss, or to hell for eternal punishment. Some Christian denominations tend to put more emphasis on eternal suffering in hell for sinful behavior. The emphasis on punishment can result in considerable fear and anxiety at the time of death among some Christians. The sacrament of last rites was developed by the early Catholic Church in order to provide Christians with peace at the time of death by reminding them of Christ's love and the promise of eternal life. This is often accompanied by two other sacraments: confession and communion. During the sacrament of the sick, a Catholic priest prays for the patient and anoints him or her with holy oils, and as death approaches, prayers are often offered for the person's soul (Kramer, 1988). Christian funeral practices vary from simple observances to elaborate rituals.

Islam is the world's fastest growing religion and is currently the belief of more than 970 million people around the world (Markham, 1996). Muslims believe that suffering is caused by deviation from the will of Allah (God) and is relieved by total surrender and commitment to Allah's will as described in the Koran (Islam's holy book). Muslims believe that creation, death, and resurrection are inseparable parts of the life cycle. Islamic teachings view death as the will of Allah, so Muslims tend to be fatalists about approaching death and often want to spend their remaining time praying and reading the Koran. Muslims believe that only other Muslims should touch the dead body of a Muslim. Non-Muslims should put on rubber gloves before touching the dead body. The dying person often wants to sit or lie turned toward Mecca. There are no official last rites in Islam; family members usually repeat prayers, read the Koran, and encourage the dying person to repeat the statement of faith, "There is no God but Allah and Muhammad is his Prophet." After death, the body is bathed at the mosque or at home and often wrapped in white cotton. Muslims are not cremated and are usually buried within 24 hours of death.

More than 730 million people around the world are Hindus. Hindus view death as mortality of the body but not the soul. They believe that the soul transmigrates from one reincarnation to another and that the ultimate reality, referred to as Brahman, is the eternal oneness. Most Hindus believe they will undergo many incarnations before achieving union with Brahman. As death approaches, religious rites and ceremonies provide support for the dying person. Family members and friends gather and sing devotional prayers, and read Hindu scriptures to comfort and reassure the dying person. After death, the body is washed, anointed, and dressed in burial clothes. Hindus believe that cremation is the best way for the soul to begin its journey.

After cremation, remaining bones are usually buried or cast into a river (Kramer, 1988).

Buddhism is the religion of more than 300 million people around the world. Buddhists believe in reincarnation and that an eternal soul, or self, transmigrates from one reincarnation to another. They also believe that the last thoughts of a person before his or her death determine the rebirth condition. If one is confused or angry at the time of death, one's soul would likely be reborn in different (worse) state than if this person had died peacefully. Family members, friends, and monks often surround the dying person, read religious texts, and repeat mantras to help the individual achieve peace. After the person dies, the body is washed, dressed in new clothes, and then cremated (Kramer, 1988).

Judaism is the religious belief of approximately 17 million people around the world (Markham, 1996). According to Jewish belief, death is viewed as a part of God's creation, not as a punishment for sins. In Jewish culture, the dying person should be attended at all times (Kramer, 1988). Surrounding family members and a rabbi frequently read specific religious texts and recites psalms. As death becomes imminent, the dying person is encouraged to make a confession, and pray for forgiveness. After death, a son or a relative closes the dead person's eyes and mouth and washes and dresses the body. Orthodox Jews are often resistant to autopsies and organ donation. Most Jews do not believe in cremation and the body is often buried as soon as possible after death. At the end of the funeral, relatives recite a mourner's prayer also known as Kaddish. The dying person's family often observes a seven-day period of mourning after the death. During that period, they remain at home, recite prayers, and welcome visitors who come to offer condolences. This period is followed by a less rigorous mourning period for up to 11 months after the funeral.

DEATH AND GRIEF IN THE WHITE AMERICAN CULTURE

The cultural practices of the White majority currently dominate the discussion of death and dying in the United States. Complicating this discussion is the fact that the White American population is a heterogeneous group of individuals. Great diversity exists for rituals and customs concerning death. Discussions of cultural practices for this group are gross generalities at best.

For most of the White American population, cultural rituals at time of death include preparation of the corpse, funeral services, and burial of the body. Surviving family members choose the articles of clothing to adorn the deceased and the setting in which final religious and sacral rites are administered. For family members and friends, these rituals can serve as an appropriate time and place to say good-bye to and pray for the soul of the deceased, while offering respects and comfort to the surviving immediate family members. Despite this culturally sanctioned process, White Americans are more likely to avoid direct contact with the corpse and the funeral process than other ethnic groups (Kalish & Reynolds, 1976).

Eleazer and colleagues (1996) studied 1193 frail older persons and reported that frail older White, African, Hispanic, and Asian Americans differ significantly in their end-of-life health care wishes. African Americans were significantly more likely to choose aggressive interventions and less likely than non-Hispanic Whites and Hispanics to utilize a written instrument for expressing health care wishes. Whites were significantly more likely to use written documents for advance directives, whereas Asians were more likely to select less aggressive intervention but were unlikely to use written advance directives. McKinley and colleagues (McKinley, Garrett, Evans, & Danis, 1996) surveyed 92 African American and 114 White ambulatory cancer patients who were over the age of 40 and found that African American patients wanted more life-sustaining treatments and were less willing to complete a living will at some time in the future than were White patients.

Death and Grief in the African American Culture

African Americans constitute a heterogeneous group that includes individuals from diverse ethnic and religious cultural backgrounds. They represent a mixture of descendents of the ex-slaves who were brought to the United States mainly from the west coast of Africa as well as the immigrants from different African countries such as Nigeria, Ghana, Liberia, Sierra Leone, Ethiopia, and Sudan. This heterogeneity complicates the discussion of cultural practices of the African American community around the time of death.

The African American community has a strong sense of spirituality that influences the grieving process. While many African Americans believe in a better afterlife, they still avoid death and have a strong instinct for survival. In one study (Kalish & Reynolds, 1976), 40% of African Americans indicated that religion influenced how they felt about death. Lincoln (1974, 1984) pointed out that some African Americans subscribe to a "Black Theology" that embraces notions of man's responsibility to work with God and of man's faith that God can handle any problem exclusively. Differing religious attitudes, promoting an attitude of resilient hope in spite of overwhelming odds, may reflect the legacy of oppression left on the consciousness of some African American patients. African Americans partially interpret the death of a loved one as a chance for that person to move on to a better place, but at the same time they feel a sense of loss in the battle against the odds.

Grief over the loss of a loved one is often expressed openly in the African American community. Funeral rituals often have exaggerated displays of emotion and grief that may extend beyond societal norms. Yelling, crying, fainting, shaking, and other somatization of emotions may be common at the time of grief when the sense of loss is overwhelming. Support during these times of intense grief usually comes from the family and community members. Family members, or extended family, friends, neighbors, church members, and other members of the community often visit the home of the grieving family to comfort them and help them cope with their grief.

Resolution and coming to terms with the loss of a loved one is often a time of celebration or coming together of family and friends. This typically begins after the funeral, with friends and family coming over to share a meal with the family of the decreased. Other death rituals in the African American community that help to resolve grief include the pouring of libations for the deceased friend or family member, setting a place at the table for a deceased family member, and visiting the grave site to place flowers and tokens of remembrance. These rituals celebrate the life of the deceased and their place in the community they once shared.

Death and Grief in the Hispanic American Culture

Hispanic Americans originally immigrated from Mexico, Cuba, Puerto Rico, Central America, and South America and represent a variety of racial mixtures and social classes. Most Hispanics place a great deal of value on family relations. Many Hispanics are socialized to believe that the needs of the family are more important than one's own needs. This cultural belief places the emphasis on cooperation and sharing and leads to the family serving as the most important support system for its older members. As with all cultural beliefs, this one is evolving. As each generation becomes acculturated to the "American" value system, in which fewer people live in extended families households, the expectations of older Hispanics are often left unmet. In these more isolated environments, support systems for grieving and coping with loss may be less than optimal for older Hispanics.

There is a wide degree of acculturation among Hispanic Americans. With each successive generation of Hispanic immigrants, cultural belief systems based in traditional Hispanic values tend to wane as individuals become more integrated in Western cultural values dominant in the United States. Traditionally, Hispanics believe that the world is inhabited by both good and evil spirits that may affect the individual in a positive and a negative way. The Mexican system of *curanderismo*, the Cuban system of santeria, and the Puerto Rican system of *espiritismo* all have beliefs related to special powers at work in the world. These systems influence health beliefs and behaviors, such as the use of alternative medicine and prayer for healing. These beliefs translate into a cultural attitude about the inevitability of death. Hispanic culture generally accepts death as a part of the life cycle (Talamantes, Gomez, & Braun, 2000). Many Hispanics view life as a temporary gift from God. *Dia de los Muertos* is an example of this type of celebration. During this Hispanic holiday, celebrated throughout Mexico and the United States, the family goes to the cemetery to place food on the grave of deceased loved ones. The practice honors the life of the deceased and brings the family together. Masses, religious services, and public announcements are often held on the anniversary of the death of a loved one. These practices reinforce the view that death is part of the cycle of life (Rael & Korte, 1988). Hispanics rely heavily on spirituality to cope with the death of a loved one. Their faith in God and the great power of God helps them cope with the death of a loved one and provides them with comfort during the grieving process (Villa, 1991; Talamantes, Lawler, & Espino, 1995). Hispanics tend to focus on the present and not the future. Subsequently, focusing on future life and happiness may not be the most effective coping strategy for older Hispanics during the grieving process.

Death and Grief in the Japanese American Culture

Among Japanese Americans there are generational differences in response to death. *Issei* (first generation) respondents are more likely to practice the customs and traditions of Japan compared to *sansei* (third generation) and *yonsei* (fourth generation) (Hirayama, 1990). In a study conducted in Honolulu (Braun & Nicholas, 1996), Japanese Buddhist participants said that death is a part of the natural process of life and is not finality. They believed that the present world is painful and unsatisfactory because of the worldly attachments people have to it, and the next world is a better place because people are relieved of those attachments and there is peace.

Japanese Buddhists feel that planning for death is a good idea. A growing number of Japanese Americans saw the usefulness of advance directives and many had already executed such documents (Braun & Nicholas, 1996). One study of advance directives among nursing home residents found that Japanese residents were more likely than other ethnic groups to request no code status (Vaugn, Kiyasu, & McCormick, 2000). Many Japanese Americans left Buddhism following Japan's bombing of Pearl Harbor in World War II, as Japanese Buddhist ministers (and others in leadership positions) were sent to internment camps. Some Japanese Americans became Christians at this time and others stopped participating in organized religion altogether.

Death and Grief in the Chinese American Culture

Chinese traditions at end of life are influenced by three religions: Confucianism, Taoism, and Buddhism. In Confucianism, it is believed that the body should be preserved in order to respect one's parents and that ancestor worship is very important. In Taoism, longevity is emphasized and stimulates discussions about the right foods to maintain health and obtain long life. The Buddhist religion teaches that one must be good in the present life to be reincarnated on a higher level in the next life. Chinese people have traditionally thought it was bad luck to talk about death. Living wills are not prompted in Hong Kong or in mainland China. Newer generations are more westernized and more open to advanced planning (Wilson & Ryan, 1990; Ryan, 1986).

Death and Grief in the Filipino American Culture

The immigration of Filipinos to the United States started after the U.S. victory over Spain in 1892, at which time the Philippines was ceded to the United States. As a U.S. territory, Filipinos were considered U.S. nationals and, therefore, immigration was unrestricted. Immigration was severely curtailed in 1935, when the Philippines were granted commonwealth status, but with the Immigration Act of 1965, Filipino immigration accelerated (Agbayani-Siewart & Revilla, 1995).

There have been several different waves of immigration to the United States from the Philippines, with each group having unique experiences and backgrounds that would influence their belief system. Catholicism had an important influence on death and dying in Filipino culture. This is not surprising given that the vast majority of Filipinos are Catholic as a result of 330 years of Spanish rule (Braun & Nicholas, 1996). Filipinos do not like to talk about death or funerals and generally do not execute living wills.

Assessment of Bereavement

Understanding an individual's cultural mourning practices is critical in the assessment of bereavement. There are very few quantitative bereavement assessment instruments available and most have only limited published psychometric data on their use with older adults. Available data is largely from younger adult Caucasian convenience samples. The Grief Experience Inventory (Sanders, Mauger, & Strong, 1985) is a 135-item scale designed to measure an individual's reaction to bereavement. Patterned after the Minnesota Multiphasic Personality Inventory, it provides a grief reaction profile score and contains three validity scales. It has been criticized as being too long for use with older adults. A second instrument, the Texas Revised Inventory of Grief is designed to measure adjustment and change over time (Faschingbauer, 1981). The instrument's 26-items assess how the respondent felt at the time of the loss and what the individual is currently feeling (Hansson, Carpenter, & Fairchild, 1993). The scale has received some criticism for the retrospective reporting of feelings and should be used cautiously with older adults experiencing memory problems. A third instrument, the Inventory of Complicated Grief, (Prigersin et al., 1995) was developed to assess grief symptoms and predict later dysfunction. Strong psychometric properties have been reported for the scale, including high internal consistency, high test-retest validity, and concurrent validity with the

Beck Depression Inventory (Bierhals, Frank, Prigerson, Miller, Fasiczka, & Reynolds, 1995–96). The short format is conducive to working with older adults.

Conclusion

Culture plays an important role in individuals' perception and interpretation of human experiences. This interplay between culture and human experience is most poignant at the time surrounding death. The experience of grief and loss across cultures is intertwined in the various meanings of life and death within each culture. It is important to note, however, that although beliefs and characteristics may be ascribed to each cultural group, there are differences within groups and there is uniqueness to each person. Thus, health care providers have to be on guard against stereotyping any person by his or her cultural affiliation and should discuss possible cultural differences directly with the patient and family. ■

Hosam K. Kamel, MD, is currently an Assistant Professor of Medicine in the Division of Geriatrics and Gerontology at the Medical College of Wisconsin and is the Medical Director of the GEM and subacute care units at the Zablocki VAMC in Milwaukee. Dr. Kamel obtained his MBBCH degree from Kuwait University in 1989, completed his internal medicine training at the State University of New York at Stony Brook, and his geriatric medicine training at Saint Louis University Hospital. He is board certified in internal medicine, geriatrics, nutrition, pain management, and wound management and home care. He has more than 100 publications covering different aspects of care of older adults. Currently he is researching geriatric nutrition, geriatric endocrinology, and utilizing interdisciplinary teams to improve outcomes in hospitalized elderly patients, falls, and hip fractures.

Charles P. Mouton, MD, is Associate Professor of Family and Community Medicine and Associate Chief of the Division of Community Geriatrics at the University of Texas Health Science Center at San Antonio. He completed his medical education at Howard University, a residency in Family Practice at Prince George's Hospital Center, and a geriatrics fellowship at George Washington University. He has also received a Master of Science in clinical epidemiology from the Harvard School of Public Health. Currently he is researching elder mistreatment, end-of-life care, health promotion in frail elders, and ethnogeriatrics.

Deborah R. McKee, PhD, is a postdoctoral fellow in geriatric psychology at the Clement J. Zablocki Veterans Administration Medical Center in Milwaukee, Wisconsin.

References

Agbayani-Siewart, P., & Revilla, L. (1995). Filipino Americans. In P. G. Min (Ed.), *Asian American: Contemporary trends and issues.* Thousand Oaks, CA: Sage Publications.

Bierhals, A.J., Frank, E., Prigerson, H.G., Miller, M., Fasiczka, B.A., & Reynolds, C.F. (1995-96). Gender differences in complicated grief among the elderly. *Omega: Journal of Death and Dying, 32,* 303-317.

Brail, A., & Mori, G. (1990). Leaving the fold: Declining church attendance. In McKie C., Thompson K. (Eds.) *Canadian social trends* (vol.1). Ottawa: Statistics Canada.

Braun, K.L., & Nicholas, R. (1996). Cultural issues in death and dying. *Hawaii Medical Journal, 55,* 260-264.

Brislin, R. (1993). *Understanding culture's influence on behavior.* New York: Harcourt Brace.

Eleazer, G.P., Hornung, C.A., Egbert, C.B., et al. (1996). The relationship between ethnicity and advance directives in a frail older population. *Journal of the American Geriatrics Society, 44,* 939-943.

Faschingbauer, T.R. (1981). *Texas revised inventory of grief manual.* Houston, TX: Honeycomb Publishing.

Hansson, R.O., Carpenter, B.N., & Fairchild, S.K., (1993). Measurement issues in bereavement. In M.S. Stroebe, W. Stroebe, & R.O. Hannson (Eds.), *Handbook of bereavement: Theory, research, and intervention.* Cambridge, England: Cambridge University Press.

Hirayama, K.K. (1990). Death and dying in Japanese culture. In J. Perry (Ed.), *Social work practice with the terminally ill: A transcultural perspective.* Springfield, IL: Thomas Books.

Johnson, C.J., & McGee, M.G. (Eds.). (1991). *How different religions view death and after life.* Philadelphia: Charles Press.

Kramer, K.P. (1988). *The sacred art of dying. How world religions understand death.* New York: Paulist Press.

Kalish, R.A., & Reynolds, D.K. (1976). *Death and ethnicity: A psycho-cultural study.* Los Angeles: University of Southern California Press.

Lincoln, C.E. (1974). *The Black church since Frazier.* New York: Schoken Books Inc.

Lincoln, C.E. (1984). *Race, religion, and the continuing American dilemma.* New York: Hill and Wang.

Markham, I. (1996). *A world religions reader.* Boston, MA: Blackwell.

McKinley E.D., Garrett, J.M., Evans, A.T., & Danis, M. (1996). Differences in end-of-life decision making among black and white ambulatory cancer patients. *Journal of Gen Internal Medicine, 11,* 651-656.

Prigersin, H.G., Maciejewski, C.F., Reynolds, C.F., Burhals, A.J., Newsom, J.T., Fascizka, A., Frank, E., Doman, J., & Miller, M. (1995). The inventory of complicated grief: A scale to measure certain maladaptive symptoms of loss. *Psychiatry Research, 59,* 65-79.

Rael, R., & Korte, A.O. (1988). El ciclo de la vida y muerte: An analysis of death and dying in a selected Hispanic enclave. In S.R. Applewhite (Ed.), *Hispanic elderly in transition: Theory, research, policy, and practice.* Westport, CT: Greenwood Press.

Sanders, C.M., Mauger, P. A., & Strong, P. N. (1985). *A manual for the grief experience inventory.* Palo Alto, CA: Consulting Psychologists Press.

Smith, H. (1991). *The world's religions: Our great wisdom traditions.* New York: HarperCollins.

Talamantes, M.A., Gomez, C., & Braun, K.L. (2000). Advance directives and end-of-life care: The Hispanic perspective. In K.L. Braun, J.H. Pietsch, and P.L. Blanchette (Eds.), *Cultural issues in end-of-life decision making.* Thousand Oaks, CA: Sage Publications.

Talamantes, M.A., Lawler, W.R., & Espino, D.V. (1995). Hispanic American elders: Care giving norms surrounding dying and the use of hospice services. *Hospice Journal, 10(4),* 35-49.

Vaugn, Kiyasu, & McCormick W.C. (2000). Advance directives preferences among subpopulations of Asian nursing home residents in the Pacific Northwest. *Journal of the American Geriatrics Society, 48,* 554-557.

Villa, R.F. (1991). La fe dela mujer. In M. Sotomayor (Ed.), *Empowering Hispanic families: A critical issue for the '90s.* Milwaukee, WI: Family Service America.

Wilson, B., & Ryan, A.S. (1990). Working with the terminally ill Chinese Americans. In J. Perry (Ed.), *Social work practice with the terminally ill.* A transcultural perspective. Springfield, IL: Thomas Books.

Chapter 26

Making Sense of Loss

Robert A. Neimeyer

Introduction: Two Cases Of Loss In Later Life

Phyllis is a 67-year-old woman who can't seem to get out of the rut she has been in since she experienced a string of losses beginning seven years ago. Soon after she turned 60, Phyllis's losses began with the chronic illness and death of her beloved father. She recalls her father's funeral and her mixed feelings of sadness and anger, of swallowing her own grief in order to answer questions about how her mother was doing. Phyllis's mother was in poor health and soon after her husband's death moved into Phyllis's home, despite the tense and distant relationship between daughter and mother. Phyllis grew to resent caring for her frail and forgetful mother, and eventually began retreating to her bed to avoid all contact with her, a pattern of depression and self-isolation that eventually cost Phyllis the office job she had held for many years. Desperate, her family finally persuaded the mother to move to an assisted living facility, which left Phyllis feeling relieved, but also guilty in relation to her mother, and directionless without the previous work role that had been a source of satisfaction for many years.

A few months later, Phyllis received a fateful phone call: her husband, Bill, had been rushed from his office to the hospital. When she arrived in the emergency room, an unknown doctor drew her aside and told her that her husband had died of a ruptured aneurysm. Phyllis then saw what became a deeply etched and horrifying sight of her husband's face—eyes and mouth frozen open as he lay on the gurney. Years later, she remains haunted by that image.

More losses came in the year that followed, including the death of a beloved older sister. Now, Phyllis says that she still finds no meaning in life, and continues to ruminate about her sister's and husband's deaths. On good days, she finds solace in remembering the good times shared with Bill, but on bad days, she feels embittered at God, as she struggles to understand the reason for her suffering. In her darkest moments, she feels that the deaths of her husband and sister were God's way of punishing her for abandoning her mother. This conflict fuels Phyllis's ambivalence about returning to church, and it is all she can manage to do just to get by day to day.

In addition to feelings of despair, Phyllis has a number of physical symptoms, including fatigue and cardiac arrhythmia. Phyllis appreciates her family's support, but she also senses her daughter's growing impatience. Although she manages to live relatively independently, Phyllis has a very restricted range of activities and hasn't been able to return to the sort of respected work position she had prior to her discharge.

■

Well established in his career as a rehabilitation counselor for the disabled, Donald had earned the respect of his coworkers and the affection of most of his patients. Although he had known his share of setbacks, including divorce from his first wife, Donald had recently remarried and had been elected president of his regional professional organization. Indeed, he was troubled by only one problem: the gradual downward spiral into depression of his only son, Chris. By his early thirties, Chris had accumulated a long list of perceived failures—at school, in relationships, and in faltering attempts at work, and he never seemed to respond to family support, professional therapy, or antidepressant medication. As a result, Chris had been living in Donald's home, until one tragic day when Donald came home to find Chris dead in his bedroom, with empty medication jars scattered around him.

Chris's suicide shook Donald's world, triggering an agonizing search for answers. Donald's quest to make sense of the event led him to register for several graduate courses in psychology at the local university. Today, Donald acknowledges that he still grieves and regrets not having been more supportive of his son, despite the reassurances of family members and professional helpers. Even with the great void he continues to feel, Donald finds a silver lining in his bereavement, as he has come to learn more about depression, psychotherapy, and mental illness in general. The effect, he states, "has been positive in my personal life, my teaching, and in my own practice" in helping people adjust to disability-related losses. Donald has also developed a new perspective regarding things that do and do not matter so much in the larger scheme. As a result, half a decade after his traumatic loss, Donald feels that he is a changed person—calmer, more reflective, and more empathic to the suffering of others. Though he would trade it all in a minute if he were able to have his son back, he views Chris's death as a kind of turning point in his life that has clearly made him a better person.

■

In attempting to understand the complex patterns of adaptation to loss in later life exemplified by the struggles of Phyllis and Donald, two questions emerge about the nature of grieving: What factors predict the longer-term outcomes of bereavement, which can either undermine or enrich the lives of survivors? What processes help people find healing and growth in the wake of these losses, reconnecting them to sustaining themes in their lives, as well as to a world shared with other people? In seeking answers to these questions, grief theorists and therapists have begun to reach toward new models of mourning, calling into question traditional assumptions that have shaped both popular and professional understanding of grieving. My goal in this chapter is to explore some of these new concepts and to consider their practical implications for those attempting to learn the "lessons of loss" in later life (Neimeyer, 2001b).

Loss And The Reconstruction Of Meaning

In our medical culture, bereavement traditionally has been understood in largely symptomatic terms. Many physical reactions to grief are, in fact, commonly associated with illness: fatigue, lack of appetite, sleep disruption, and pangs in the heart or abdomen (Rando, 1995). More subtly, the progressive deterioration of health that often attends bereavement has prompted the study of grief in physiological terms (Hall & Irwin, 2001). This focus on physical symptoms is accentuated in later life, when age-related illnesses serve as a continuing reminder of the body's diminishing capacity (Moss, Moss, & Hansson, 2001).

Despite our improved medical understanding of grief, anyone who has survived the loss of a loved one knows that grieving is more than simply managing the physical symptoms of loss. Such a loss can also undermine the psychological, social, and spiritual foundations of the bereaved person's world. In keeping with this effort to broaden the frame for understanding post-loss adaptation, we will consider one emerging approach which views *grieving as a process of reconstructing a world of meaning that has been challenged by loss* (Neimeyer, 2001).

In a sense, all of us are the "authors" of our lives, striving to construct a life story that makes sense of the events we confront, the relationships we cultivate, and the people we become (Polkinghorne, 1988). Far from being an abstract principle, this narrative impulse is evident in daily life, as people immerse themselves in countless stories on television, in books, and in the theater and share accounts of their day with friends and loved ones. This same effort to make sense of life in story form is perhaps most compelling in the troubled tales that come in the wake of tragedy as people strive to find meaning in events radically at odds with the course they assumed their lives would take (Neimeyer & Levitt, 2001). When we are profoundly dislocated from the narrative structure of our lives, we may even lose a sense of who we are as persons, as we are thrown into an unpredictable future that seems to contradict our past. Faced with this sort of narrative disruption, we are confronted with the task of sifting through our lives to find what remains viable and reinventing our sense of self and purpose (Neimeyer, 2000). Bereavement often prompts just this kind of adaptation (Viney, 1991).

For both Donald and Phyllis, the death of their loved ones profoundly shook the foundations of their life stories. For Phyllis, the successive losses of her father, husband, and sister were compounded by her own illness, the loss of her career, and the distressing psychosocial transitions that placed her failing mother under her care. For Donald, a relatively stable life narrative was disrupted by a single, traumatic loss—the suicide of his son. For each, traumatic changes triggered a far-ranging attempt to make sense of life differently, a process that met with a very different outcome in each instance. Phyllis's and Donald's struggles to reconstruct the meaning of their lives provide a helpful vehicle for understanding three of the primary processes involved in re-authoring life narratives: *sense-making, benefit-finding,* and *identity reconstruction.* Following a brief presentation of each of these processes, I will close with a few concrete suggestions for facilitating this meaning reconstruction process, and fostering the integration of loss.

Sense-Making

Of all the dimensions of meaning reconstruction, sense-making is perhaps the most fundamental. In its most concrete form, this involves making sense of the death itself—finding satisfying answers to the question of why the loved one died, at levels ranging from the physical (What kind of aneurysm was it? Did he suffer long?) to the philosophical (How could God permit such a thing? What could explain such a self-destructive act?). Still more abstractly, it involves fitting bereavement into the broader framework of the grieving individual's experience and philosophy of life. Phyllis, for example, struggled to understand God's intentions in taking both her husband and sister in the wake of her father's death, never arriving at a satisfying answer. Indeed, in her darkest moments Phyllis believed that these losses were a kind of divine retribution for her selfishness, a conclusion that only reinforced her suffering.

Research by Davis, Nolen-Hoeksema, and Larsen (1998) suggests that prolonged questioning regarding a loss is associated with protracted anxiety, anger, and depression and diminished well-being. In contrast, those who are able to integrate a loss into their existing belief system (for example, by viewing it in terms of a stable and unquestioned core of spiritual convictions) are more likely to grieve less intensely (Braun & Berg, 1994), at least in the early months of bereavement (Davis et al., 1998). Likewise, the effort to augment one's meaning system to make sense of a previously incomprehensible event—as in Donald's quest to grasp the psychology of his son's suicide—helps one come to terms with the loss (Neimeyer, 2001a).

Sense-making may be an especially important resource in later life, as research by Barnes, Harvey, Carlson, and Haig (1996) indicates that older adults spend more time constructing meaningful accounts of loss than do younger persons. This tendency might represent a more reflective, contemplative form of coping that remains available to persons of advanced age, as other more active forms of adaptation (e.g., investing in one's career, forming new relationships) become less feasible. Seeking meaning in loss in later life might also be a natural outgrowth of the wisdom that can come with maturity (Carlsen, 1989) and the growing acceptance of death that is typical of relatively healthy older persons (Fortner & Neimeyer, 1999). Whatever the explanation, current research is consistent in suggesting that sense-making is the single most powerful predictor of well-being after loss, vastly outweighing such factors as objective relationship to the deceased (e.g., as parent, partner, child, or friend) and the length of time since the death. This conclusion holds across different samples of several hundred bereaved persons studied by my research group, including Nancy Keesee, Adam Anderson, and James Gillies. The generality of this finding underscores the primacy of meaning-making as a cardinal feature of grieving, rather than an incidental coping tool, as it has sometimes been considered.

BENEFIT-FINDING

Another feature of meaning reconstruction is the capacity to find some benefit, an unexpected silver lining, in loss (Davis, Wortman, Lehman, & Silver, 2000). What sort of gains might result from such tragic losses? Our research on hundreds of bereaved persons in the two years following loss suggests that substantial percentages of grieving people grow closer to family and friends, develop a deeper sense of the spiritual dimension of life, or consciously adopt a healthier lifestyle. Others find a bittersweet benefit in the end of their loved one's suffering, and a few even describe a keener existential awareness of death as an eventuality in their own lives, one that is accepted with equanimity (Neimeyer, 2001d). These results are echoed by the findings of Frantz, Farrell, and Trolley (2001), and are reflected in Donald's reordered life priorities in the aftermath of his son's suicide. In contrast, Phyllis has not yet found compensation for the train of losses she has suffered, each of which has only reduced rather than enriched her life.

Current evidence suggests that benefit-finding differs from sense-making in its relationship to the outcomes of bereavement. Whereas the ability to understand a loss seems to predict favorable adaptation even in the early months of bereavement, the capacity to convert loss into gain typically unfolds slowly and is associated more strongly with long-term outcomes (Davis, Nolen-Hoeksema, & Larson, 1998). In Donald's case, for example, learning the lessons of loss in a constructive sense required five years of diligent effort on cognitive and emotional levels, suggesting that Phyllis, too, might harvest a sense of purpose or renewed priority from her losses if she were to cultivate them over a longer span of time. Experience with bereaved persons suggests the need for patience on the part of professional helpers and the bereaved themselves, as the unique silver lining associated with any given loss must be sought *within* that loss, not given to the survivor from an outside source.

One particularly important dimension of benefit-finding is revisiting the story of the relationship with the deceased in order to winnow sustaining themes of connection that can provide longer-term comfort and consolation. This is evidenced in the comfort many bereaved people find in reminiscing about their loved ones in the presence of caring friends and family. Simulating this situation, Maercker, Bonanno, Znoj, and Horowitz (1998) invited 44 bereaved spouses to talk for 18 minutes about their relationships with their deceased spouses, six months following their loss. The researchers then recorded and coded these reflections, looking for both positive and negative themes in the reminiscing and using these to predict the intensity and complications in the bereaved spouses' grieving eight months later. The results were revealing: the number of positive themes—of relational trust, intimacy, and positive characteristics of the deceased—predicted less debilitating grief in the future. Spouses who told predominantly positive stories of their life with their partner had fewer later reports of intrusive and distressing thoughts about the death or inclinations to avoid reminders of the loss. On the other hand, those whose stories revolved around negative themes of anger, despair, and regret tended subsequently to experience more intense grief and avoidance of reminders of the loss. This suggests the healing power of positive reminiscence as one means of finding benefit—if not in the loss itself, then in the life shared with one's own. Such a process would seem to be especially important in later life, when spouses commonly have lived the better part of their lives together.

Identity Reconstruction

If life is a story, then it is certainly one in which we show character development as the plot progresses, when we as protagonists encounter and overcome challenges and adversities. The loss of a loved one is surely among the most telling of these challenges, and the path to integrating such a loss into one's future life is one of the most powerful catalysts to personal growth. This is evident in the gradual evolution of Donald's identity following his son's suicide. As Donald grew to be calmer, more empathic, and more psychologically minded, he found new opportunities to apply his understanding of human suffering in his life and work with people with disabilities. A similar pattern of developing greater sensitivity to others, and acquiring a stronger and more mature sense of self as a "survivor" is reported by a substantial minority of the grieving people we have studied (Neimeyer, 2001d). For these people, weathering the storm of bereavement left them battered, but also unbeaten, giving rise to or reinforcing a "coping narrative" of themselves as resilient (Neimeyer & Levitt, 2001). In a sense, living a long life—one that is necessarily fraught with many losses—provides repeated opportunities to cultivate such personal growth or hardiness. Of course, less favorable outcomes are also possible: in our ongoing research, 12% of the bereaved speak of being sadder or more fearful people, and 6% describe themselves as more self-protective, unwilling to risk further hurt by reinvesting in relationships with others (Neimeyer, 2001d). Thus, the way in which we integrate our losses into our sense of self may be a major determinant of whether we experience "post-traumatic growth" or only "post-traumatic stress" in the wake of bereavement (Tedeschi, Park, & Calhoun, 1998).

Some Words Of Advice

Approaching bereavement as a process of reconstructing meaning (Neimeyer, 2001c) carries fresh implications for adapting to loss that are not as easily extracted from the traditional focus on the symptoms and stages of bereavement. Thus, I would like to close with a few thoughts of a practical kind, suggesting some ways of facilitating the sort of sense-making, benefit-finding, and identity reconstruction that is associated with constructive adaptation to loss.

To Each Its Own

In later life, losses tend to come in clusters, with the deaths of a spouse, siblings, and friends often occurring within the space of a few years. Moreover, these recognized losses often occur against the backdrop of others less visible, such as the loss of meaningful work, health, and home. It was this sort of bereavement overload (Parkes, 2001) that compromised Phyllis's ability to adapt. Still reeling from her father's death, Phyllis in quick succession lost her job, her husband, and her sister, while also contending with degenerating health. When losses overlap in this fashion, the grief and disorientation that attend one is compounded by the next, instigating a cycle of confusion, helplessness, and hopelessness that is difficult to break. Moreover, the stigmatization of older adults, in part as an expression of our widespread cultural death anxiety (DePaola, Neimeyer, & Ross, 1994), means that older people grappling with a sequence of losses may receive less support in their grief than their younger counterparts.

One response to the concentration of losses in a short period is to take care to grieve each loss in its own way, and in its own time. Of course, general support is valuable, but it is also helpful to reserve some quiet time to reflect on each loss in turn, asking, "What is it, most basically, that I have lost in connection with _______?" and "Who or what can help me most with what I need right now?" Sometimes this attempt to name the loss yields surprising answers. Reflecting on each of her losses, Phyllis realized that a common theme was the loss of unconditional love, which took different but related forms in her relationship with her father, work, husband, and sister. She then began considering how she might once again feel such love, perhaps through participating in a foster grandparent program, getting a pet, or spending more time with her daughter and new grandchild. Individuating losses can also help the grieving person explore the unique meanings, hidden lessons, and prompts to personal growth entailed in each loss. Donald, for example, had learned through his divorce that he needed to develop greater autonomy as an adult, being less dependent on his partner for traditionally female functions such as keeping house, cooking, and so on. The death of his son, however, prompted a rather different learning, centering on his need to slow down and deeply open himself to the feelings of others. Of course, life will not slow down just to allow a grieving person to finish grief work for one loss before undertaking another, but working on each loss individually can clarify the emotional and practical work that each loss requires.

Sustaining Bonds

Contemporary grief theory recognizes that the goal of grieving is not to let go so much as to find ways of preserving bonds to the lost loved one that help to sustain the bereaved person (Klass, Silverman, & Nickman, 1996). In fact, many researchers are now reporting what bereaved people often understand intuitively, that a sense of a deceased loved one's continued presence in their lives, even in vivid, sensory ways, is not only common but also welcome (Datson & Marwit, 1997). Of course, unsettling memories are also possible, especially if the death was traumatic or the relationship was conflicted. Phyllis, for example, seems to experience both the positive and negative aspects of this sense of presence; she is troubled by flashbacks to the horrific scene of her husband's death in the hospital, but she also has begun to access more comforting memories. Thus, the question is not *whether* to reconnect with the memory of lost loved ones, but rather how to do so in a way that gives solace rather than stress.

Fortunately, there are many practical ways of sustaining meaningful connection to a shared life story. The most common way is to reminisce with others, especially those whose lives were also touched by the deceased. More palpable connections are also possible, such as carrying forward projects that were important to both the deceased and the survivor (Attig, 2000). Moreover, there are several narrative methods for exploring and preserving the connection, including tracing the impact of the loved one's life on the survivor's own life, developing a biographical sketch of the deceased, or even exchanging "correspondence" by having the bereaved write to the deceased and then write back to him- or herself as if from the loved one's perspective (Neimeyer, 2001b). All of these methods have a common aim: to restore a sense of continuity to a shared history disrupted by death.

A Family Affair

One of the failings of traditional grief theories is that they have too often situated grief within individuals, rather than recognizing that it also plays out between people, on an intricately social level (Neimeyer, 2001b). At their worst, families can constrain the forms of grief expression and the patterns of adaptation available to the bereaved (Neimeyer & Keesee, 1998), assigning to some members a kind of second-class status. For example, families often exclude older persons from the circle of discussion and decision making about the illness and impending death of a member. Likewise, frail elders might be encouraged not to play a role in the funeral or memorial service for a loved one, out of a misguided attempt to protect the older person from an emotionally demanding situation (Walsh & McGoldrick, 1991). Although well intentioned, these efforts marginalize older persons, in essence devaluing both their emotional reactions and their potentially healing role in helping the family grieve their loss.

At their best, however, families represent the natural context for integrating a loss through shared conversation and ritual practices. Nadeau (1997) has documented the fascinating ways in which family members discuss, debate, and sometimes disagree as they struggle to come to terms with the meaning of a joint loss. Such collective efforts at sense-making can consolidate a comforting story of the death ("At last she is at peace." "I think she was asking permission to let go.") and help fix the meaning of the person's life ("He always had such a great sense of humor. I'll never forget the time he....").

Ritual forms of recognition are often an extension of such conversation. Donald, for example, following his son's suicide, arranged a memorial service in his home to which he invited not only his friends, but Chris's as well. Playing some of the CDs that his talented son had composed, Donald helped those who loved Chris to reach across generations and affirm their caring for him and for each other. Such rituals extend our sense of family beyond blood relatives and simultaneously draw on the social system to assist with our mutual grieving.

The Write Stuff

As critical as it is to grieve together, there are some features of loss that can only be experienced and integrated alone. Indeed, even in the closest of families and broader social networks, the same loss never translates fully into the same grief for different survivors (Gilbert, 1996). This reflects the irreducible individuality of grief (Neimeyer, 2001b), producing an inevitable gap in the grieving of family members. This kind of gap probably exacerbated the pre-existing tensions between Phyllis and her mother, as her father's death carried quite different significance for the two women. In such instances, it may be important for each person to attend to unique features of the loss for him- or herself, before attempting to reach out empathically to another.

One means of doing so is to encourage the grieving person into "conversations" with him- or herself, perhaps by keeping a journal. Pennebaker (1997), for example, has encouraged adults of all ages who are struggling with painful life events to write privately and vividly about them, particularly those they have never mentioned in the presence of others. Across a series of studies Pennebaker has consistently found that writing in a journal, even for as little as 20 minutes per day for a few successive days, promotes psychological healing, helping the writer to overcome a tendency toward limiting activities and even fostering improved physical health. In our own work, we are finding that people who find new meaning in their losses through keeping a journal make the greatest gains in mastering their grief symptoms. Encouraging reflective, emotionally resonant writing can be helpful, particularly when losses are multiple or grief is overwhelming (Neimeyer, 2001b).

Conclusion

Contemporary theories of bereavement are evolving to embrace the complex needs of people who grieve and are struggling to find meaning in their loss. This growing understanding offers several useful frameworks for grasping the subtle social and personal processes by which people come to terms with the loss of loved ones at all points in the life cycle. In this chapter, I have tried to sketch some of these evolving understandings, as they pertain to our attempts to make sense of the realities of loss, to find existential gifts even as something precious is taken away, and to cultivate new possibilities in a way that promotes growth. I hope that some of the themes touched on here offer encouragement to both bereaved persons and those who help them as they seek to reconstruct meaningful lives in the wake of loss. ■

Robert A. Neimeyer, PhD, holds a Dunavant University Professorship in the Department of Psychology, University of Memphis, where he also maintains an active clinical practice. Since completing his doctoral training at the University of Nebraska in 1982, he has published 18 books, including Meaning Reconstruction and the Experience of Loss, *and* Lessons of Loss: A Guide to Coping. *He serves as Editor of the journal* Death Studies *and is the author of more than 200 articles and book chapters. He is a researcher and a member of the American Psychological Association's Task Force on End-of-Life Issues. In recognition of his scholarly contributions, he has been granted the Distinguished Research Award by the University of Memphis, made a Fellow of the Clinical Psychology Division of the American Psychological Association, and given the Research Recognition Award by the Association for Death Education and Counseling.*

References

Attig, T. (2000). *The heart of grief.* New York: Oxford.

Barnes, M.K., Harvey, J.H., Carlson, H., & Haig, J. (1996). The relativity of grief. *Journal of Personal and Interpersonal Loss, 1,* 375-392.

Braun, M.L., & Berg, D.H. (1994). Meaning reconstruction in the experience of bereavement. *Death Studies, 18,* 105-129.

Carlsen, M.B. (1989). *Meaning making: Therapeutic process in adult development.* New York: Norton.

Datson, S.L., & Marwit, S.J. (1997). Personality constructs and perceived presence of deceased loved ones. *Death Studies, 21,* 131-146.

Davis, C.G., Nolen-Hoeksema, S., & Larson, J. (1998). Making sense of loss and benefiting from the experience: Two construals of meaning. *Journal of Personality and Social Psychology, 75,* 561-574.

Davis, C.G., Wortman, C.B., Lehman, D.R., & Silver, R.C. (2000). Searching for meaning in loss: Are clinical assumptions correct? *Death Studies, 24,* 497-540.

DePaola, S.J., Neimeyer, R.A., & Ross, S.K. (1994). Death concern and attitudes toward the elderly in nursing home personnel as a function of training. *Omega, 29,* 231-248.

Fortner, B.V., & Neimeyer, R.A. (1999). Death anxiety in older adults: A quantitative review. *Death Studies, 23,* 387-412.

Frantz, T., Farrell, M.M., & Trolley, B.C. (2001). Positive outcomes of losing a loved one. In R.A. Neimeyer (Ed.), *Measuring reconstruction and the experience of loss.* Washington, DC: American Psychological Association.

Gilbert, K.R. (1996). "We've had the same loss, why don't we have the same grief?" Loss and differential grief in families. *Death Studies, 20,* 269-284.

Hall, M., & Irwin, M. (2001). Physiological indices of functioning in bereavement. In M.S. Stroebe, R. Hansson, W. Stroebe, & H. Schut (Eds.), *Handbook of bereavement research* (pp. 473-491). Washington, DC: American Psychological Association.

Klass, D. Silverman, P.R., & Nickman, S. (Eds.) (1996). *Continuing bonds: New understandings of grief.* Washington, DC: Taylor & Francis.

Maerker, A., Bonanno, G.A., Znoj, H. & Horowitz, J.J. (1998). Prediction of complicated grief by positive and negative themes in narratives. *Journal of Clinical Psychology, 54,* 1117-1136.

Moss, M.S., Moss, S.Z., & Hansson, R. (2001). Bereavement in old age. In M.S. Strobe, R. Hansson, W. Stroebe, & H. Schut (Eds.), *Handbook of bereavement research* (pp. 241-260). Washington, DC: American Psychological Association.

Nadeau, J.W. (1997). *Families making sense of death.* Newbury Park, CA: Sage.

Neimeyer, R.A. (2000). Searching for the meaning of the meaning: Grief therapy and the process of reconstruction. *Death Studies, 24,* 541-558.

Neimeyer, R.A. (2001a). The language of loss. In R.A. Neimeyer (Ed.), *Meaning reconstruction and the experience of loss.* Washington, DC: American Psychological Association.

Neimeyer, R.A. (2001b). *Lessons of loss: A guide to coping.* New York: Brunner Routledge.

Neimeyer, R.A. (2001c). *Meaning reconstruction and the experience of loss.* Washington, DC: American Psychological Association.

Neimeyer, R. A. (2001d). Reauthoring life narratives: Grief therapy as meaning reconstructions. *Israeli Journal of Psychiatry, 38,* 171-183.

Neimeyer, R.A., & Keesee, N.J. (1998). Dimensions of diversity in the reconstruction of meaning. In K.J. Doka & J.D. Davidson (Eds.). *Living with grief: Who we are, how we grieve* (pp. 223-237). Washington, DC: Hospice Foundation of America.

Neimeyer, R.A., & Levitt, H. (2001). Coping and coherence: A narrative perspective. In C.R. Snyder (Ed.), *Perspectives on coping.* New York: Wiley.

Parkes, C.M. (2001). *Bereavement* (3rd ed.). London & New York: Brunner Routledge.

Pennebaker, J. (1997). *Opening up.* New York: Guilford.

Polkinghorne, D.E. (1988). *Narrative knowing and human sciences.* Albany, NY: State University of New York.

Rando, T.A. (1995). Grief and mourning: Accommodating to loss. In H. Wass & R.A. Neimeyer (Eds.) *Dying: Facing the facts* (pp. 211-241). Washington, DC: Taylor & Francis.

Tedeschi, R., Park, C., & Calhoun, L. (Eds.). (1998). *Posttraumatic growth: Positive changes in the aftermath of crisis.* Mahwah, NJ: Lawrence Erlbaum.

Viney, L.L. (1991). The personal construct theory of death and loss. *Death Studies, 15,* 139-155.

Walsh, F., & McGoldrick, M. (1991). *Living beyond loss.* New York: Norton.

Chapter 27

Counseling Later-Life Families

Janice Winchester Nadeau

It is better to go to a home where there is mourning than to one where there is a party, because the living should always remind themselves that death is waiting for us all. Sorrow is better than laughter; it may sadden your face, but it sharpens your understanding. Someone who is always thinking about happiness is a fool. A wise person thinks about death.

—Ecclesiastes 7: 2–4

Introduction

Grief is a family affair. Families with a preponderance of older members face particular loss and grief issues. Aging involves change, and change brings loss. Families do not remain static. As family members age and change, the group also moves through developmental stages. Grieving the loss of what was is natural and, perhaps, necessary in order to embrace the present and move forward. Experiences of loss are prevalent in later stages of family development. There is much to understand and appreciate about later-life families who are grieving. This chapter explores some of the challenges of later-life families, discusses concepts that may be useful in understanding them, and suggests some approaches to counseling.

Socrates said that the beginning of wisdom is the definition of terms. What is meant by the term *later life*? When speaking of individuals, it is often said that age is more about attitude than it is about calendar years. When discussing families, rather than individuals, we have to consider that most families have members of all ages. So, what characterizes a family in *later life*? For lack of a clear definition and for the sake of clarity and emphasis, let us assume that families in later life are those who have a preponderance of older members. In such families losses are myriad and demands on family resources are great.

What follows is a brief outline of types of loss that later-life families may experience as well as a summary of family concepts that will prove useful in the subsequent discussion of counseling families in later life.

Loss in Later-Life Families

David Peretz, (1970) defined loss as the experience of being without something (or someone) that one once had. I would add to this the notion that people also experience loss when we lose something we *thought* we possessed and would continue to possess. In later-life couples, for example, if one of the couple dies sooner than expected, the wished for or anticipated retirement years together are lost.

Peretz's (1970) categories are helpful in considering the myriad losses that challenge later-life families: *loss of possessions, developmental loss, loss of self, and loss of significant others.* Loss of possessions refers to the loss of concrete objects that give meaning to life. A striking example is the not uncommon pattern of an older family member's moving from a family homestead to a senior living apartment or residence, to a nursing home, and finally to a point where everything the older family member possesses can be contained in one bag. An image comes to mind of an older woman carrying every thing she owns in a canvas bag attached to her walker: the nursing home "bag lady," as some have described this phenomenon.

Peretz's second type of loss is developmental loss. This type of loss is experienced as family members move from one developmental stage to another. The stage of old age is characterized by learning to cope with losses of all kinds. The role reversal that occurs between the generations, sometimes referred to as the stage of parenting parents, is peppered with loss for all players. The effect of such changes can be overwhelming to families in terms of family structure and interaction patterns, the need for increased resources, including time and money, and the sense of loss as younger generations witness their elders becoming more and more frail. Younger family members must adjust to the absence of a functioning older generation and eventually to becoming the older generation themselves. Even if one is 70 and has a 90-year-old parent, one is not yet "orphaned."

A third type of loss is the loss of self. By that, Peretz means the loss of some aspect of the self, some mental representation or image of one's person and body. Later-life losses include loss of physical faculties, the loss of independence, and loss of the ability to work and contribute to society. Families struggle with such emotionally charged issues as what to do when they think that an older family member is no longer safe driving a car. Caring family members may be torn between the conflicting needs to protect family members (and others on the highway) and the need to preserve the aging member's independence. The aging member may fear the dependency that could accompany such a loss and object vociferously. Loss is a family affair.

Other losses of self that older members may experience include loss of life roles such as worker, provider, and caretaker. I remember my own father complaining of how differently he was treated at an animal feed store when he was no longer active in his role as a dairy farmer. He felt as if he had become invisible, since he was no longer the customer he had been in years past. His sense of identity and worth were threatened.

Many elders experience the loss of safety, including doubts or fears about financial security, going out alone, particularly at night, living alone, and trusting the health care system and/or their family to be there when they need help. Loss of health becomes more likely in later life. Family members are affected to greater or lesser degrees depending upon the particulars of the family structure, family dynamics, and the nature of the losses.

The fourth type of loss identified by Peretz is the loss of others. This type of loss may occur through divorce, by death, or through the "death" of a relationship, the loss that occurs when people stay in marriages or relationships that are no longer life-giving or have changed from relationships of give and take to caretaker-care receiver relationships. A classic example is when a disease such as Alzheimer's afflicts a family member. While care taking and care receiving may be meaningful on a number of levels, it remains true that the relationship as it once was has been lost. The prototypical loss of other, however, is by way of death. Issues related to this type of loss are emphasized in the remainder of this chapter.

Finally, the important assumptions of this chapter are that any change by its essential nature results in loss and that the human response to loss is grief. Later life is fraught with change, loss, and grief, and later-life families face many challenges.

Systems Concepts Used In Counseling Later-Life Families

Since the early 1950s family scholars have borrowed ideas from systems theory to better describe certain features of the family. Hall and Fagan (1956) defined a system as "a set of objects together with relationships among the objects and between their attributes." In family systems theory the "system" is a set of family members and the relationships among them and among their attributes.

Family grief can be thought of as family restructuring, which means changing family roles, rules, and boundaries. Roles are the behaviors, responsibilities, and privileges that are associated with certain positions in the family, such as parent, grandparent, child, and sibling (Stryker, 1972). Roles are also continuously created and maintained as family members interact with one another and, therefore, may include roles such as scapegoat, family star, peacemaker, black sheep, "family therapist," mascot, sick one, and so forth.

When a family member dies, the family is bereft not only of the person lost but also of the roles that that member played within the family. In its attempt to survive as a system we can expect, according to family systems theory, that a family will attempt to fill the vacuum left by the missing role. Noticing what roles the dying or deceased family member played and how a particular family goes about filling the lost roles will go a long way toward understanding a grieving family's behavior. Such understanding can help us tailor interventions if intervention is indicated. Many grief helpers are familiar with the worrisome phenomenon of the "parentified" child. This occurs when a child, sometimes at a remarkably young age, attempts to assume the role of a deceased parent. The child may be encouraged and praised by well-meaning others to assume such responsibility, but by assuming adult responsibilities at so early an age the child loses his or her own childhood.

Rules are the unspoken family understandings that govern all of family life. Role function as discussed above is a good example of the governing function of family rules. When a family member is dying or has died, a broad spectrum of family rules is needed. Flexible families, those with the required range of rules, are thought to survive best. For example, a flexible family would be one in which roles are interchangeable. Behaviors are not rigidly assigned to any one member. On the occasion of a member's death there are others who can assume his or her roles in the family.

Conversely, it is not uncommon even in this day and age for later-life families to have more rigid role assignment. A surviving spouse may have little or no experience with the roles his or her partner played. A widower may have no idea of how to do a load of wash or where the Christmas decorations are, or a widow may have no experience with balancing the checkbook or changing the furnace filter. Relationally, the one who died may have been the "emotional glue" in the family and without this person the family may become disconnected.

Boundaries delineate the elements belonging to the system and those belonging to its environment (Broderick & Smith, 1979). Family boundaries most relevant to grieving families include the boundary that delineates who is in the family and the boundaries around subgroups within the family. Critical changes occur in family boundaries when a family member is dying or has died. At such times family boundaries may become more open. Families who generally do not welcome outsiders into their family may, of necessity, allow others in to help them. Because of this boundary dynamic hospice workers or home health providers may gain access when most others would not be welcome.

The question of who is in the family and who is not in the family is not a simple one. Even in later-life families who have had years to work out such matters, some family members may be more "in" than others. Differences will play out at the time of terminal illness and death. Noticing boundary characteristics and shifts will help helpers to be more sensitive and to know whether to intervene. It is by way of these boundary shifts that families restructure themselves following the death of a member or members.

Other boundary features that are important to notice are the boundaries around subgroups in the family. They may be made of groupings of two or more within a family. Often, the family member likely to be most bereaved is one who had previously been in a two-person alliance or coalition with the one who has died. Others in the family can carry on with their fellow subgroup members and thereby experience relatively less disruption. I call this phenomenon being "left hanging from the family tree." It is a family dynamic likely to be more intense in later-life families where there are fewer resources and greater needs. The one "left hanging" may require more or different forms of support.

Special Issues: Closeness and Asynchronous Grieving

In addition to the systems concepts described above, there are two other family grieving patterns that are noteworthy: changes in the degree of emotional closeness and asynchronous grieving. The degree of emotional closeness among family members usually changes in times of loss and grief. Clinically, what I have observed is that family members become closer than usual around the time of death and then drift back to their pre-loss level of closeness over time. Some family members experience an additional loss when this drifting apart occurs, while others are relieved at having regained their familiar emotional distance. Families seem to be helped by having these changes acknowledged and having support tailored to their varied reactions.

The second family systems issue, asynchronous grieving, is bound to occur but when families have unspoken rules calling for synchronizing their grief, distress is increased. Differences may be in terms of timing, intensity, duration, or style. At the root of differences are such factors as relationship to the deceased, gender, age, previous experience with loss, and a multitude of personal characteristics. One of the differences acted out most often is between males and females in the family since, historically, female ways of grieving have been the "gold standard." Because of traditional gender roles and stereotypes, later-life families may have more problems with asynchronous grieving than do younger families.

Counselors can help by normalizing the diversity of grieving behaviors and doing so in the presence of as many other family members as possible. Family grief counseling and therapy is well suited to such work.

Family Meanings And Counseling Later-Life Families In Grief

While family systems thinking is useful in understanding some aspects of family grief, it cannot capture how families make sense of their experience. Systems theory also fails to reveal how the meanings that families attach to a death influence their grieving. For such understanding we turn to social constructionist theories such as symbolic interaction theory (see the further reading list for this chapter). The main idea of symbolic interaction theory is that people make sense of their experience by interacting with each other, and families are the primary sites of such interaction. Rosenblatt and Fischer (1993) point out that from a symbolic interactionist's perspective it is less important to know whether or not an event actually happened then whether or not people believed it happened.

Thomas (1923), a social interactionist most well known for his self-fulfilling prophecy theory, contends that if people define situations as real, then those situations are real in their consequences. Grieving families make sense of the dying and death of a family member by using certain methods called family meaning-making strategies. The meanings they make with these methods greatly influence how they will grieve (Nadeau, 1998). For example, if a family construes the death of an older family member as a relief because he or she was in acute pain, they will grieve differently than if they construe a loved one's death as the result of a medical error and, therefore, untimely.

Paying attention to the ways families make sense of the death of a family member and tracking their meanings over time provide a focus for grief counseling. Some meanings are associated with higher levels of distress than are others. Intervention, which is discussed below, consists of working with the processes by which families struggle to make meaning. The struggle may be intensified in later-life families in which losses are likely to occur more frequently and draw heavily upon family resources.

Approaches To Counseling Later-Life Families In Grief

Keeping the Family Context in View

First and foremost, the greatest challenge is to focus on the family as the "unit of care." This has been a goal in hospice care from the start. So much of what we know about grief is about individual grief, not family grief. I find it helpful to start the first family encounter by drawing a genogram, which is a graphic depiction of the family showing relatedness, gender, ages, and multigenerational patterns of connection, conflict, and former losses (see the further reading list for this chapter). This is a relatively nonthreatening way to join the family and to collect data that will be invaluable in either short- or long-term counseling. I keep the genogram in view for each subsequent meeting to bridge current events and the family's history. I also expand the genogram with new information as it emerges.

Helping the Family Make Sense of Its Loss

Much of what is important about family grief can be seen through the lens of family meaning-making, that is, the actual interactive processes used by families to make sense of their loss (Nadeau, 1998). This approach is one of helping families enhance behaviors that appear to support meaning-making and reduce factors that seem to inhibit it. To the degree that this approach is successful, families are more likely to construct meanings that will be congruent with their family values, style, and beliefs. The goal of such an approach is to reduce the overall level of family distress and promote family well-being. It is most important that a would-be helper starts by noticing the natural ways a given family goes about making sense of the experience.

Some interventions described below will apply more to longer term counseling, but keeping some of the basic ideas in mind may be helpful even in the briefest of family encounters.

Helping Families Tell Their Story

Most families attempt to make sense of the death of a family member by telling the story of how their loved one died (Nadeau, 1998). When there is a diagnosis of terminal illness or when an older member is obviously becoming frail, family members begin to construct the story by talking among themselves and with others. If the death is sudden or unexpected the story begins with the circumstances of the death event. After someone dies, the funeral rituals provide time-limited opportunities for storytelling and meaning-making, but most families run out of opportunities to tell their story before they run out of the need to tell. Later-life family members have more history to recall, and former losses are likely to be revisited with each subsequent loss. Losses occur more frequently. Some later-life families may have more time for storytelling than their younger counterparts.

Simply *listening* to family stories, as ordinary as it may sound, is our most powerful intervention. Meanings are embedded in family stories, and it is in the repeated telling of their stories that families come to new meanings (Nadeau, 1998). Intervention consists of helping a family to find family-specific ways of telling the story over and over again. Critical times such as the anniversary of the death, the deceased person's birthday, and holidays provide good opportunities for gathering family members in community to elicit storytelling.

Listening becomes a more difficult task if the death has been sudden or traumatic or there have been multiple deaths. The family may want help in reviewing media releases, autopsies, medical examiners' records, and pictures of crime scenes. They may want to revisit the horrific events of the death again and again. In such cases, special therapy skills are required: knowing how to limit the amount of stimuli the family is exposed to at any one time, how to deal with one death at a time, how to deal with emotional flooding and the like. Psychotherapy techniques not unlike those used for the treatment of post-traumatic stress disorder may be indicated in such cases.

Listening may be more of a problem for the counselor or therapist whose own loss or losses could be recent or may not have been grieved. When this is the case, counselors tend to unconsciously draw back and some families in pain seem to be very sensitive to the helper's uneasiness with their story and may even begin to "take care of" the counselor.

Creating a Safe Environment and Taking a Neutral Stance

Family members are most likely to share with one another if they feel emotionally safe (Nadeau, 1998). The need for a safe environment may be even greater for later-life families who grew up in an age when people in general were less likely to turn to strangers, such as grief counselors, for help with their emotional pain. They may see needing grief counseling as a sign of weakness. A sense of security is enhanced when the counselor maintains a sense of wonder and curiosity as the family members interact about their loss. Safety is enhanced when the counselor can maintain a nonanxious presence, explore the meanings families present, and resist the temptation to impose his or her meanings upon the family. It is helpful in family grief therapy to notice differences in the meanings that family members make and how they go about making them interactively. Validating diverse meanings as they emerge goes a long way toward helping families come to meanings that promote their well-being.

Gathering the Family

Family meaning-making is enhanced when multiple family members are present, when multiple generations are represented, and when in-laws are included (Nadeau, 1998). The generations are likely to connect with one another and bring different information. This helps the family as a whole to make sense of what has occurred. The presence of in-laws stimulates the making of meaning in that they are not subject in the same way as immediate family are to any taboos about what can be discussed, and they can ask innocent questions. In later-life families there may be limits to how many members can be gathered together at one time; in which case, inviting peers to the sessions can invigorate the interactive processes. The system can be expanded further if members are asked what missing members, both absent and deceased, would say if they were present. This effectively expands the system, enriches the storytelling, and facilitates making sense of what has occurred.

In-Session Techniques That Can Facilitate Meaning-Making

In a study of multigenerational grieving families (Nadeau, 1998) some "natural" strategies that families used to make sense of a death in the family emerged. Using what families tend to do as a starting point for intervention is a reasonable way to proceed. Family strategies include talking about dreams, comparing the current death with other deaths, characterizing the lost member, and giving meaning to so-called, coincidences. The first of these strategies, talking about dreams, introduces meanings that otherwise might be outlawed by family rules. Encouraging family members to tell about their dreams and their interpretations of them acts as a catalyst to family meaning-making.

Comparing the current deaths with others is a strategy that helps families establish themselves among their reference group of all grieving families (Nadeau, 1998). Directly asking families to compare their current loss with other deaths, both within and outside the family, usually results in productive conversation. Families shed their self-consciousness and constructive meaning-making can progress.

Characterizing the deceased nearly always occurs in some form or another. It may begin at the time of diagnosis of terminal illness or immediately upon hearing of a sudden death. Characterizing the deceased is woven into funeral rituals, including the eulogy, and it continues for as long as the family tells the story. Characterizing plays a critical role in what meanings the family will attach to a given death (Nadeau, 1998). In later-life families, there may be long life histories to review and grief counseling can include these reviews using a variety of personal belongings, pictures, or articles to help families attach meaning to their loved one's life and death.

Giving meaning to so-called, coincidences associated with the death is a commonly used family strategy that I have referred to as, "coincidancing" (Nadeau, 1998). Sometimes families attribute the events to acts of the deceased or acts of God. Asking families whether they have noticed any so-called, coincidences and if so, what they make of them will generally reveal the terrain of the family meaning system and enable the counselor to help them navigate the rough spots.

Conclusions

Later-life families grieve many losses and grief is a family affair. Hospice has traditionally cast the family as the unit of care When counseling families of any stage of life it is important to remember that in order to understand and intervene well, we must pay attention to the particulars of a given family. This includes collecting information on their history, their multigenerational patterns, changes in family roles, rules, and boundaries, listening to the family story, and ferreting out the family meaning system. This is what it means to focus on the family, rather than the individual.

Later-life families have particular needs and deserve our special attention. As counselors of later-life families, we must keep the family context in view. We must be prepared to function as travel guides, suggesting alternative routes, and noticing bumps in the road and potential potholes. We have to recognize that we bring to the counseling situation our own family rules and sense of how things ought to be. To the degree we have come to terms with our own family grief, we will be capable of entering in and helping in times of great emotional pain and family turmoil. Counselors who work with families who are grieving know how rewarding such "entering in" can be, both for the families and for the counselors themselves. ■

Janice Winchester Nadeau, PhD, is a licensed marriage and family therapist, psychologist, and nurse. She has been active in the death and dying field for 25 years. Her book, Families Making Sense of Death, *won the National Council on Family Relations and Sage Book Award. She is a member of the International Work Group on Death, Dying and Bereavement and a clinical member of the American Association of Marriage and Family Therapy. She also serves on a scientific advisory panel at the Center for the Advancement of Health in Washington, DC, for a study sponsored by the Project on Death in America. In 2000 she received The Distinguished Service to Families Award from the Minnesota Association of Marriage and Family Therapy for her work with grieving families. Nadeau is in private practice at Minnesota Human Development Consultants in Minneapolis.*

References

Hall, A.D., & Fagan, R.E. (1956). Definitions of systems [Revised introductory chapter of *General systems*]. New York: Bell Telephone Laboratories. (Reprinted from *General systems, 1, 18-28*).

Nadeau, J.W. (1998). *Families making sense of death.* Thousand Oaks, CA: Sage.

Peretz, D. (1970). Development, Object-Relationships, and Loss. In B. Schoenberg, A.C. Carr, D. Peretz, & A.H. Kutscher (Eds.), *Loss and grief. Psychological management in medical practice.* (p.5). New York: Columbia University Press.

Rosenblatt, P.C. & Fischer, L.R. (1993). Qualitative family research. In P.B. Boss, W.J. Doherty, R. LaRossa, W.R. Schumm, & S.D. Steinmetz (Eds.), *Source book of family theories and methods: A contextual approach.* New York: Plenum.

Stryker, S. (1972). Symbolic interaction theory: A review and some suggestions for comparative family research. *Journal of Comparative Family Studies, 3* (1), 17-32.

Thomas, W.I. (1923). *The unadjusted girl.* Boston: Little, Brown.

Additional Reading

Broderick, C.B. (1993). *Understanding family process.* Newbury Park, CA: Sage. Includes information on family systems theory.

Cooley, C.H. (1909). *Social Organization.* New York: Scribner. Historical readings from the Chicago School of Sociology on Symbolic Interaction Theory.

James, W. (1890). *Principles of psychology.* (Vol.2). New York: Holt. Historical readings from the Chicago School of Sociology on Symbolic Interaction Theory.

McGoldrick, M. & Gerson, R. (1985). *Genograms in family assessment.* New York: Norton & Company. Includes technical information on genograms.

Mead, G.H. (1936). *Movements of thought in the nineteenth century.* Chicago: University of Chicago Press. Historical readings from the Chicago School of Sociology on Symbolic Interaction Theory.

Nadeau, J.W. (1998). *Families making sense of death* (Appendix). Thousand Oaks, CA: Sage. Includes a list of questions that may be used to elicit family stories.

Walker, A.J., Manoogian-O'Dell, M., McGraw, L.A., & White, D.L.G. (Eds.). (2001). *Families in later life. Connections and transitions.* Thousand Oaks, CA: Sage. Includes empirical selections and literary pieces on later-life families.

CHAPTER 28

Expressive Therapies: Piecing Together the Quilt of Life

Virginia Lynn Fry

In the weeks after the terrorist attacks of September 11, 2001, I visited many older cancer patients and bereaved survivors. They offered their own perspectives on this national tragedy and the grief that has followed. An 80-year-old woman said, "Ever since my diagnosis of cancer, I have felt like I have been living in another world, apart from the rest of the world. Only my sister crosses between the two worlds because she has to take care of me. But now, since the attacks, I feel like our worlds are closer together." Another terminally ill patient said, "I don't feel so lonely now."

Being alone in grief and loss is devastating at any age. It is particularly difficult for older persons, who may be more physically and socially isolated than the rest of us. In the aftermath of the terrorist attacks, many older persons found solace in the sharing of stories of human suffering, compassion, and community. Such emotional support and sense of connectedness were significant responses to those attacks.

Similar responses are evoked when people recall earlier experiences of shared national trauma. I collected stories from patients describing where they were when Pearl Harbor was bombed, when Nagasaki and Hiroshima were bombed, and when President Kennedy was killed. Through remembering these events, people relived their shock, horror, and doubt about the future of such a violent world, as they wove their personal histories into this moment in time. Some of my patients literally pulled the pieces out from under the bed, where the yellowed newspaper clippings had been living a forgotten dusty life. The patients cut and pasted the clippings into place, surrounding this new terror with a history of survival and faith that life will again be healed.

The actual cutting and piecing together of broken pieces of our lives into a new whole is an age-old practice of what is now called *expressive therapy,* but was then just good common sense. A hundred years ago, if a loved one died, the bereaved gave away the person's clothes to those who cherished him or her and could use them. The remaining clothes were cut into pieces and stitched together into memory quilts. Others would join in this task, which took many hours over many months, and many stories would be told about the missing loved one. Thus, people grieved in community and gave their grief meaning—and they got a warm quilt to wrap around themselves just when they were missing those loving arms the most. It was good sense to express grief through handiwork.

For the past 20 years, I have traveled from hospitals to homes to schools, helping people understand grief and the time and creative actions it takes to heal. It usually makes sense to people at a gut level—when you feel things strongly, you have to move the emotions out of your body or you get sick. If you use a medium, such as a memory quilt or a personal-history collage, it serves to relieve the emotional intensity and transform the feelings into something bearable. This process often results in a symbol, ritual, object, or something that adds meaning to the pain. Victor Frankl, a survivor of Auschwitz concentration camp, wrote of this in *Man's Search for Meaning.* Suffering without meaning is intolerable. Only when meaning is found does the pain of grief become tolerable.

Grieving people sometimes don't know the meaning of their suffering until they use an expressive therapy to explore it. Another survivor of unimaginable torture was led through this process by her therapist, who helped her to blow up balloons and name her antagonists and draw faces on each balloon. Then she decided to destroy each balloon/person. At first she was too timid to strike, and the pin the therapist gave her just bounced off the balloon's stretched rubber. When she was reminded of what this balloon/person had done to her, she was able to stab and destroy her nemesis.

With each balloon's death, she became bolder, finally dropping the end of the couch on the last one! Breathless, she looked around at all the balloon carcasses and decided that she needed a symbolic funeral for them. She gathered them into a shoebox and dug a hole in the backyard. After she shoveled the dirt over the dead ones, she said a few words of compassion and forgiveness and forgave herself for being a victim, as well. Her final act in this life-healing ritual was to plant a flower on the grave so that something good might grow from all the pain she had endured. This was all quite spontaneous and surprising but a truly organic expression of grief that led to great peace at the end of her life.

The Buddhists have an ancient saying that describes this grief work: "You cannot prevent the Birds of Sorrow from flying over your head. *But* you can prevent them from building nests in your hair!" In fact, that is an apt job description of what many bereavement counselors do—we just keep those Birds of Sorrow moving!

Sometimes, *music* is the most effective means of connecting because it is a subliminal and powerful medium. You don't have to pay attention or even know that music is on for it to affect your blood pressure, pulse rate, and stress level. I once met an older Austrian woman in a nursing home and brought her Vivaldi's music to transform the sterile environment. But she hated it! So I asked her what music she had loved in her childhood. Austrian waltzes, she answered.

I went to the library and recorded waltzes on a cassette. Then I played the tape for her. Her wrinkled, cranky face transformed into an excited child's as she described the dancing of kings and queens swirling in ball gowns as she watched from the balcony of her parent's chateau. When the waltzes ended, I asked what music came next in her life? Military marches—it was war! A sample of these enabled her to relive that time. Then we added "that crazy flapper music" that greeted her immigration to America. We taped the jazz that played as she dated, her wedding music, and so on. She ended up with a 90-minute cassette tape of her whole life—a personal musical history, which she used to time-travel out of that sick body and the isolation of a nursing home to happier times in her life.

Another hospice patient used needlework to express her history in an *embroidered family tree.* She and I drew a tree with roots to represent her mother, three brothers, and three sisters. Across the base of the tree she drew lines that blocked the connection to each sister because she said she had to protect herself from each of these relationships. As she named each brother's root, she relived their meaning in her life and their deaths. The closest one to her trunk had lived with her for 10 years and then died of a heart attack in her home. Her mother was the center taproot, which grew around a large black hole in the roots. This hole she named her father because he had died when she was a baby, but his absence had been a central and dark presence in the life of her family.

The trunk was strong and surrounded by wisteria, a beautiful, but deadly, purple flowering vine that overcomes and kills other vegetation and even destroys buildings. She said, "I am the trunk of my family tree, and the wisteria is the cancer that is choking the life out of me. But it has brought me some beautiful things too!"

Her branches were her family—her ex-husband was a broken branch, her children the strong branches, with animals and nests for spouses and grandchildren. But one lower branch was broken with the end dangling. She explained, "This is my son who drowned 10 years ago. I didn't identify his body because the police told me that his face had been eaten by fishes! But I have regretted that decision ever since, because I have dreamed a hundred nightmares of different ways his face could look. How much worse could the one truth have been than a hundred fears?"

That dangling branch symbolized her unreconciled grief, which she hid most of the time. Seeing it clearly on her embroidery made her determined to do something about it. She wanted to write a poem but was afraid and didn't know how to begin. So we wrote a grief poem together, "I Light a Candle for You," and she embroidered that too. Then she created a small ritual space on a shelf between the family tree and her poem, where she could light a candle from her recliner and be with her memories of her son in the long and lonely evenings.

Many cultures encourage the creation of *personal shrines* in the home to remember those the family has lost or is worried about. In America, this is often frowned upon and seen as a failure to move on in life by focusing on the dead. In fact, it has the opposite effect—it enables us to recognize the ties to the past as we incorporate the loss and love into our present lives.

Expressing the grief in *memory boxes* frees the grieving person from having to carry the burdens of the past, while also containing the grief so that it does not spread destructively all over his or her present life. Memories, both good and bad, can be symbolized in objects small enough to fit into a box, yet poignant enough to represent a multitude of recollections. My mother-in-law created such a box for my children; it included Grandpa's World War II medals and ribbons from three invasions, which he would never talk about. It also included his ski medals from 70 years of skiing, of which he was very proud.

The Circle of Life is a powerful Native American symbol that shows life, as we know it, to represent only half of the circle. After death is the second half, and it includes the possibility of reunion with loved ones, spiritual fulfillment, and movement toward rebirth. Drawing personal *life circles* with grieving people can help them express their own spiritual beliefs and hopes for the future.

One older widow drew a different life circle by using a paper plate, after realizing that her husband's death had left too big a hole in her "Pie of Life." She divided the paper plate into slices representing other aspects of her life: friends, church, bingo, hobbies, animals, music, and theater. As she surveyed her work, she realized that if she put her attention and time into each of these, it would shrink her husband's hole in her pie to a livable slice. She commented, "I will always miss him, but I can still have my pie and eat it too!"

Paper plates were a useful tool of expression for another grieving person, who had difficulty naming the jumble of confusing emotions he was experiencing. Using paints, he created a color key—blue for sadness, red for anger, orange for worry, green for fear, black for regrets, purple for loneliness, yellow for happiness, and so on. Then he filled the plate with colors as if it were his body filled with feelings. The innermost colors and largest areas of colors were the most important at that moment. Each week he painted his "Map of Feelings," as he came to call them, and he could see the problem areas, brainstorm action to take, and chart his progress through acute grief to a less painful and more fulfilling life.

Coping with feelings of regret, shame, and blame makes bereavement extremely difficult. I often bring an old iron pot with me to such visits and invite the grieving person to write out these feelings—in total privacy, with candles and music sometimes to help get in touch with the feelings. This is especially useful for expressing disenfranchised grief—the kind of pain that is difficult to admit in this culture, like the loss of a pet or a loss through suicide, AIDS, or even divorce. People who think they have nothing to say will write pages, while crying, then set fire to the lot. You can see the weight of such feelings lift from their shoulders as the flames leap into the air. Finding the right spot to distribute the ashes is the last step in this simple cleansing-by-burning ritual, which allows one's personal garbage to become manure and enables something good to grow from such pain. Our bereavement groups always end with this burning ritual, and it provides powerful healing for all.

Sometimes the pain of loss is overwhelming, and all we want to do is lie on the floor and moan. This is a fabulous thing to do for grief, and it is called *yoga*. It is as simple as that—no human pretzels necessary. My yoga teacher is over 60 years old, as are many of the participants. After the terrorist attacks on New York City and Washington, DC, and the heroic plane crash in Pennsylvania, not only were the churches full, so were the yoga classes. Learning to let out the pain through deep breathing and connecting to open-hearted compassion is the most healing expressive therapy I know. It is not uncommon to hear sniffs, sobs, and sighs in our group as we stretch our contracted bodies, which are weary from carrying the weight of the world.

Yoga homework consists of remembering to breathe into our bellies whenever we feel stress, anger, hate, fear, frustration, or desire for revenge, and to recognize the potential terrorist that lives inside each of us. "I am that too" is a powerful meditation for finding compassion. We have discovered that healing is possible when such a meditation is combined with this final expressive assignment: "Now, do five deep sighs from my door to yours!"

All of these expressive therapies ease the loneliness of bereavement. The key to all of them is creating a connection with others through some medium that can help bereaved persons express themselves and thereby ease their pain. This is especially important for older persons, who may be physically or socially isolated. This kind of emotional support and connectedness is one way to revive the lost tradition of grieving as a community. ■

Virginia Lynn Fry is Director of the Hospice and Palliative Council of Vermont and Bereavement Coordinator for Central Vermont Home Health and Hospice. She is the author of the award-winning Part of Me Died Too, *and the forthcoming* Will There Still Be Birthdays?, *which includes the use of detailed expressive therapies for all ages.*

References

Chodron, P. (1997). *When things fall apart: Heart advice for difficult times.* Boston: Shambala Publications.

Epstein, M. (1988). *Going to pieces without falling apart. A Buddhist perspective on wholeness.* New York: Dell Publishing.

Morehouse, J. (Director). (1995). *How to make an American quilt* [Film]. Produced by Amblin Entertainment, Los Angeles, CA (Distributor: Universal Pictures).

Remen, R.N. (1994). *Kitchen table wisdom: Stories that heal.* New York: St. Martin's Press.

CHAPTER 29

Rituals and Stories: Creative Approaches to Loss in Later Life

D. Elaine Tiller

INTRODUCTION

Throughout all of life, from the day of birth until the moment of death, humans deal with change and transition. Life is about going through transitions and finding meaning in what we are leaving and where we are going, even during the transition period of grief. Another, more personal, way of looking at this is to say that we search to make sense out of who we have been, who we will be, and who we are in between.

Older persons, because of their longevity and wealth of experiences, have gone through more transitions, more grief, than younger persons. Older adults who have learned to adapt to change and find meaning in the midst of change can provide wisdom about growing through transitions. If we honor older persons by asking them to teach us through sharing their stories and history, and if we listen carefully, they become our elders. The word *elder* doesn't mean simply an old person—it means one who teaches, one who has knowledge and understanding. Our elders can become models for transition—for adjusting to and incorporating change.

One of the main ways people adjust to and incorporate change is through rituals and stories. These are some of the most sacred resources we have, and they need to be treated with respect, shared appropriately, and cherished personally. Life stories and rituals are ways we humans have of making sense out of our lives and finding meaning in our experiences.

Rituals

Through work with bereaved family members, I hear about rituals that help to bring a sense of meaning and acceptance during mourning. Funerals and memorial rites can help the grieving family by rallying a community of support around them during the initial period of grief. In the beginning of grief, people are numb, not feeling much, just operating on autopilot, so to speak. They manage to get through the funeral or memorial service but barely remember it afterwards or remember it as if it were a dream.

Rituals conducted some time after the death may be even more significant to the intensely bereaved. Often, bereaved family members spend much time and energy on planning and carrying out memorials and rituals. Perhaps this is another key to why these rituals are so significant in healing. By taking an active role in developing a ritual to remember and honor their loved one, the bereaved also take an active role in healing some of their own grief. Following are examples of persons who developed rituals to honor their deceased loved ones, enabling them to move further in their own grief work:

- A widow recently told me about a memorial service she planned for her deceased husband nine months after his death. The idea started forming for her because she wished to take his ashes to the seashore that he had loved so much. This woman had worked extensively on her grief by writing down many of her feelings and thoughts over those nine months. While putting together the service, she reread those writings, which helped her to do the planning for this special memorial ritual. She invited both her family and his to take part in this "interment" in the sea. As part of the ceremony, she gave each family member who wanted it a gift of some of his ashes. It was a special time of remembering and honoring her husband, as well as a special time for receiving and giving support within the extended family.

This woman reported feeling much more reconciled to her deep loss after the ceremony. She was able to begin looking to her future. Among other things, she began to look for a new job, and she hired a contractor to plan some changes in her home. Previous to this time of remembering and honoring her deceased husband, she was unable to look to the future with a sense of openness and hope. This memorial ritual time was a point of transition in her grief.

- A large Italian family developed many rituals throughout the year after the death of the father, to honor him and to incorporate their loss of him into their family traditions. On special holidays they would share stories of Dad from previous holidays, and on the first anniversary of his birthday after his death, they gathered to celebrate his life. They had all of the food Dad loved and would have wanted, including his favorite birthday cake. On the anniversary of his death, they gathered to go to the cemetery together, had a prayer and told stories about Dad, and then shared a meal at one of their favorite restaurants. They plan to continue these traditions as a way of honoring Dad and of teaching the next generation about him. These times together have been very important to this family in working through their grief.

- A family made up of a widow, her four grown children and their spouses, and her eight teenage grandchildren wanted to remember their husband, father, father-in-law, and granddad on the first Father's Day after his death. He had been an avid outdoorsman, with a deep love of camping, hiking, canoeing, and backpacking. The widow and her family decided that the best way of remembering Dad would be to take a family hike on Father's Day—a hike that he would have loved and shared joyously. One of the teenage grandsons decided to wear one of Grandpa's old sweat-stained T-shirts for the hike, creating another way of having Grandpa's memories with them.

- A widow wanted to include her husband in the holiday celebrations the first Christmas after his death. She decided to do this by decorating his urn of cremains, which was in the living room, with Christmas decorations. He had always loved Christmas decorations and had decorated the house elaborately, so this seemed a fitting way of incorporating him and the family's loss into the Christmas holidays. The whole family could laugh and enjoy the humor, but it also lessened their pain by helping them talk with each other about Dad and include their memories and their grief in the family holiday celebrations.
- An older woman ritualizes and honors the life of her deceased mother by buying flowers and a birthday card each year on her mother's birthday. She puts these with a candle on a small table in her living room and remembers her mother and all she meant to her throughout her life. She spends time thinking about their relationship and the love given and received, and how this has affected her own life as well as those of her children and grandchildren.
- An older parent whose adult child died remembers and honors her daughter by organizing, planning, and carrying out a fund-raising concert in honor of her daughter. She donates the proceeds to a hospital that was very involved in giving care to her daughter during her terminal illness. Other persons have found meaning in rituals honoring their deceased loved ones by taking part in fund raisers for a particular cause, such as the search for a cure for Alzheimer's, cancer, ALS, and others. Remembering and honoring are important in finding meaning in the life and death of our loved ones, thus incorporating their life and death into our own being and meaning.

Rituals provide ways to make the transition from what was and is now gone, to what will be. Rituals give hope for the future while they honor the past. Humans are ritual-creating beings. Rituals help to heal us, sustain us, comfort us, guide us, and reconcile us. Throughout the course of a lifetime, we use traditional rituals to mark major transition times in life—births, graduations, birthdays, weddings, retirement parties, anniversary parties, and funerals or memorial services. As life expectancy expands and as more and more people live longer, we should continue to develop rituals to acknowledge other turning points.

Creating new rituals helps to bring order out of chaos and begins the process of grieving the losses brought by transitions. Many people are beginning to develop rituals of acknowledging and dedicating persons to grandparenthood; leaving midlife and entering later life; acknowledging the losses and blessings in moving to a retirement home, assisted living home, or nursing home; and giving up a driver's license and becoming more dependent on family and community for transportation and mobility. These are some of the significant changes that most people go through if they live long enough, and rituals can help in acknowledging them and working through the transition times.

Best and Brunner's *Memories of Home: A Keepsake You Create* (1994) has many ideas for older persons and their families to use to ritualize the move from a home with cherished memories and to carry these memories with them in written and visual form. The book suggests taking a walk through the house one last time and sharing favorite memories in each room and in the yard, rather than just walking out without acknowledging what this final closing of the door means.

A major transition is the move from midlife to later life, which occurs for most people at about age 60. When the teenage checkout clerk at the Hallmark store automatically gives us the senior discount, we come face to face with the fact that we are entering our final stage of life.

Some women going through this transition have developed rituals and ceremonies to help them acknowledge the significance of this time of change in their lives. Instead of a traditional birthday party or retirement party, they have a "Croning Ceremony." This ceremony recognizes a woman's entrance into a new time of life and honors the gifts of wisdom she has gained by having lived and learned for six or more decades. These women are returning to the old meaning of the word *crone*, which many years ago was used to describe a wise old woman (Wall & Ferguson, 1998). It was a term used to honor those who had achieved a level of distinction by being among the oldest. In more current usage, the word has come to mean "an ugly, withered old woman; a hag" and has been used to denigrate older women (*American Heritage College Dictionary*, 1993). A Croning Ceremony is a time for honoring the female elder's wisdom, which in our society is often ignored at best or even denied.

Rabbi Cary Kozberg, Director of Spiritual Care at Wexner Heritage Village, a senior care center in Columbus, Ohio, has developed a service for older persons moving to a nursing home. He calls it "Let Your Heart Take Courage: A Ceremony of Hope and Welcoming" (1992). This service begins as follows:

> We gather today to consecrate a moment of transition. In the journey of life, it is a significant milestone. Much time has been spent in preparing for this moment. Amidst this preparation, there have been feelings of hope and fear, anticipation and anxiety, sorrow and perhaps relief. Embarking on this new phase of the journey, we pause to reflect on the continuance of life and its progression, and to contemplate both the changes and the challenges to be faced. With hearts full of emotion, we turn to the words of our Tradition, seeking faith in the midst of uncertainty, comfort in the midst of despair.

This kind of service can easily be adapted to any religious tradition. It is a ritualized way of acknowledging the need for this move, the security and hope that it brings, but also the sadness, sorrow, and sense of abandonment at giving up a home, a community of many years, and a previous life. This ritual is meant to enable the new resident to continue the process of redefining who he or she is apart from the life that is permanently changed by this move.

Rituals are born of our need to mark significant persons and events in our lives. Sometimes these rituals are spontaneous, as when many mourners take flowers and other gifts to the scene of a fatal accident. At other times these rituals are well-planned, organized and orchestrated, such as the service at the National Cathedral in Washington, DC, after the events of September 11, 2001.

Some rituals are communal events involving a family, a church community, a membership organization, a neighborhood, a city, or a nation. Others are personal and carried out alone. Rituals grow out of a need to comprehend and make sense of our lives and the lives of others and to acknowledge significant people and events. We have a need to remember and to be remembered, and by taking part in rituals we enable our grief work through the inevitable transitions and changes of life (Feinstein & Mayo, 1990).

An older woman who was diagnosed with a terminal illness just months after losing her husband of many years reported that she felt a great need to be with her children and grandchildren after the events of September 11, 2001. As the matriarch of the family, she called all of them and told them that she needed them to come to her home on the Saturday evening following this tragic day. They all showed up as requested. She fed them around the family table and then explained that she needed to be with them and to share her fears, pain, sadness, and hope with them and to hear theirs in return. They talked and then they lit candles and paraded through the streets of her neighborhood, singing songs of hope, encouragement, and national solidarity to uphold them during this time of crisis. This wise woman felt a need and reached out to her family to fulfill that need in a ritualized form in which they could share some very important feelings and hopes with each other. This is what rituals are for—healing, supporting, comforting, transitioning, guiding, reconciling, sustaining, and sharing. Let us use rituals, both personally and communally, in abundance.

STORIES

Each of us has stories to tell about our lives. We have stories about the hard times and the good times, about family, about learning to drive, about a first date or a first job, about the death of a close friend or family member, about an ethical decision. All of these stories make us who we are. They make us interesting and distinct. Sharing stories can be one way of transmitting the wisdom we have gained, not just passing on the knowledge we've learned.

According to Erikson's (1963) theory of the eight stages of life, the last stage or challenge of life is one of integrity versus despair. People in their later years look back at who, where, how, and what they have been in order to integrate and make sense of the total of their life—the good and bad, the ups and downs, the successes and failures, the mistakes and accomplishments. When they are able to accept all the parts of their lives, they find integrity rather than despair. Telling stories, sharing wisdom with other generations is one of the important ways of coming to integrity.

In later life, stories become even more important to remember. By reliving events, older persons sort out what has been important to them, what they are proud of, and what they would do differently if given another chance. This life review is a normal part of aging and should be encouraged. Older persons are fortunate if they have friends or family members who listen to their stories and ask questions to encourage more storytelling. The listeners also are fortunate because they learn what it is about the storytellers' lives that has made a difference and kept them going through life's challenges. Both tellers and listeners learn in this process (Bandler & Grinder, 1979).

Often an older person tells the same story over and over again. By listening to repeated stories rather than tuning out, we learn new things about the storyteller and about ourselves. Having a listener may help the storytellers with transitions in their lives. For 13 years, my office was on the ground floor of a continuing care retirement center. I was on the staff of the corporate organization that ran the center and had no professional responsibilities to the residents. My connections to them were informal. Over time, several residents adopted me as a person they would visit once or twice a week. They shared their stories with me, and I learned much through these relationships. I worked hard at listening in order to understand what meaning they had found throughout their lives.

One man visited me for four years. I watched him deteriorate physically and mentally. He shared many stories about his life, but at least once a week he told me one particular story. For most of his professional life he had lived in New York City, and over that 30-year period he became friendly with many well-known personalities in politics and publishing. He told me about the exciting parties he attended and the important people he met there. I always responded that the parties must have been fun or exciting. Yet nearly every time he returned to my office, he told me this same story. Each time I wondered what it was that he was trying to tell me with this story that I was not getting. I knew there was something. I felt that if I got it, and let him know I got it, then he would not have to keep telling me.

Finally, as I was listening to him one day, I did not listen to the details of the story and the parties, but focused instead on the gentleman himself. At the end of his story, I looked at him and said, "You were really an important person." He looked at me with a twinkle in his eye, and said, "Yes." It was so simple and yet so profound, and it had taken me years to get it. He was important with important people in an important city for many years. He needed someone to understand this, particularly at this time in his life when he was growing frailer, more vulnerable, more dependent on others, and less in control. He needed someone to understand and confirm that he had been very important. I needed to understand his story in order to think more about my own story and what gives meaning to my life, both now and in the future.

Our stories are important for ourselves and for others. Another person who came by often to talk was a woman in her 90s. She told me many stories of her life, but one she told regularly was that she had read the Bible from cover to cover five times. She was very proud of this. I acknowledged that it was an incredible accomplishment and asked her how long it took. One day, I finally got the real meaning of what she was telling me. I said, "You are a very religious person with deep beliefs." She responded with an emphatic "Yes!" and I knew that I had finally heard her story and the meaning behind it. The meaning she had found in her life challenged me to think about my own religious or spiritual self—what gives me meaning spiritually?

Many people have written extensively on the importance of life review or life storytelling, particularly in the later years (Birren & Deutchman, 1991; Butler, 1977; Hateley, 1985; Kaminsky, 1984). But some older persons find the idea of writing their stories intimidating. Others have no one to listen to their stories when they want to share them orally. Thus, many of them sort out their stories and make meaning out of their lives in their own heads, alone, instead of sharing the meanings with others.

In Maclay's (1977) wonderful short story, "The Occupational Therapist," the reader hears the internal life review of an older woman in a nursing home. An occupational therapist comes by regularly to urge the woman to take part in the activities rather than sitting and doing nothing. Of course, she knows that what she is doing inside her own head and soul is of ultimate importance:

> Oh, here she comes, the therapist, with scissors and paste.
> Would I like to try decoupage? "No," I say, "I haven't got time."
> "Nonsense," she says, "you're going to live a long, long time."
> That's not what I mean, I mean that all my life I've been doing
> things for people, with people, I have to catch up on my
> thinking and feeling. About Sam's death, for one thing…

Like the occupational therapist, we too often miss opportunities to listen to and learn from our elders. But how do we get others to talk to us about important things in their lives? Most people will share stories if they have an attentive listener. It usually takes only a few questions and attentive listening. "Who or what most influenced and shaped your thinking as you were growing up?" "What do you think were the most important historic events you have lived through?" "How did you take part in these events personally?" Questions like these are a way to begin.

When a friend or relative enters a nursing home, it is important to communicate his or her stories to the staff. This helps the staff perceive the newcomer as an individual with a unique personality and history, not just another resident. Studies have shown that sharing the histories of residents can significantly and positively influence the attitudes of nursing home aides (Pietrukowicz & Johnson, 1991). Aides who have been given a sense of a resident's life history tend to see that resident as more capable.

Some persons who move to a nursing home are able to tell their own stories, but many are too ill, incapacitated, or depressed to do so. In this situation, it is important that friends and relatives do it for them. One way to do this is orally, by telling the staff about the resident, where he or she comes from, and where he or she has been.

Most family and friends usually do not see the night shift of aides and nurses or the housekeeping staff. There are other ways of communicating the stories to these staff members. One way to communicate the uniqueness of the resident is to make a collage of pictures from different periods of his or her life. The collage could show an older woman in her teens, as a new bride, young mother, middle-aged professional, and a retired person enjoying family, friends, and life in general. A poster telling events of the person's life chronologically, perhaps adding pictures for each event, is another way of communicating. This could also introduce significant family members and friends to the staff. One family, for example, took the time to make a picture collage on poster board, which hung on the wall in the resident's room. Next to the collage they placed a short note about her to the staff. It read:

> To All Staff:
> Hello, my name is Edna Liverett, I was born and raised in Washington, DC. The picture on the dresser is my Mom, Lottie. I am now 82 years old. I married Jim Liverett from Asheville, NC, and we had 5 children (their pictures are on the wall). I stayed home and raised my children. Jim then built us a house in Arden, NC. Jim died shortly after our 50th wedding anniversary. For the past three and a half years,

> I have been living with my daughter, Arlene and her husband, Hank, in Rockville, MD. My other children live in various states across the country.
>
> I enjoy listening to tapes and hearing piano and organ music. I also like to put cream on my face and hands each morning and at bedtime. A special treat for me is to have someone say the Lord's Prayer with or for me each evening. The afghan on my bed is special to me also. I enjoyed making it.

A few nursing homes around the country are now encouraging this kind of storytelling about residents, and making available the ideas and tools to residents, families, and friends. If there are no family members around to do this story-sharing with the nursing home staff, then friends or members of congregations and organizations involved with the resident might take on this responsibility.

My own mother is a very shy person and finds it easier to listen to others than to talk, but she has many stories to tell and much wisdom to pass on to her family and friends. We wanted to celebrate her 85th birthday by coming together as a family to honor her, hear her stories, and celebrate her years. Because she is shy, we knew we had to plan a way to allow her to tell her stories that would be comfortable for her. One day of the celebration was spent just with children, grandchildren, and one great-grandchild. We did a simple ritual to allow Mom and the rest of us to share stories about her life. The whole family sat around a table in the living room on which we put nine candles, each candle representing a decade of her life. As we lit the first candle, we told stories of the first ten years of Mom's life. We got Mom started by sharing the stories that we remembered being told. It worked and pretty soon we were hearing other stories from her. Everyone asked questions and joined in as the spirit moved them. The candles took some of the focus off Mom and allowed her to be less self-conscious. We talked and listened as we lit the candle for her second, third, and subsequent decades. The ninth candle represented the last five years of her life and her future and led us into discussions of what is to come.

This was a very special day for all of us as we laughed and cried together, sharing the transitions and the losses and gains of Mom's 85 years of living. It ended with the grandchildren receiving candles to take home as reminders of Grandma and the stories they had heard. We also tape-recorded the stories told that day, and each family member later received a copy of the tape.

The second day of the celebration was a more public celebration with Mom's lifelong friends, neighbors, and extended family. We asked that no presents be brought. We suggested instead that guests might bring stories of Mom's life to share with everyone else. People did bring stories to share, and the stories are cherished by all of us.

Aristotle once said, "They are continually talking of the past because they enjoy remembering." This is true, but remembering the past goes beyond enjoyment. We need to remember in order to find significance and meaning in the lives we have lived. Remembering is at times painful because parts of our lives have been painful. Reminiscing is the process of integrating the joy and pain of the past to enrich the present and the future.

Each of us has a story to tell about our life and how we lived it. That story needs to be shared with younger generations. Let us think back on the struggles we have faced and how we have handled them. Let us remember the simple things in our childhood that gave our lives meaning and direction. People are unique because of the experiences they have had and how they have handled them; sharing these experiences with others helps both teller and listener to grow. ■

D. Elaine Tiller is a gerontologist, bereavement counselor, and author of numerous articles in both fields. She is currently the Bereavement Care Coordinator of Montgomery Hospice in Rockville, Maryland. In 1981, she developed and implemented the first Bereavement Care Program at the Hospice of Northern Virginia. She has served as chair of the National Interfaith Coalition on Aging of the National Council on Aging, and presently serves on the Governing Council of the Forum on Religion, Spirituality and Aging of the American Society on Aging.

References

Bandler, R., & Grinder, J. (1979). *Frogs into princes: Neuro linguistic programming.* Moab, Utah: Real People Press.

Best, R.J., & Brunner, J.A. (1994). *Memories of home: A keepsake you create.* New York: Paulist Press.

Birren, J.E., & Deutchman, D. (1991). *Guiding autobiography groups for older adults.* Baltimore: The Johns Hopkins Press.

Butler, R.N. (1977). Successful aging and the role of life review. *Journal of the American Geriatric Society, 22*, 529-535.

Costello, R.B. (Executive Ed.). (1993). *The American Heritage college dictionary* (3rd ed.). Boston: Houton Mifflin Co.

Erikson, E.H. (1963). *Childhood and society*, (2nd ed.). New York: W.W. Norton & Co.

Feinstein, D., & Mayo, P.E. (1990). *Rituals for living and dying: How we can turn loss and the fear of death into an affirmation of life.* New York: HarperCollins.

Hateley, B.J. (1985). *Telling your story, exploring your faith: Writing your life story for personal insight and spiritual growth.* St. Louis, MO: CBP Press.

Kaminsky, M. (Ed.). (1984). *Uses of reminiscence: New ways of working with older adults.* New York: Haworth Press.

Kozberg, C. (1992). Let Your Heart Take Courage: A Ceremony of Hope and Welcoming (unpublished).

Maclay, E. (1977). *Green winter: Celebrations of old age.* New York: Reader's Digest Press distributed by McGraw-Hill.

Pietrukowicz, M.E., & Johnson, M.M.S. (1991). Using life histories to individualize nursing home staff attitudes toward residents. *The Gerontologist, 32*, 102-106.

Wall, K., & Ferguson, G. (1998). *Rites of passage.* Hillsboro, OR: Beyond Words Publications.

Conclusion

Kenneth J. Doka

As a whole, the chapters in this book affirm two significant points. The first is that older bereaved persons do, in fact, have unique needs that professionals must address in order to provide effective services. Professionals must take into account the varied perspectives of each aging cohort or generation. There are private and public experiences that have shaped each generation's relationships and views of the world. Naturally, these perspectives will also shape their sense of loss. For example, among the present oldest cohort, women may not be as likely to have worked outside the home. The loss of a spouse may then have severe financial repercussions and produce specific fears that may not necessarily appear in younger generations.

Professionals should also consider the individual circumstances of older clients and the ways that these factors may complicate the experience of grief. For example, the frailty of very old persons may inhibit their participation in rituals or other forms of grief support. It may be disruptive to social relationships and networks and make them far more vulnerable to stress. In some cases, they may have been dependent on a now-deceased spouse, causing secondary losses of their remaining independence and ability to remain in their own home. They may experience other forms of multiple losses, such as a number of significant deaths within a short span of time. They may be distant from their support system—residing in retirement communities or nursing homes, inaccessible to their closest confidants. Or it may be that it is their closest confidants, loved ones, and friends who are inaccessible or who have died.

Our chapters also affirm the significant strengths of older persons. Most likely they have experienced some sort of loss earlier in their lives that gives them a sense of understanding of grief, an appreciation of the grief process, and recognition of their own resilience. They can often draw informally from their networks, giving and receiving support. In a sense, their very awareness of finitude may insulate them from the extreme shock of sudden loss. It could be said that their age, in itself, suggests that they are survivors.

The above factors should not deter professionals from offering sensitive support. As we have shown, the needs of older persons who experience grief are significant and affect the lives of all generations. Most of all, professionals should understand one essential truth: Even as we help, we can learn much from the wisdom and the strength of our elders.

Resources

As the aging population increases, so does the number of people who face caregiving responsibilities and the issues of loss that inevitably follow. In response, many organizations offer support and resources to meet both personal and professional needs. The following list provides a guide to these organizations and the services they offer.

AARP
601 E Street, NW, Washington, DC 20049
(800) 424-3410
www.aarp.org
e-mail: member@aarp.org

AARP is a membership organization dedicated to shaping and enriching the experience of aging by helping individuals make the most of their lives after age 50. AARP provides education and information about caregiving, long-term care, and aging, including publications and audiovisual aids for caregivers.

Administration on Aging (AoA)
330 Independence Avenue, SW, Washington, DC 20201
(202) 619-7501 Fax: (202) 260-1012
www.aoa.gov
e-mail: aoainfo@aoa.gov

AoA is the federal focal point and advocate agency for older persons and their concerns. AoA works to heighten awareness among other federal agencies, organizations, groups, and the public about the valuable contributions that older Americans make to the nation and alerts them to the needs of vulnerable older people. Through information, referral, and outreach efforts at the community level, AoA seeks to educate older people and their caregivers about the benefits and services available to help them.

Aging Network Services
4400 East-West Highway, Suite 907, Bethesda, MD 20814
(301) 657-4329 Fax: (301) 657-3250
www.AgingNets.com
e-mail: ans@AgingNets.com

Aging Network Services provides counseling, consultation, psychotherapy, and care management to elders and their family members.

Alliance for Aging Research
2021 K Street, NW, Suite 305, Washington, DC 20006
(202) 293-2856
www.agingresearch.org
e-mail: info@agingresearch.org

The Alliance for Aging Research is a nonprofit organization dedicated to improving the health and independence of Americans as they age. The Alliance works to stimulate academic, governmental, and private sector research into the chronic diseases of human aging. The Alliance produces many educational brochures and reports for both consumers and professionals.

Alzheimer's Association
919 North Michigan Avenue, Suite 1100, Chicago, IL 60611-1676
(800) 272-3900 or (312) 335-8700 Fax: (312) 335-1110
www.alz.org
e-mail: info@alz.org

The Alzheimer's Association, a national network of chapters, is the largest national voluntary health organization committed to finding a cure for Alzheimer's and helping those affected by the disease. The Association seeks to advance research and to enhance care and support for patients and their families and caregivers.

Alzheimer's Disease Education and Referral (ADEAR) Center
National Institute on Aging
P.O. Box 8250, Silver Spring, MD 20907
(800) 438-4380 or (301) 495-3311
www.alzheimers.org
e-mail: adear@alzheimers.org

The ADEAR Center is an information service sponsored by the National Institute on Aging. The Center distributes information about all aspects of Alzheimer's disease to health professionals, patients, their families, and the general public. In addition to a wide variety of information about Alzheimer's and other dementias, the Center provides information about caregiving and can help locate information and resources to deal with the grief and loss associated with the disease.

American Association of Homes and Services for the Aging (AAHSA)
2519 Connecticut Avenue, NW, Washington, DC 20008
(202) 783-2242 Fax: (202) 783-2255
www.aahsa.org
e-mail: info@aahsa.org

AAHSA consists of more than 5,600 not-for-profit nursing homes; continuing care, assisted living, and senior housing facilities; retirement communities; and community service organizations. AAHSA's members include faith-based and community-sponsored providers. AAHSA serves its members by representing before Congress and federal agencies the concerns of not-for-profit organizations that serve older people.

American Geriatrics Society (AGS)
The Empire State Building, 350 Fifth Avenue, Suite 801,
New York, NY 10118
(212) 308-1414 Fax: (212) 832-8646
www.americangeriatrics.org
e-mail: info.amger@americangeriatrics.org

AGS is a professional organization of health care providers dedicated to improving the health and well-being of all older adults. With an active membership of more than 6,000 health care professionals, the AGS has a long history of effecting change in the provision of health care for older adults.

Americans for Better Care of the Dying (ABCD)
4125 Albemarle Street, NW, Suite 210, Washington, DC 20016
(202) 895-9485 Fax: (202) 895-9484
www.abcd-caring.org
e-mail: info@abcd-caring.org

ABCD seeks to improve end-of-life care by focusing on social and political changes that will lead to enduring, efficient, and effective programs.

Association for Death Education and Counseling (ADEC)
342 N. Main Street, West Hartford, CT 06117
(860) 586-7503 Fax: (860) 586-7550
www.adec.org

ADEC is a multidisciplinary professional organization dedicated to promoting excellence in death education, bereavement counseling, and care of the dying. ADEC provides its membership and the public with information, support, and resources based on theory and quality research.

Center to Improve Care of the Dying
1200 South Hayes Street, Arlington, VA 22202
(703) 413-1100, extension 5451 Fax: (703) 414-4717
www.medicaring.org
e-mail: info@medicaring.org

Part of RAND Health, the Center to Improve Care of the Dying focuses on health care services research and quality improvement. The Center has helped lead the call to improve end-of-life care. Its website provides a resource of professional and private organizations working on a range of important issues.

Children of Aging Parents (CAPS)
1609 Woodbourne Road, Suite 302-A, Levittown, PA 19057
(800) 227-7294
www.caps4caregivers.org
e-mail: caps4caregivers@aol.com

CAPS assists caregivers of older persons with information and referrals, a network of support groups, and publications and programs that promote public awareness of the value and the needs of caregivers. CAPS is dedicated to assisting caregivers of older adults in all aspects of caregiving.

Compassion in Dying Federation (CIDF)
6312 SW Capitol Highway, Suite 415, Portland, OR 97201
(503) 221-9556 Fax: (503) 228-9160
www.compassionindying.org
e-mail: info@compassionindying.org

CIDF is a charitable organization that works to improve care and expand choices at the end of life. CIDF provides national leadership for client service, legal advocacy, and public education to improve pain and symptom management, increase patient empowerment and self-determination, and expand end-of-life choices to include aid-in-dying for terminally ill, mentally competent adults. CIDF provides client services, legal advocacy, and public and professional education.

Compassionate Friends
P.O. Box 3696, Oak Brook, IL 60522
(630) 990-0010 Fax: (630) 990-0246
www.compassionatefriends.org

Compassionate Friends is a self-help organization that offers friendship and understanding to families following the death of a child. There are 580 chapters nationwide that provide monthly meetings, phone contacts, lending libraries, and grief-related literature. The Compassionate Friends also provides training programs and resources for local chapters and answers referral requests.

Eldercare Locator
National Association of Area Agencies on Aging
927 15th Street, NW, 6th Floor, Washington, DC 20005
(800) 677-1116 or (202) 296-8130 Fax: (202) 296-8134
www.eldercare.gov

Eldercare Locator provides referrals to area agencies on aging via zip code locations and offers information about many eldercare issues and services in local communities.

Foundation for Health in Aging (FHA)
The Empire State Building, 350 Fifth Avenue, Suite 801,
New York, NY 10118
(212) 755-6810
www.healthinaging.org
e-mail: staff@healthaging.org

FHA was established to meet the health care needs and concerns of older adults and their caregivers through public education, research, and public policy. FHA aims to build a bridge between geriatrics health care professionals and the public, and to advocate on behalf of older adults and their special needs: wellness and preventive care, self-responsibility and independence, and connections to the family and community.

Generations United (GU)
122 C Street, NW, Suite 820, Washington, DC 20001
(202) 638-1263 Fax: (202) 638-7555
www.gu.org
e-mail: gu@gu.org

GU is the only national membership organization focused on promoting intergenerational strategies, programs, and public policies. GU advocates for the mutual well-being of children, youth, and older adults. It serves as a resource for educating policy makers and the public about the economic, social, and personal imperatives of intergenerational cooperation. GU provides a forum in which those working with children, youth, and older adults can explore areas of common interest while celebrating the richness of each generation.

Gerontological Society of America (GSA)
1030 15th Street, NW, Suite 250, Washington, DC 20005
(202) 842-1275
www.geron.org
e-mail: geron@geron.org

GSA is one of the oldest and largest multidisciplinary scientific organizations devoted to the advancement of gerontological research in the country. GSA's primary missions are to promote research and education in aging and to encourage the dissemination of research to other scientists, decision makers, and practitioners.

Growth House, Inc.
www.growthhouse.org

Growth House, Inc. is a website dedicated to improving the quality of compassionate care for people who are dying. It seeks to accomplish this mission through public education about hospice and home care, palliative care, pain management, death with dignity, bereavement, and related issues.

HealthandAge
www.healthandage.com

The HealthandAge website provides articles and other resources on health, illness, and aging.

Hospice Association of America (HAA)
228 7th Street, SE, Washington, DC 20003
(202) 546-4759 Fax: (202) 547-9559
www.hospice-america.org

HAA is a national organization representing more than 2,300 hospices and thousands of caregivers and volunteers who serve terminally ill patients and their families. HAA advocates hospice interests before Congress, the regulatory agencies, other national organizations, the courts, the media, and the public.

Hospice Foundation of America (HFA)
2001 S Street, NW, Suite 300, Washington, DC 20009
(800) 854-3402 or (202) 638-5419 Fax: (202) 638-5312
www.hospicefoundation.org
e-mail: hfa@hospicefoundation.org

HFA is a nonprofit organization that provides leadership in the development and application of hospice and its philosophy of care. The Foundation produces an annual award-winning national bereavement teleconference and publishes the companion *Living With Grief* book series. HFA also provides a variety of other resources, including *A Guide to Recalling and Telling Your Life Story*, a tool to assist people in writing their autobiographies. *Clergy to Clergy: Ministering to Those Facing Illness, Death, and Grief* is an audiotape series developed to help clergy of all faiths minister to their communities. HFA also publishes *Journeys*, a monthly newsletter for the bereaved, and offers brochures on topics from *Choosing Hospice to Supporting a Friend Through Illness and Loss*. HFA is a member of the Combined Federal Campaign through Health Charities of America.

Last Acts Campaign
c/o Barksdale Ballard, 1951 Kidwell Drive, Suite 205, Vienna, VA 22182
(703) 827-8771 Fax: (703) 827-0783
www.lastacts.org

Last Acts is a national campaign to engage both health professionals and the public in efforts to improve care at the end of life. Last Acts comprises more than 400 partner organizations that believe that every segment of society—employers, clergy, voluntary health organization leaders, medical and nursing professionals, and counselors, among others—has a role to play as a part of a larger movement that addresses end-of-life concerns at the national, state, and community levels.

National Academy of Elder Law Attorneys, Inc.
1604 North Country Club Road, Tucson, AZ 85716
(520) 881-4005 Fax: (520) 325-7925
www.naela.org

The National Academy of Elder Law Attorneys, Inc. is a nonprofit association that assists lawyers, bar organizations, and others who work with older clients and their families. The Academy provides a resource of information, education, networking, and assistance to those who must deal with the many specialized issues involved with legal services to older and disabled clients. Request a copy of "Questions and Answers When Looking for an Elder Law Attorney" by sending a self-addressed, stamped envelope.

National Asian Pacific Center on Aging (NAPCA)
1511 Third Avenue, Suite 941, Seattle, WA 98101
(206) 624-1221 Fax: 206-624-1023
www.napca.org
e-mail: angelo@napca.org

NAPCA serves as a national advocacy organization committed to preserving the dignity, well-being and quality of life of Asian Pacific Americans in their senior years. NAPCA recruits and places persons who are 55 and over in support, technical, and engineering positions in Environmental Protection Agency offices through the Senior Environment Employment Program. NAPCA provides low-income persons who are 55 and over with opportunities to gain meaningful part-time paid work experience in community service agencies and assists them in obtaining unsubsidized jobs in public or private sectors through the Senior Community Service Employment Program. It conducts roundtables, town meetings, and conferences where elders are able to voice their needs and concerns in their native languages.

National Association for Hispanic Elderly (Asociación Nacional Por Personas Mayores)
234 East Colorado Boulevard, Suite 300, Pasadena, CA 91101
(626) 564-1988 Fax: (626) 564-2659

The National Association for Hispanic Elderly is a national, private, nonprofit organization providing a variety of services for older Hispanic people. Its resources include a national Hispanic research center, research and consultation for organizations seeking to reach older Spanish-speaking people, and dissemination of written and audio-visual materials in English and Spanish. The Association administers Project AYUDA, a program providing employment counseling and placement services.

National Association for the Support of Long Term Care
1321 Duke Street, Suite 304, Alexandria, VA 22314
(703) 549-8500 Fax: (703) 549-8342
www.nasl.org
e-mail: member@nasl.org

The National Association for the Support of Long Term Care provides a national communication forum, as well as legislative and regulatory representation, for long-term care industry professionals; serves as a source of information in the development of health care policy; and joins the nursing home community in promoting a realistic national program for the provision of the highest quality services to patients receiving long-term care.

National Association of Professional Geriatric Care Managers
1604 North Country Club Road, Tucson, AZ 85716
(520) 881-8008 Fax: (520) 325-7925
www.caremanager.org

Geriatric care managers (GCMs) are health care professionals, most often social workers, who help families deal with the problems and challenges associated with caring for older people. This organization provides referrals to state chapters which, in turn, can provide the names of GCMs in a particular area.

National Caucus & Center on Black Aged, Inc. (NCBA)
1220 L Street, NW, Suite 800, Washington, DC 20005
(202) 637-8400 Fax: (202) 347-0895
www.ncba-blackaged.org
e-mail: Health@ncba-aged.org

NCBA, founded in 1970, is the only national organization dedicated exclusively to improving the quality of life for African-American elders, particularly those of lower socioeconomic status.

National Hospice and Palliative Care Organization (NHPCO)
1700 Diagonal Road, Alexandria, VA 22314
(703) 837-1500 Fax: (703) 525-5762
www.nhpco.org
e-mail: info@nhpco.org

NHPCO is the oldest and largest nonprofit organization in the United States devoted exclusively to hospice and palliative care. It operates the Hospice Helpline (800-658-8898) to provide the general public and health care providers with information about hospice and palliative care.

Older Women's League (OWL)
666 11th Street, NW, Suite 700, Washington, DC 20001
(202) 783-6686 or (800) 825-3695 Fax: (202) 638-2356
www.owl-national.org
e-mail: owlinfo@owl-national.org

OWL, a grassroots membership organization that focuses on issues unique to women as they age, strives to improve the status and quality of life for midlife and older women.

Partnership for Caring
1620 Eye Street, NW, Suite 202, Washington, DC 20006
(202) 296-8071 Fax: (202) 296-8352
Hotline: (800) 989-9455
www.partnershipforcaring.org
e-mail: pfc@partnershipforcaring.org

Partnership for Caring is a coalition of individual consumers, consumer organizations, health care professionals, and health care organizations advocating for needed changes in professional and public policy and health care systems to improve care for dying persons and their families.

Project on Death in America
Open Society Institute
400 W. 59th Street, New York, NY 10019
(212) 548-0150 Fax: (212) 548-4613
www.soros.org/death/index.html
e-mail: pdia@sorosny.org

The mission of Project on Death in America is to understand and transform the culture and experience of dying and bereavement through initiatives in the provision of care, public education, professional education, and public policy.

■

This list was compiled by the American Geriatrics Society Foundation for Health in Aging, with additional information from Hospice Foundation of America and Americans for Better Care of the Dying.